SPI
EGE
L&G
RAU

The

Long Journey
Home

The
Long Journey
Home

A Memoir

Margaret
Robison

Spiegel & Grau

New York | 2011

The Long Journey Home is a work of nonfiction. Some names
and identifying details have been changed.

Published in the United States by Spiegel & Grau,
an imprint of The Random House Publishing Group,
a division of Random House, Inc., New York.

Spiegel & Grau and Design is a registered
trademark of Random House, Inc.

Portions of Chapter 24 were originally published in "Begin by Remembering," *Common Journeys*, Fall,
1995. The following were originally published in *Kaleidoscope: International Magazine of Literature, Fine Arts,
and Disability*: an earlier version of Chapter 2 appeared as "The Headache" (Spring/Fall, 1998);
Chapter 5 was originally published as "Common Bonds" (Summer/Fall, 1999); and portions of
Chapter 7 were originally published in "Renascence" (Winter/Spring, 1993).

Grateful acknowledgment is made to the following for permission
to reprint previously published material:

Harvard University Press: "There is a pain so utter" from *The Poems of Emily Dickinson: Variorum Edition* by
Emily Dickinson, edited by Ralph W. Franklin (Cambridge, MA: The Belknap Press of Harvard
University Press, 1998), copyright © 1998 by the President and Fellows of Harvard College.
Copyright © 1951, 1955, 1979, 1983 by the President and Fellows of Harvard College.
Reprinted by permission of the publishers and the Trustees of Amherst College.

Alfred A. Knopf, a division of Random House, Inc., and Harold Ober Associates Incorporated: Four lines from
"Dreams" from *The Collected Poems of Langston Hughes* by Langston Hughes, edited by Arnold Rampersad
with David Roessel, Associate Editor, copyright © 1994 by the Estate of Langston Hughes. Print
rights in the United Kingdom and worldwide electronic and audio rights are administered by
Harold Ober Associates Incorporated. Reprinted by permission of Alfred A. Knopf, a division
of Random House, Inc., and Harold Ober Associates Incorporated.

Library of Congress Cataloging-in-Publication Data
Robison, Margaret.
The long journey home: a memoir / Margaret Robison.
p. cm.
ISBN 978-1-4000-6869-2 (hardcover)—ISBN 978-1-58836-922-2 (ebook)
1. Robison, Margaret. 2. Robison, Margaret—Childhood and youth. 3. Robison, Margaret—
Family. 4. Robison, Margaret—Health. 5. Women artists—United States—Biography.
6. Artists—United States—Biography. 7. Women authors, American—Biography.
8. Young women—Georgia—Biography. I. Title.
CT275.R7435A3 2011
975.8'043092—dc22   2010029327
[B]

Printed in the United States of America on acid-free paper

www.spiegelandgrau.com

2 4 6 8 9 7 5 3 1

First Edition

Book design by Elizabeth A. D. Eno

For Pat King

"Why are you here?"

A young psychiatrist sat across from me, clipboard propped against his crossed leg. My friend Helen and Dr. Turcotte's daughter June sat beside me, silent. My son Chris stood in the doorway, his adolescent face earnest and distressed.

"Because the Amherst water is polluted," I replied flatly. "Because the rain is poisoned."

Dr. Turcotte sat across from me, sleeping, his chin resting on his chest. Lamplight glistened on his thick white hair. It was he who had driven me to this psychiatric hospital, who had driven us all, me in the backseat silent.

"Because I have a therapist I wouldn't recommend to the devil," I said.

The young psychiatrist wrote something on the questionnaire clamped to the clipboard.

I did not tell him that a bomb as large as the one that leveled Hiroshima was about to go off anytime.

My son shifted his weight. Behind him, in the hall, a nurse pushed a cart full of medications past the open door.

The doctor looked up from his questionnaire. "Religion?"

With my breath I lifted a hot-air balloon off the ground and was keeping it afloat at a safe height. The balloon basket was sturdy and well insulated. If I can keep my son, friends, and myself in the air until the danger is past, we'll all be safe, I thought.

"Religion?" the doctor asked again.

"I take the best from each and throw the rest away," I answered sullenly. *I don't remember how long I kept the balloon aloft, but I was exhausted from the effort.*

"What day of the week is this?"

"I don't know."

I looked down at my bandaged fingers and left wrist. I had burned my fingers by holding them against the coils of a small electric heater in my kitchen. Before or after this I had pressed a burning cigarette into the flesh of my left wrist. But I have no memory of doing these things, only a memory of lying on a table in the hospital's emergency room while a doctor dressed the wounds. Self-inflicted wounds. I looked down at the bandaged evidence, feeling a mix of incredulity and shame.

"What's today's date?"

"I don't know."

The doctor scribbled something on the paper again.

"My mother never knows the date when she's writing or painting," Chris said. His statement sounded like a plea. What he meant was that I didn't keep up with the date even when I wasn't crazy.

The bomb didn't go off. How hard I worked, using my breath to keep us so high for so long.

Now I was in a decompression chamber. People came and went, saying nothing. No one understood what was happening to me. It didn't matter. I didn't expect them to.

Breathe, I told myself. *Just breathe.*

My son and friends left the hospital for the night.

I stood before a mirror, talking to myself, gesturing with both hands. But when I try to remember what I was telling or asking my image in the mirror, when I try to go back to enter this experience again, I am able only to stand outside my body. Like someone floating above a car accident, looking down at her crushed and mangled limbs, I can only observe. I feel nothing. But when I look into my eyes, what I see there is terror.

PART ONE

The Early Years

Chapter One

MOTHER STOOD AT THE TOP OF THE LADDER, SCRAPING WALLPAPER OFF the living room walls with a putty knife. Uncle Frank's wife, my Aunt Mary, came through the unlatched screen door without knocking.

She looked up at Mother.

"Louisa, I just want you to know that you'll never have a house as nice as mine." Mother looked down at Aunt Mary, who stood with her hands on her hips, a white leather handbag looped over one arm. She was dressed in a red-and-lavender polka-dotted dress and white sling-backed shoes. "I tell you this now so you get all such thoughts out of your head from the start," Aunt Mary continued.

Mother—married three months and already six weeks pregnant with me—was wearing a sweat-drenched cotton housedress. Scraps and curls of wallpaper lay around the ladder. All afternoon she'd been soaking down the layers of old, stained paper and scraping them off; rose-colored stripes and rosebuds, formal bouquets and baskets of violets, bits and pieces of Richter family history were now strewn on the floor.

Aunt Mary was much older than Mother, who had married the youngest of the three sons in the Richter family. Daddy and Uncle Frank were partners in a produce business. With their sister Bama—

her real name was Alabama Margarete—living miles away in Columbia, North Carolina, Aunt Mary was reigning matriarch, and according to Mother she intended to keep it that way.

Mother climbed down the ladder. "Why, Mary," she said in what must have been that sweet tone of hers—ice water running just beneath the words—"a new house is the farthest thing from my mind. I'm just trying to get this dirty old place clean and decent before the baby comes."

She offered Aunt Mary a glass of mint tea.

Aunt Mary declined. Hers was not a social call.

This was one of the first stories Mother told me, and she retold it again and again. This, and how Aunt Mary somehow manipulated herself into the delivery room to watch Mother's manners and restraint dissolve into one scream after another as I wrestled my way out of her tortured body while lightning lit the sky and thunder rumbled like an angry god. "Your birth was the most terrible thing that had ever happened to me," she repeatedly told me.

Mother was twenty-four years old when I was born.

She never stopped talking about what she referred to as the humiliation of Aunt Mary's shocking invasion of her privacy. She claimed that the sight of my aunt's face over my carriage was enough to send me into a fit of screaming. I don't know if Aunt Mary actually scared me or if I picked up on Mother's controlled but ever-present and powerful emotions. I have no memories at all of Aunt Mary in my infancy. Nevertheless, I grew up with Mother's stories of her a part of me as surely as the genes that gave me green eyes and a prominent nose like my father's.

Growing up I had a pleasant relationship with Aunt Mary until Uncle Frank died in a house fire in 1945 and Daddy and Aunt Mary had a dispute about the division of property and the business. After that Aunt Mary forbade her children to relate to us, though her son Peyton and I continued our friendship in secret and her daughter Roberta remained fond of Mother.

As an adult, on a trip back to my hometown—I believe it was in

1970—I decided to ignore the tension of the years and visit Aunt Mary. I phoned first, and her daughter-in-law said it would be fine for me to visit. Aunt Mary welcomed me warmly. She was lying in bed, smoking a cigarette. Holes from cigar and cigarette burns dotted her lavender satin comforter. Beside the bed a wicker clothes basket held a pile of paperback murder mysteries.

I bent down to hug her, and she opened her arms eagerly.

"I'm so glad to see you, Margaret. Here, sit on the bed beside me," she said as if the past twenty-five years of silence and distance between us had never existed. And in a sense that's true, for that brief visit seemed to erase the past as easily as my teachers had erased numbers and letters from the blackboards in the elementary school around the corner from her house.

Mother and Aunt Mary had a contentious relationship from the time Mother married Daddy until the evening Aunt Mary called her not long after my visit. Mother told me that the two of them talked for nearly two hours, finally making their peace. According to Mother, my aunt died shortly after hanging up the phone.

There were other stories Mother told me about the four years we lived in The Old Home Place before Granddaddy died and we moved to the new house up the street. She told me Daddy was often away on business trips, leaving her alone with Granddaddy and me, and Bubba, my first brother, the new baby who kept her awake with his earaches. One night, when especially tired, she picked him up from the crib in the dark and—missing the rocking chair altogether—fell down hard on the floor beside it. "I just broke down and cried and cried," she said each time she told the story, and each time my own eyes filled with tears. Mother seemed so fragile that I wanted to protect her.

She also told me about the way Daddy always put Granddaddy before her. "He made me sit in the backseat of the car while that old man sat up front with him. Even when I was pregnant." And she told me that after Granddaddy died Daddy kissed the glass over his photograph every day before leaving for work and the first thing on coming home. There was also the framed eight-by-ten photograph of Uncle Frank that stood on a table in the living room of our new house after Uncle Frank was killed in the fire. I would walk away from the picture, then turn around quickly to see if those eyes were still watching me. They always were. They followed me all around the room. I swallowed my fear and told no one.

I don't remember when or how she managed it without Daddy's resistance, but I was relieved when Mother took Uncle Frank's photograph, along with the large-framed photograph of my Aunt Bama's house in Columbia, and buried them under the bedsheets and blankets in the linen closet.

Mother had married into a more eccentric family than she'd realized. I suspect that Daddy had married into a more conservative family than he'd realized. Both had little tolerance of the other's parents and siblings. Grandmother Ledford's voice at our front door was enough to send my father, her son-in-law, fleeing through the back door to his car, and then to the safety of the produce warehouse.

Mother too had difficulty with Grandmother Ledford. Though in her later years she referred to her mother—at that point long dead—as a wonderful person, the tension between the two of them when I was young, until Grandmother's death when I was fifteen, was thick and constant. Mother felt Grandmother to be cold and domineering, and closer to her other daughters. As the fourth daughter in a family with no sons, Mother felt unwanted. She told me how, when she was a young child, Grandmother would sometimes rock her in a rocker on the front porch in the evening. Packs of wild dogs skirted the town, howling. When Mother fussed and wouldn't settle down to sleep quickly enough, Grandmother would threaten: "Hush! If you don't go to sleep, I'll feed you to those dogs."

Mother was also upset about Uncle Frank's cursing and drinking, and Aunt Bama's intrusion into her life. She did more than complain about the occasional beer that Daddy drank at a drive-in restaurant. My birth finally gave her adequate ammunition to fight this rare in-dulgence. The three of us were together when Daddy reached for the beer he'd ordered. Mother announced firmly: "If you take one sip of that alcohol, I'll give it to the baby as well. I intend to make the baby drink whatever you drink."

Her voice filled with pride. "That was the end of your father's drinking."

Then there was Fanny McClure. Fanny had a long, thick neck and dark wavy hair that spilled down her back. To me she always looked like a merry-go-round horse. My cousin Peyton told me that Fanny had been determined to capture Daddy for her own until Mother came into the picture and altogether eliminated what—if any— chance Fanny ever had. Nevertheless, according to Peyton, for several years after my parents' marriage, Fanny devoted many Sunday after- noons to riding back and forth in front of their house in her dark green Chevrolet sedan. Uncle Charlie, Daddy's middle brother, of- fered to take Fanny off Daddy's hands. He not only did that, he mar- ried her as well. Mother never mentioned anything about Fanny chasing Daddy. I don't know if she was even aware of it. But she did tell me that for some reason Fanny didn't like her and had once tried to run her down with her car when Mother was crossing the street from Mizell's Drugs to Roddenbery Hardware Store. But these things happened after Granddaddy died, after we moved into the new house up the street.

It was into The Old Home Place, the wood-framed house that Granddaddy had built, that Mother—who by her own account was immature, naïve, and timid—moved after marrying Daddy, bringing her clothes and her few treasured books. She looked forward to a life of financial plenty after all the penny-pinching necessary in her fa- ther's family, one of the most respected families in town but one lacking in financial abundance. The reason, Mother always explained with pride, was because her father, Mercer Ledford, was one of the rare honest lawyers. He also served as state senator and later as state treasurer; national senators and representatives were his friends. As child, Mother was impressed that Senator Russell wore silk paj?

THE LONG JOURNEY HOME · 7

dulgence. The three of us were together when Daddy reached for the beer he'd ordered. Mother announced firmly: "If you take one sip of that alcohol, I'll give it to the baby as well. I intend to make the baby drink whatever you drink."

Her voice filled with pride. "That was the end of your father's drinking."

Then there was Fanny McClure. Fanny had a long, thick neck and dark wavy hair that spilled down her back. To me she always looked like a merry-go-round horse. My cousin Peyton told me that Fanny had been determined to capture Daddy for her own until Mother came into the picture and altogether eliminated what—if any— chance Fanny ever had. Nevertheless, according to Peyton, for several years after my parents' marriage, Fanny devoted many Sunday afternoons to riding back and forth in front of their house in her dark green Chevrolet sedan. Uncle Charlie, Daddy's middle brother, offered to take Fanny off Daddy's hands. He not only did that, he married her as well. Mother never mentioned anything about Fanny chasing Daddy. I don't know if she was even aware of it. But she did tell me that for some reason Fanny didn't like her and had once tried to run her down with her car when Mother was crossing the street from Mizell's Drugs to Roddenbery Hardware Store. But these things happened after Granddaddy died, after we moved into the new house up the street.

It was into The Old Home Place, the wood-framed house that Granddaddy had built, that Mother—who by her own account was immature, naïve, and timid—moved after marrying Daddy, bringing her clothes and her few treasured books. She looked forward to a life of financial plenty after all the penny-pinching necessary in her father's family, one of the most respected families in town but one lacking in financial abundance. The reason, Mother always explained with pride, was because her father, Mercer Ledford, was one of the rare honest lawyers. He also served as state senator and later as state treasurer; national senators and representatives were his friends. As a child, Mother was impressed that Senator Russell wore silk pajamas when he stayed overnight with the family. As an adult, Mother, who hated asking favors of anyone, called Senator Russell and reminded him that she was Mercer Ledford's daughter when she asked him for help in bringing my brother Mercer back to the States after he became psychotic while serving on a ship stationed off the coast of Vietnam. Senator Russell responded immediately and had a helicopter pick my brother up and take him to the Philippines, then to Bethesda Naval Hospital.

Mother spoke with adoration about her father, but she told me only a few stories about him. One is how he gave her sister Curtis a dollar for every A she made in math, while he gave Mother a dollar for every time she *passed* math. She also told me how he sometimes bought ice cream for his daughters on his evening walks home from his courthouse office, during which he stopped to say hello to so many friends along the way that he often arrived home with the ice cream melting, cones gone soft in his large hands.

Because he never learned to drive, Mother at thirteen began to drive him around the county for his law practice. She took great pride in that role and was grateful for the time they spent together. He worked to send all four of his daughters to college and lived to see them all become teachers. He died from a heart attack the year before Mother's marriage.

Mother had suffered another loss, but a loss she acknowledged aloud only after Daddy's death. While her father was serving as state treasurer, she became involved with the son of an ambassador from Brazil. She said that her father had given the relationship his blessing, but shortly after her father's death, the young man was killed in an automobile accident.

Other than the fact that she was glad Daddy's family had money, Mother said little about her feelings toward him before they married. It was Daddy who told me how he dressed mornings in suit, tie, and spats and sat at the window watching until he saw Mother walking past his house on her way to teach Latin classes in the high school across town. He would rush out the front door and offer to drive her to school. This daily ritual continued for some time before he dared to ask her out on a date.

Daddy played the piano by ear. Although he couldn't read a note of music, he composed a love song to Mother and had a musician write the notes down for him. When she went to New Orleans to summer school at Tulane, he arranged with her host and hostess to take her to a nightclub where the band played the song dedicated to her. Her father and boyfriend dead, Mother finally accepted Daddy's romantic overtures.

They were married on New Year's Day, 1935. And though they fought often and bitterly as I was growing up, Mother and Daddy ended many of their days walking hand in hand through the flower gardens. And they spent most Sunday mornings of my childhood in bed rubbing each other's feet.

II

I remember the house when it was white and the steps held you up when you stood on them. The porch columns were white, solid, and straight. The kitchen cabinets glistened buttery yellow, and the linoleum glowed with wax. The furniture was dusted and polished, the paper on the walls new. But the floors in every room were slanted like a ship tossed at sea, and cracks crisscrossed the ceilings and traveled from wall to wall like roads on maps of places I'd never been.

Mother, Daddy, and I lived with Granddaddy in the The Old Home Place, where Daddy, his two brothers, and his three sisters were born and grew up. It was there, sixty-eight years later, that Daddy died. By that time, his sister Bama had inherited the house. She did little to take care of the place. After several renters defaced the house before moving on, she let it stand vacant for years. Kudzu vines took over what had been Mother's flower beds and covered the abandoned heart-shaped fish pool she had dug from the hard earth.

After Uncle Earnest died, Aunt Bama and their son, Earnest

Junior—who must have been in his forties by then—stayed in the house with their parakeet when they came down from Columbia, North Carolina, several times a year. The usual pretense for their visits had something to do with house repairs, but Bama's real reason was to visit Daddy and check up on, and criticize, Mother. Though Aunt Bama was the only family member left with wealth, instead of staying in a hotel she, Earnest Junior, and the bird always stayed in the living room of The Old Home Place, where they'd set up army cots for sleeping and hang sheets over the windows for privacy.

It must have been on one of those cots that Daddy died. Mother told me he'd been complaining of being cold all that evening and that he'd said he wished his sister hadn't come that weekend. Mother said that he fed the birds before briefly visiting my brother Wyman and his wife, Anne. Then he went to see Aunt Bama and Earnest Junior in The Old Home Place.

Within the hour Earnest Junior was banging on Mother's locked door yelling, "Uncle Wyman's dead, Aunt Louisa! Uncle Wyman's dead!"

Earnest Junior had been reading the book of Revelations aloud, he told Mother, when Daddy just fell back dead. At breakfast on the day of the funeral, I was about to ask Earnest Junior what verses he'd been reading and why, when he leaned over me and began stroking the satin binding of my robe with his fingers. Then he gave me that creepy look that had always made me feel uncomfortable. I got up and moved across the room. I've said nothing to him since. The last news I heard about him was that he was in federal prison someplace in the South.

Earnest Junior was always peculiar, and his parents' behavior toward him was equally so. One family story went that when he was a little boy in public school, Aunt Bama would go each day at recess to stand and peer at him through the schoolyard fence until the bell called the children back into the building. Even as an adult, Earnest Junior wasn't allowed out of his parents' sight. A trip out to their car to retrieve a sweater or suitcase required an entire family expedition.

cessant smoking, and constant complaining about being at death's door while refusing to go to a doctor.

"Someday, Wyman, you're going to drop dead!" she'd scream shrilly again and again. And he did, of course, still smoking cigarettes, and with a heart so enlarged that you could sometimes hear it pumping if you were quiet enough.

Aunt Bama was also full of complaints about Mother's cooking. "This Jell-O has a peculiar taste to it," she would say, poking tentatively with a fork prong at a quivering lime-green blob. Or she would push her almost empty plate away, announcing: "I can't eat any more of this food, Louisa. Something's just not right about it." Livid, Mother would do everything she could do to pretend that my aunt wasn't there in her dining room at all, that the irritation was nothing more than a gnat that had slipped in through a snag in a window screen.

Daddy tried to ignore both women, dumping so much catsup on his food that his plate looked like a miniature replica of one of the bloodiest battles in the Civil War. With Aunt Bama present, Daddy knew that Mother wouldn't let her manners go and scream at him with her usual "You ruin everything I cook by pouring catsup on it, Wyman! Absolutely everything!"

Earnest Junior loved Mother's cooking and ate helping after helping. Well satiated after one dinner of baked ham, sweet potato soufflé, and green peas in white sauce, he pushed his chair back from the table and announced with a rare sparkle in his eyes: "When Mama and Daddy die I'm going to be as rich as a king."

"When your Daddy and I die all our money is going to foreign missions. That's stated in our wills," Aunt Bama said severely, glaring across the table at her son. "The Lord will take care of you, Earnest Junior."

"The Lord, my foot," Mother snorted when the two of us rehashed the dinnertime conversation privately later. "She means the law."

Then once again she expressed her frustration with Aunt Bama for not telling her more about Earnest Junior's condition. Mother felt it unfair, since she, by far the youngest of the whole bunch, would probably be left to deal with him. In a way, that's exactly what happened. In her old age, when Earnest Junior called Mother collect from a prison, or some other place when he was an escapee on the run, she always accepted his calls. She said it made her feel safer to know where he was. She grimly referred to him as "my inheritance from your father."

But it was Earnest Junior who ended up inheriting The Old Home Place.

I have few memories of Daddy during the first four years of my life. While we lived there he was either at the warehouse supervising the workers or traveling in the northern states drumming up trade for his and Uncle Frank's lucrative produce business. I do remember his striking image when, like Uncle Frank, he dressed up in his white linen suit on special occasions, pausing at the garden during rose season to snap off a red rosebud for his coat lapel.

Granddaddy is a giant in my first memory of him. I am sitting on the floor, looking up and up into his teasing face under his straight dark hair. The whole house was filled with his presence, his voice, and his smell, a mixture of talcum powder and cologne, both of which he used liberally because he never bathed. He just splashed a little water on himself like Daddy did and depended on the toiletries to do the rest. But Granddaddy never smelled bad, unless you didn't like the aroma of Prince Albert pipe tobacco that clung to everything he wore and permeated his skin. I loved its smell because his pipe, and the smell of it, were part of him, and he was as much a welcome part of my world as the sun, the pecan orchard, and the flower garden in the backyard with its row after row of blossoms.

I think of Granddaddy in a dark, pin-striped gabardine suit. Even at breakfast he wore a suit. After breakfast he'd sit on the front porch in one of the high-backed rocking chairs, cross his legs, and smoke his pipe. After a while Daddy would come out of the house and ask, "Are you ready to go to work, Daddy?" Granddaddy would get up and go with him, though he hadn't worked in years.

Mostly I remember Granddaddy, still dressed in his pajamas, on mornings when I went to his room to play with him. I always gave him the baby doll whose glass eyes shut with a clanking sound and whose wooden head was covered with brown, carved curls. I pretended to give him the baby doll because she was best, but the real reason was that I loved my brown bear more.

Our play together was a daily ritual. Mother told me that Granddaddy was "a nice old man, but senile." Lucille Williams, the African American woman who worked for my family from the time I was three months old, called him a "friendly old fellow." "His mind had been out of order for so long," she told me several years ago, "that they treated him like a little child." Whatever the condition of Granddaddy's mind, his heart and mine were of one accord in the early morning when the baby doll and the brown bear played together among the rumpled bedclothes.

Then one morning, when I was three years and nine months old, Granddaddy wasn't in his room waiting for me. His bed had been stripped down to the mattress, and the smell of him was hardly there at all. Baby doll and brown bear dangled useless from my hands.

Later Mother held me in her arms in the living room as she stood over Granddaddy's casket. Granddaddy looked odd and artificial, with his lips painted, rouge on his cheeks, and his mouth stitched into an expression I'd never seen before. Daddy had been mostly absent from my early childhood, and Mother had been distracted and distant. Only Granddaddy had been warm and welcoming, and he'd died and hadn't taken me with him. More than half of my world was gone.

"You shouldn't show him to her," Daddy wailed to Mother. Daddy sat in a straight chair by the secretary, pressing his bald head hard against its dark wood, sobbing. When Mother put me down on the floor, I ran out of the living room and out the back door. Just across the fence, my friend June was playing in her yard. "June!" I called. "June! I have a dead Granddaddy in the living room!"

Lucille came and stood at the back-door screen. She'd mistaken my announcement to June as bragging, not the hysteria it was.

"Shame on you, Margaret Richter!" she yelled. "Shame on you!"

I fastened my eyes on the pecan grove, while I felt my heart heavy in my chest and mockingbirds called from the trees.

Chapter Two

I

1939

NOW WE WERE LEAVING THE OLD HOME PLACE. FOR MONTHS ON Sundays Daddy had taken us two blocks up the street to the new house to see the progress the builders had made that week. "Finest oak flooring money can buy," he'd boom proudly as we walked through the rooms that weren't rooms at all but spaces divided by beams. I always walked in a daze trying to imagine that place, with its sawdust and nails, as home. But I couldn't. It didn't matter. With Granddaddy gone, home itself wasn't home anymore.

Despite my grief, the day we moved up the street to the new house I was excited. Men came and went, hauling pieces of furniture and boxes out of the house. The front yard was filled with bureaus and dressers and chairs stacked one atop the other. Mirrors leaned against the palm trees. Boxes of dishes, pots and pans, clothes, books, photographs, canned food, bags of flour, cornmeal, and sugar stood among the shrubs.

Mother and Daddy's bed, stripped of its linen, stood in the middle of the walkway. Wildly excited and nervous, I climbed up onto the bed and began to jump on the bare mattress. Granddaddy was dead and buried in the cemetery across the road from the pickle plant. A speeding car had smashed my dog Spot. And we were leaving the fig tree and my rope swing forever. But the higher I jumped, the more my sadness was replaced by the joy of pure motion. Higher and higher I jumped, giddy with a head full of blue sky and furniture. A bus pulled away from the station across the street. A dog barked. The town clock rang out the hour. Still I jumped.

Then Mother came racing out the door, screaming, "Stop! Stop that, Margaret! Stop!"

I stopped.

Even so, my feeling of freedom was so great that nothing could diminish its vivid memory. For those few minutes I spent jumping on Mother and Daddy's bed I was utterly joyous.

II

I was filled with wonder when I looked into the shoe box of tiny pine trees that Mother held in her hands. They were a whole miniature forest.

The yard of the new house was broad and deep. To one side of the backyard were four pecan trees. An old oak stood near the back door. Thick wisteria vines hung from its branches, their blossoms lush and abundant. Except for the pecan trees and the oak, the yard spread its two acres flat and blank without another tree to catch the sunlight or create patches of welcome shade.

Sometime after I was four Mother planted other trees—the maple near the front porch, the mimosa with its pink puffs and tiny leaves that folded together at evening like praying hands, Japanese magnolias, dogwood along the sidewalk, and a crab apple and a pear tree out back. Though I watched her plant many of them, it was watching her plant the shoe-box forest of pines that most filled me with wonder.

Mother set the box down on the grass and beside it dug a hole with her spade, chopping and chopping until the dirt was loose and soft enough to receive the tender roots that she pushed into it. Then she patted the dirt around the little tree with her hands and watered the earth with drizzle from the hose that she dragged around from where it lay coiled under the faucet. The tree looked small and vulnerable—not like a tree at all, just a small sprig of pine in the grass. "Are you sure this is going to grow into a real tree?" I asked.

"It will grow into a tree as tall as the house and taller," Mother assured me. Then she carried the box to another spot, dug a hole, and planted another tree. She repeated the process all over the front and long side yard while I followed her, dragging the drizzling hose and its long extensions.

I couldn't imagine the long-leafed pines they would grow into, tall and glorious, yielding enormous pinecones that were used to start the Christmas fires in the living room fireplace, or how many pine needles would be shed each year to be raked into the driveway to make it a carpet of golden brown. I don't remember being aware of when the trees changed from looking like twigs and began to look like trees, or when I began to look up and not down at them. I don't remember when I looked out at the yard and realized that we lived in a grove of pines. What I do remember is that walking around the yard with Mother, watching her plant the trees, taking them one by one from the shoe-box forest, was one of the happiest, most thrilling experiences of my childhood.

III

"Hold him up and look at me," Mother said, backing me up against one side of the new house. She stood my brother Wyman—I've always called him Bubba—in front of me. I caught hold of his hands.

"Be still," Mother said, bending her head over her Kodak box camera.

The sun hurt my eyes.

"Be still, I said!"

Bubba squirmed his determined sweaty hands free from my grip and toppled to the grass.

"I told you to hold him up!" Mother screamed.

"I didn't mean to let him fall, Mama," I pleaded. "I didn't mean to."

"I told you!"

"Mama!" I cried. But there was no way for me to reach my mother through her fury.

Bubba was special, even with his earaches and his bawling. Though I was three years and eight months old when he was born, I still remember how proud Mother was of him. She would get all dressed up afternoons and push him in the wicker baby carriage back and forth in front of the house for everyone to see. One day I sat at my rolltop desk and drew a picture of Mother pushing Bubba in the baby carriage. I worked a long time on the drawing, bearing down hard with my pencil.

When I went out to the sidewalk to show it to her, she didn't even notice me. I had to pull at her skirt to make her look down. "Mama, I've done a drawing for you." She glanced at my picture and said, "That's nice," in a tone of dismissal. Then she went back to pushing Bubba's carriage. It was around this time that I stopped saying "Mama" and began to say "Mother" instead.

IV
1944

Bing Crosby sang "White Christmas" on the Stromberg-Carlson radio that stood in the living room by the love seat. The whole house was filled with the aroma of turkey and dressing baking in the oven, fresh cranberries bubbling in the pot, yeast rolls rising on the stove. Bubba and I sat on the living room carpet watching his new electric train running around its track, the engine hooting and hooting. I felt sick with envy. I could hardly bear to look at the handsome engine with its fine wheels turning, smoke puffing out of the smokestack.

I wanted an electric train of my own. I wanted to feel the cool metal of the engine in my hands. I wanted to touch each detail of window, door, step, and wheel with my fingers. I wanted to fit the sections of track together to create my own loops and curves. I wanted to bring my train to life by switching the switch on the transformer. I watched, furious with wonder, as Bubba fumbled with the mysterious wires that sparked and sputtered.

Bing Crosby crooned as the train turned a curve. His words mixed with the hooting of the train and with my horrible feeling of shame; girls were not supposed to want electric trains. Girls were supposed to want tea sets, dolls, play kitchens, and stuffed animals. Wanting an electric train was just one more indication that something was wrong with me, that I was terribly flawed.

The Atlanta Journal crackled in Daddy's hands as he sat reading in the wingback chair by the fireplace. The fire crackled too, but inside I felt cold. I looked across the room at the bride doll abandoned under the Christmas tree, along with its wrinkled wrapping paper and tangles of bright ribbons. The doll was terribly expensive. I'd seen her price tag in Rich's, the big department store in Atlanta that we went to around Christmastime. I knew that Mother had made some sacrifice to buy such an expensive doll for me. The doll had a hole in her head for each hair—dishwater blond, hair the same color as mine—and pale blue eye shadow delicately suggested on her eyelids. Her full lips were painted a warm rose color. She was elegant and beautiful, and I hated her. I hated her most because I was supposed to love her.

"She's very beautiful," I said to Mother. She was a large, stiff wooden doll, and when I tried to bend her straight legs to make her sit down, I pushed too hard and she cracked from one end of her torso to the other. Thankfully, her body stayed in one piece so that the crack was covered by her white wedding dress. Mother wouldn't know.

The train continued tooting and puffing. Bubba added his own sounds to those of the train as it entered a long tree-covered tunnel and came back out again.

Bing Crosby continued his crooning.

I walked to my room and got my notebook and pen. Then I went back to the living room, curled up on the love seat, and wrapped the afghan around me. I was lonely for Miss Brown, my fourth-grade teacher. I thought about how just before Christmas, her boyfriend came home from fighting the Germans overseas and walked right into the principal's office and asked to see her. The principal sent a fifth-grader to our classroom to give Miss Brown the message that her boyfriend was there.

She rushed from the room, wordless, her hands trembling. I imagined her in his arms, oblivious to the principal and his secretary, Miss Muriel Adams, with her tight, thin features and her bony fingers tapping and tapping at the typewriter keys.

I tightened the afghan around my shoulders. "I love you Miss Brown," I wrote on the first line in my best penmanship. "I love you Miss Brown," I wrote again. My breathing relaxed. "I love you Miss Brown," I wrote again, and no longer felt cold. "I love you Miss Brown," I wrote until I reached the bottom of the page, then turned the paper over and continued writing the same words until the paper was filled. I imagined so hard that it was almost as if I were there, in the principal's office, hugging them both and being hugged back. I felt like we were in a circle of love, complete and safe.

"Margaret, you can set the table now."

Mother's words shattered my bliss. My face flushed with shame. I wasn't certain why, but I knew that if Mother read what I'd written, my words would upset her. "Just a minute, Mother."

I ripped the paper out of my book, crushed it, and threw it into the fire.

I went to the dining room, lifted the heavy plates from the china cabinet, and set them at their places on the special white linen table-cloth. Then I put the silver beside each plate. The handles of the ster-

ling silverware were covered with tiny flowers of all sorts like miniature gardens.

I loved the table setting and the story of how Daddy had seen a
dining table all set up in a window at Rich's. He'd liked it so much
he'd just marched into the store and bought everything—tablecloth,
napkins, plates, bowls, cups and saucers, salad and dessert plates,
serving bowls, silver, and glasses—just as he'd seen it in the department store's window. He brought the whole thing home to Mother.
From that time on, this replica of Rich's window was on our dining
table every Christmas, Thanksgiving, and Easter, and every other
special-occasion dinner.

Mother brought the turkey in and set it on the table, its plump
thighs high in the air, breast browned with butter, juices leaking out
through the holes where she'd punctured the skin to test its doneness.
The turkey, as always, lay on the enormous ironstone platter that had
belonged to Daddy's mother, and had held all the Thanksgiving and
Christmas turkeys of my childhood. The platter had a long, dark
crack down its middle, a flaw like the flaw I felt in myself.

V

I don't know what ruined me. I thought about it as I walked home
from fourth grade alone. I thought about it on my way to school as
I walked past the sandspur patch where Marty the bully crouched,
waiting to fling sandspurs at me. Sometimes they left bloody
scratches on my legs. Sometimes they buried their sharp points in my
socks and hems. It hurt my fingers to pull them out.

I walked, thinking about how I had to hide my flaws from
Mother. She'd go crazy if she found out about them. Mother always
talked about going crazy, going to pieces. "Just to pieces," she would
scream, hitting her head with her fists.

I thought about how ruined I was as I walked past Uncle Frank's house. Sometimes he forced me to stand on the sofa in his sunroom and rub his bald head. "If you stop, wild horses in the basement will trample you," he threatened. I thought the sound of the wild horses was really the sound of the fire rumbling in the furnace. But what if I was wrong, what if it was really the hooves of horses, restless and wild to escape? I hated rubbing Uncle Frank's head. Aunt Mary was never around when he asked me to do this. She was in the kitchen, cooking, or down at the creek, fishing. Aunt Mary loved to fish.

Sometimes Uncle Frank asked me to spend the night at his house. He always let me sleep in his daughter Roberta's room. It was all plush and satin, lavender, white, and purple. Even the toilet, tub, and washbasin in her bathroom were lavender. She was married and gone now. Daddy told me that Uncle Frank was terribly upset that Roberta had married a man almost as old as Uncle Frank himself. Daddy said the man owned a nightclub, someplace in Florida. Now there was only a photograph hanging over the bed, a close-up of her head. She was lying on a rug with her long hair spread around her. She was movie-star glamorous like Lauren Bacall. I wished I was beautiful like Roberta.

I loved being in her room. It felt like being in Hollywood. But even sleeping in Roberta's room, I didn't really like to spend the night at Uncle Frank's. Only I felt guilty if I didn't. He was Daddy's brother, and Daddy loved him more than anything. Uncle Frank wore pajamas with stripes—white stripes and stripes the color of Welch's grape juice. "Come here and sit on the bed with me," he'd say. "Rub my head."

I walked past the Dunns' house, with its strange tropical fruit tree that looked like a palm tree. Long woodlike things grew from it that looked like round-bottomed canoes stuck face-to-face. When the fruit was ripe the canoes burst apart; the orange fruit inside was about the size of a kumquat. Mr. and Mrs. Dunn were old, white-haired, and kind. They liked children and told me that I could come into their yard any time and eat the fruit. Sometimes I did, but not often. The fruit had a strange taste and texture, but I loved sucking on its smooth black seeds, rolling them over and over with my tongue.

Once Roberta's younger sister, Marybell, caught me walking along the sidewalk just past the Dunns' house. I was making up a play and saying all the parts aloud. I was so caught up in being those characters that I didn't realize I was talking aloud, or how loud I was talking. I felt like dying when I saw Marybell on her horse, riding beside me, listening to every word I was saying. I'd not even heard the footsteps of her horse, an old white horse retired from Barnum & Bailey's Circus, a horse with one pink eye and the other one blind. I didn't want Marybell to know that I saw her. That would just make me feel worse. I clamped my mouth shut and walked on, looking straight ahead, trying hard to forget what had just happened.

I remember the exposed roots of the oak tree that grew beside the dirt sidewalk where Mother pushed Bubba up and down in his carriage when he was a baby. I remember the fig tree from which my rope swing hung at The Old Home Place. I remember sunlight through the fig leaves. I remember the first time I saw my cousin Hugh's butterfly collection—all those beautiful butterflies, dead, their exquisite wings forever pinned down in that box.

But try as I do, I can't remember what caused me the dreadful shame I felt. Maybe it's just such a part of me now that I don't need to remember what caused it any more than I need to remember that I have arms, legs, and feet.

VI

My cousin Margaret, and her brothers, sisters, and parents, lived with her grandmother just down the street from us. Aunt Wyche, Margaret's grandmother and my great-aunt, had an enormous two-story Greek revival house with tall white columns that rose magnificently just like those on Tara in *Gone with the Wind*. The yard was broad and had few flowers, only shrubs. Margaret and I played with our dolls on the grass in the cool shade of the old oak tree near the house. She had a Scarlett O'Hara doll with pale skin, a long yellow dress, pantaloons, and lips that Margaret had painted red with nail polish.

Except for the bride doll that I hated, all of my dolls were boys. I had Hans, the Dutch boy with blond hair, blue pants, and real wooden shoes. There was Robin Hood, with his green tunic and a feather in his cap. Pedro, my Mexican doll, had a real straw sombrero and leather sandals. He was beautifully made, with stitching to define each toe and finger in the fabric of his dark skin. His body was stuffed with sawdust, his hair was black fuzz. A bright pink circle was painted on each cheek, and a cigar was stuffed in his open mouth.

Margaret loved her Scarlett O'Hara doll.

The role of Rhett Butler and those of the other leading men in our plays were reserved—comic as it might seem—for the Raggedy Andy doll Mother had sewn for me. His body was made from unbleached muslin, and he wore the bright blue pants and red-checkered shirt as illustrated in the series of Raggedy Andy and Raggedy Ann books. Mother embroidered his features by hand.

Looking back, I believe I chose to play with him most often in the many romantic stories that Margaret and I made up because he felt soft to touch, and because he, more than any other doll, felt most like a part of me. I'd had him since I was very young. He slept with me every night, my arms hugging him tightly to my chest, his coarse wool curls against my face. He shared my dreams and was with me much of the day. He was the constant observer, his wide unblinking eyes staring at everything that went on in the family, and at night staring out into the darkness.

"Rhett," Scarlett of the nail-polish-painted lips said with a sigh. "Oh, Rhett!"

"Scarlett!" exclaimed Rhett of the bright orange hair and embroidered face. Then he caressed Scarlett's smooth, pale face with his muslin, pawlike hand, and together they tumbled to the grass in a passionate embrace while cars passed slowly on North Broad Street.

VII

Bubba smashed the sharp edge of a small glass truck against the bridge of my nose. It was one of those glass trucks that you bought at the five-and-dime, filled with tiny colored candy balls. You turned the truck upside down, pried up the cardboard bottom, and ate the candy. Then you were left with a clear glass truck, or a car, a puppy, or a phone.

Blood spurted from the gash in my nose, but I didn't go running to tell Mother. I couldn't. I'd been teasing him unmercifully, telling him that the spirit of his sister had left my body, which was now inhabited by a wicked witch. I crooked my fingers like claws at him and cackled.

Bubba wasn't buying my witch act at all. Maybe I was a poor actress, or maybe he was too smart to believe it. Maybe he was too old to be as gullible as I'd been when Mother had done the same thing to me. I'd not been more than a year and a half old when I began to learn the Mother Goose nursery rhymes by heart. Mother was so proud. She told me how she would misquote lines so that I would correct her. A couple of years before her death in 1986 she brought up the nursery rhymes on the phone. It was then that she told me about how she used to change her voice, claiming that she'd left her body and that a wicked witch inhabited it. "You were such a smart little thing, I couldn't believe I could fool you like that," she said with what sounded like mild amusement as she remembered my fear and gullibility.

My mother had just told me something I'd had no memory of, but which I'd done to my brother. I felt sick. Even after nearly half a century, it was still just a joke to Mother. To me it was an example of harmful behavior that had been passed down through the generations. How many other damaging things had been done to me that I'd mindlessly reenacted on my brother and—later—my sons because Mother had taught me by her own actions when I was so young that I didn't remember? To even think about it hurt.

But the day Bubba slammed the truck against my nose I had no idea that it was Mother who'd taught me that teasing way of retaliation, for something I no longer remember. Maybe my disagreement with Bubba had to do with picking up toys. Often, enough building blocks to erect a small city lay scattered on the living room floor, along with battalions of plastic soldiers with their machine guns, rifles, and hand grenades clenched in their fists, the tin aircraft carriers that Daddy had brought from Macy's in New York City, and dozens and dozens of tiny plastic planes, almost obliterating the wool flowers woven into the carpet.

While Bubba and I were fighting, Mother was screaming that she didn't know what she'd done to deserve such children. Now she was sitting on her bed banging the back of her head against the wall, screaming, "I'm going crazy! I'm going crazy!"

I rushed to her room and stood in the doorway, watching. Remembering the scene now, I see that she looked like an enormous child having a temper tantrum, not unlike those that Bubba had when he beat his head on the floor as a toddler. But looking at Mother from the perspective of a child, I saw her as frighteningly fragile, while Bubba and I had the power to shatter her.

Maybe this time, I thought, *she is really going crazy.* As young as I was, I'd already been filled with horror stories of the state insane asylum in Milledgeville—bloodcurdling screams heard in the street, and inmates shouting scary things while pacing behind barred windows for passersby to see.

"I'm going crazy!" Mother screamed, beating her head on the wall. I felt like a lead weight was pressing against my heart and lungs, suffocating me with the fear that someone would take Mother away to Milledgeville, leaving us forever abandoned.

Finally she stopped banging her head and began to collect herself. But another attack could start at any moment. I persuaded Bubba to come with me to our bedroom, where I knelt down with him on the floor and prayed aloud to Jesus, asking him to please help Bubba and me to be good and not drive Mother crazy.

VIII
1945

ABSOLUTELY NO DIGGING FOR BURIED TREASURE. This message, painted on a board and nailed to a pine tree, was the first thing I looked for after Daddy turned off the Tallahassee highway onto the narrow dirt road that cut through the woods to Wakulla Springs. The sign was nailed to a live oak, followed by another sign, signs scattered through the woods. I looked at the sandy soil with renewed wonderment each time we went to Wakulla, where Bubba and I swam in the clear springs and the family had picnics in the woods near the water and ate ice cream at the soda fountain in the Lodge. We went often in the summer.

Daddy parked the car behind the Lodge, and Bubba and I went to the bathhouse and changed into our bathing suits. Then we walked down the path to the springs. In front of us, glass-bottomed boats for the Wakulla Springs Cruise and boats for the Jungle Cruise on the Wakulla River were tied up at the dock. Thick vine-filled woods grew on the other side of the springs. Alligators slept along the cypress-lined bank. I watched one slide into the water and swim slowly near the shore with only its snout and eyes above the surface.

Bubba and I turned to the left of the dock and walked down to the beach. Mother and Daddy were already sitting in low wooden chairs at the edge of the sand in the shade of trees hung heavy with Spanish moss. Baby Mercer was parked in his stroller beside Mother, squirming to get out. Mother picked him up, gave him his tin bucket and spade, and set him on the sand in front of her. Bubba and I spread our towels on the sand and then raced to poke our feet into the water that was always as cold as the coldest ice water imaginable.

Farther down the beach, enormous old cypress trees rose from the shallow water. Cypress knees erupted from the sand and water around the base of the trees. Farther down still stood the diving tower with its three levels. Neither Bubba nor I dared to jump from even the first level. At two he was too young, and at nine I was too afraid. Mostly we played in the water across from Mother and Daddy. Or, after our lips had turned blue from the icy water, we sat in the sun making sand castles.

When I swam, I swam back and forth in the shallow water where the bottom was sandy. Swimming out to the raft meant leaving the security of the sandy bottom and swimming over long grasses, which frightened me, for I couldn't see what might be swimming through them. Swimming anyplace where my feet even threatened to brush along the top of the grass made my heart pound.

This turned out to be our most wonderful day at Wakulla. Part of a Tarzan movie starring Johnny Weissmuller was being filmed there. And while we didn't see it being made, just knowing that someplace in the jungle a cast and crew were busy creating another Tarzan movie thrilled me. Wakulla was supposed to be someplace in Africa. The Wakulla, a relatively straight, narrow, and short river flowing from the springs to Saint Marks, Florida, was supposed to be the Congo.

We happened onto the living evidence of the movie being made on our way back to the Lodge. There, in the shade, was a newly erected pen made of logs. On its straw-covered floor two elephants stood swinging their trunks and swatting flies with their tails. Dust rose from their hides with each swat. Bubba and I followed as Mother pushed baby Mercer over to see the elephants. Their keeper, a thin, unshaven man, stood nearby with a small group of people clustered around him listening to him talk about the movie. I waited until the crowd left and there was just the man and my family. Then hesitantly I said: "Sir?"

"Yeah?" He looked at me, his friendly face bolstering my courage.

"Where are the other elephants?" I asked.

"What other elephants?"

"The other elephants for the movie."

"Ain't none." He spat a dark stream of chewing tobacco on the ground.

"But what about all those herds of elephants stampeding through the jungle?"

"Them things are done with camera tricks."

"Camera tricks?"

"Camera tricks."

He dug into one pants pocket, drew out a pocketknife, and opened it. With the blade he began to scrape at the dirt under his fingernails.

I swallowed my disappointment. But at least, I comforted myself, Johnny Weissmuller had ridden those very elephants who stood just feet from me, batting their lashes to chase away the gnats clustered around their runny eyes. Or at least he'd *probably* ridden one. I didn't dare ask the man if this was true. I'd accepted without a problem that Wakulla was supposed to be a jungle in Africa; Wakulla was mysterious and junglelike. But until my conversation with the elephant keeper, I hadn't been aware of the possibility of camera tricks to create the appearance of what wasn't there at all. It was too much for me to accept that the herds of elephants were like the magic tricks that a magician had performed one day in the school auditorium. I stood in the shade of a moss-covered live oak, looking at the elephants and feeling miserably betrayed. I didn't want to find out that Johnny Weissmuller hadn't even laid eyes on those elephants.

Daddy thanked the elephant keeper for his attention, and we walked on up the path toward the Lodge, a 1930s stucco Spanish-style building with arched windows and doors and a red tile roof. Mother, Daddy, and Mercer went into the Lodge, where swimsuits and bare feet weren't allowed. Bubba and I went back to the bathhouse and changed into shorts, T-shirts, and sandals before going to the soda shop for ice cream.

The Lodge always felt magical to me, with its long marble soda fountain, marble floors, and staircases. The large color photographs of cypress trees, water, and boats on opaque glass, bordered in deep frames and lit from behind, enchanted me. After having ice cream with our parents at the soda shop, Bubba and I headed to the lobby to play a game of checkers before going home. Usually there were at least a few well-dressed adults in the lobby sitting on sofas or chairs, smoking and talking softly, but that one late afternoon my brother and I were the only people there. It was more a sense of a presence than a sound that caused me to stop in midmove and look up from the checkerboard and across the broad expanse of floor. Just yards from where I sat, Johnny Weissmuller was striding silently across the lobby, bare feet on the marble floor, his tan and muscular body naked except for a loincloth.

It felt like time itself had taken note of his arrival and had slowed everything to the slowest slow motion possible. Johnny Weissmuller looked even taller and larger in person than he looked in the movies. With his dark hair and eyes, long legs, and large hands, he seemed to fill not only his body but the entire room. Here was the man who was inseparable in my mind from the Tarzan I adored, the Tarzan who roamed free in the jungle and called it home, who called to the wild animals as if they were his own family, who defied the rules of the Lodge and walked through the lobby barefooted and nearly naked, as if the Lodge was as much home to him as the jungle and the only rules were those that nature made. Here was the Tarzan who was not afraid to swim where the grasses grew long and thick; who was not afraid to dive down into and through the grasses themselves, willing and able to face whatever he might find there.

Then he turned and walked up the marble staircase and was gone.

Chapter Three

I

I DON'T REMEMBER WHAT I DID TO MAKE MY FRIEND JENNY ANGRY, BUT the way her eyes grew calm and cold under her thick, straight bangs told me that she'd come up with a way to get back at me. I braced myself.

"You're nothing but a Jew, Margaret Richter," she announced. "Nothing but a Jew."

Then she turned and walked briskly away. I stood watching her back as she disappeared down the street.

Nothing but a Jew?

I felt the August heat through the soles of my sandals. No one had ever told me we were Jews. Certainly we didn't go to a synagogue—we went to the First Baptist Church, with Jesus in the stained-glass windows and a steeple on top. Mother's side of the family was mostly Scotch-English, and Daddy's was German.

But were we German Jews?

Heat waves rose from the cars parked in front of Mizell's Drugs, where Jenny and I had just eaten ice cream cones. I walked home slowly. *What's wrong with being a Jew anyway?* I thought.

When Daddy came home from work, I asked him: "Daddy, are we Jews?"

He didn't answer, but he got that secretive, evasive look he got when I asked him something about his disowned sisters, Bessie and Kate. Then he turned his eyes from mine.

"Daddy, are we Jews?" I repeated pleadingly, but again he looked away. I knew there was no hope of an answer from him. For all his weakness, Daddy was iron-willed when it came to what he would and wouldn't talk about. But because of Jenny's statement and Daddy's refusal to confirm or deny it, I spent the remaining years of my childhood examining family behavior and information for evidence of the truth. I desperately wanted to know who I was.

A part of me decided that because he wouldn't say we weren't, we must be Jews. Also, though I heard Daddy talk about African Americans in racist language, I never heard him say a single negative word about a Jew. *Doesn't that tell me something?* I asked myself. Daddy was prejudiced against a lot of people: Yankees, Catholics, people he called "white trash," Gypsies, people who rented their houses, and the lawyer who said to him, "I'd have done it for the blackest nigger," when Daddy thanked him for a favor.

My conviction that our family had to be Jewish strengthened when Mr. Louie Steiman was turned down for membership in the country club in a nearby town and Daddy stopped work early and drove over there to support Mr. Steiman's appeal. Why would he have done that when he and Mr. Steiman were hardly friends? And country club membership was one of the last things to interest Daddy. His defending Mr. Steiman felt almost like a family affair, like the way he acted when he, Uncle Frank, and Aunt Bama would rush to one another's aid when the need arose. And what about the Yiddish words the three of them used with one another?

After Daddy's death I asked Mother the same question: "Mother, was Daddy's family Jewish?"

"I really don't know," she replied. "I remember people referring to your father's people as 'those rich Richter Jews,' but whether they said that because they had money or because they were Jews, I don't know. They certainly acted like Jews, the way they kept so to themselves."

My cousin Peyton, a college professor in the humanities, told me—it must have been the seventies by then—that old Dr. Walker in Cairo said on his deathbed that my father's family was Jewish. Peyton and I were eating lunch at the Lord Jeffery Inn in Amherst, Massachusetts. He'd come to visit me, and to deliver a lecture at one of the area colleges. I don't know what brought Dr. Walker to Peyton's mind, but whatever it was, there we were once again talking about our Southern family.

Many years later, when I asked Peyton about our conversation in the Lord Jeffery, he swore he'd never said anything about the family being Jews. Peyton was as adamant in his denial of our previous conversation as Daddy was in turning his eyes away when I asked him a question he didn't want to answer. The subject was forever closed. Closed for Daddy and Peyton, but it has never been closed for me.

When we were in our early sixties, I had a conversation with Jenny in which I asked her what she knew about my family being Jewish. She responded with surprise at the question, saying that she knew nothing at all about it. I didn't remind her of our childhood conversation. But after we talked, I sat a long time, remembering how burdensome the not knowing had been all my life. More than anything, my family felt weighed down by secrets—secrets about Daddy's sisters, secrets about Earnest Junior, and all the secrets Mother and Daddy discussed in their complex private language combining a few German words and Southern English, together with common words spelled at machine-gun rapidity, creating a code that I finally gave up trying to decipher.

When I was young, I desperately wanted the family to be Jewish. If the Richters were Jews, I reasoned, their behavior of clinging so closely together would have made sense to me, and would have made them seem heroic, or at least rational, rather than merely peculiar. Maybe being a Jew was the thing that made me feel so different from other children. The thought of having a clear reason outside myself for my feelings of alienation was comforting. And I didn't want to be a German like the Germans spreading their monstrous cruelty throughout much of Europe.

"*Heil Hitler,*" Uncle Frank would bark as my little brother did the goose step up and down his lawn. Uncle Frank applauded and laughed his loud, deep laugh, encouraging Bubba to perform that deadly prance across the grass. Then he would again show us his collection of enameled buttons with swastikas, and the Nazi flag he kept folded in a drawer. It was much more comfortable to think of us as being a family of Jews rather than a family of Nazis.

At the Zebulon Theater, watching *The March of Time* newsreels, I saw many of the atrocities the Nazis were perpetrating. In the woods someplace in Europe, a building burst into flames. The newscaster said the building was filled with the crippled and the insane. I remember his exact words. Later I saw corpses of Jews bulldozed into a mass grave, and how they tumbled on top of one another. I'd have covered my eyes with my hands, but it was too late. I'd already taken the images into my soul. All those naked bodies knocking against one another. What if they'd been people from my own life? My timid and fearful father. My modest mother. Miss Sarah with her cats and kittens. The postman with his friendly face. The iceman. That forced nakedness, that unasked-for intimacy of bodies, that ghastly intrusion of flesh against flesh, bone against bone.

I could hardly breathe in the still air of the picture show. The EXIT sign glowed red in the front of the room, but there was no exit from what I'd just seen. Without their stories, clothes, or names, these people would nevertheless always be a part of my life. There was no way I could get them out of my memory.

No, I didn't want to be related to the Nazis.

II

It was difficult and confusing to be a Richter. But it was the Richter side of the family I identified with, more than my mother's family. They were the misfits in the community, echoing my own feeling of not belonging. Daddy's family also represented the arts to me. I had a cousin who Peyton said wrote novels, and both Daddy and Aunt Bama played the piano. Peyton wrote short stories, though he never tried to get them published. He was also artistic and made wonderful puppets and models of sailing ships. His sister Roberta painted portraits, while his sister Marybell was an actress and his older brother, Ashton, was a photographer.

Daddy wrote music and did pencil drawings. As a small child I watched with fascination while he drew profile after profile on pieces of typing paper. When I was older, I began to copy him and draw profiles, as he had, though not with his skill and confidence. Throughout grade school I spent many hours drawing those faces while making up stories to go with them. When I was drawing, I could escape everything I didn't want to see or feel. When I was drawing, I was suspended in a state of timeless contentment.

Mother and her family represented respectability, sociability, class, manners, law, and education. Her father had been a lawyer and state treasurer. Mother's sister Sarah taught high school English and was married to a lawyer who practiced with their father and later became the county judge. Her sister Ina was a teacher married to a minister who was president of a small Baptist college. And Curtis, unmarried until middle-aged, was a math professor. Mother herself taught high school Latin before her marriage.

Then there was my great-uncle Gerard Christopher, a retired Baptist preacher who, when visiting from a nearby town, would stand and pray in our church for an unbearably long time. His tall, imposing frame towered over the Sunday-morning congregation, while church members shuffled in the pews and fanned themselves with paper fans with pictures of Jesus on one side and advertisements for the funeral homes on the other. Mother's family was conventional and respected, a solid part of the system. They clearly belonged. The Richters were a puzzle, but I was far more interested in them.

The Richter who captured my imagination most was my great-grandfather, who immigrated to this country from Germany. I remember a few family stories about him: that in his old age, after his first wife died, he married a woman who'd advertised in a newspaper for a husband, and that one of his wives made soap by boiling rats. I don't know how many wives he had. I do know that he fought in the Mexican-American War, participating in the bloody conquest of Veracruz in 1847; and that he served in the Confederacy during the Civil War.

Along with the question of whether or not he was a Jew, there was one other story that gave him a prominent place in the whole of my life. It was a short human-interest story from a Baltimore newspaper, brittle and yellowed with age. I found the newspaper in the bottom drawer of Mother's mahogany secretary that stood by the front door in the living room. The article told the story of how my great-grandfather had missed his ship to America because his baggage had failed to arrive at the dock on time. The ship, *Johannes*, left without him. It and its three hundred or more passengers were never heard of again. He then booked passage on the *Copernicus* and landed safely in Baltimore after a stormy crossing of fifty-one days. Three hundred people or more had drowned in a stormy sea, while my great-grandfather had lived to fulfill his dreams in America. I read and reread the story, trying each time to take in the truth of it: I owed my very existence to the late arrival of my great-grandfather's luggage.

It seemed to me that whole generations of human beings must be alive because of some seemingly insignificant event or circumstance. Nothing, however small, could ever be dismissed as trivial. I thought of the many people who would not have lived had my great-grandfather drowned. I imagined the many other people who would have never felt the effects of his presence on this earth, or my presence, and that of my children. The connections seemed endless.

But was my great-grandfather a Jew? Over the years I've found nothing to prove it. But after all the years of focusing on my heritage, a part of me will forever be a Jew, imagined, real, or borrowed.

III
NOVEMBER 25, 1945

I slept through everything.

I woke to find Daddy sitting on the edge of my bed, dressed in a dark suit and tie. His hands were clasped between his knees, and his head was bowed. His eyes were red and swollen, and as he began to talk, tears streamed down his face.

Uncle Frank was dead.

A fire had started in his basement and climbed the stairs to the kitchen, just like the stampeding horses he'd always threatened would climb the stairs and trample me to death if I stopped rubbing his bald head. *The horses got Uncle Frank instead of me,* I thought, then tried to take back the thought that came with its flood of guilt. Hadn't he invited me to spend that very night at his house? Hadn't I told him no? Now I was alive while Uncle Frank was dead.

The night of the fire Aunt Mary had gone to Albany to pick up a new suit for him. She'd backed her Buick out of their driveway and headed north while the furnace rumbled and the flames even then were getting ready to break free, those thunderous horses, their wide nostrils snorting fire and smoke, hooves blazing.

I was dimly aware of people talking in the living room, wandering up and down the hall, all with hushed voices. It was as if the house had become a library or a church.

"That Frank's dead is no excuse to not eat a good breakfast," Mother announced as she set a plate of bacon and eggs and grits in front of Daddy at the breakfast table.

Mother's command to Daddy jerked me out of my struggle with guilt to focus my attention on him. I could hardly bear what I saw. All of the light had drained from his eyes. Without a word, he picked up his fork and began to eat one mouthful after another, slowly chewing each bite, his movements mechanical, like those of a child with his spirit broken to silent obedience. Looking at him, I knew with painful certainty that much of Daddy had died along with Uncle Frank.

Daddy would no longer take Uncle Frank to the special hospital where he went when his drinking got especially bad. He would no longer go and bring him home after he had—as Daddy called it— "dried out." Uncle Frank had been outgoing, boisterous, and profane. Daddy was hesitant, timid, and private. Both men drove a hard bargain in business. Each clung to the other as if an invisible cord joined them from one incomplete heart to the other. Now Daddy was left with half his life source gone. Though it took twenty-two years for him to follow his brother to the grave, those years were lived with chronic depression, the onset and progression of both diabetes and heart disease, the downfall of a once prosperous business, loss of confidence, loss of self. "Only a shell of a man," he would mutter. "I'm only a shell of a man."

He slumped in the wingback chair in the living room, fists crammed hard against his eyes.

"Pull yourself together, Wyman," Mother said to him. "Here come the Maxwells."

Aunt Bama went to open the door. More people crowded into the house, but no one with whom I felt comfortable. I wandered among them feeling lost and alone. Daddy didn't get up to greet anyone but sat silently. Aunt Bama pulled a chair over next to him, while he stared at the flowers in the rug.

A young black man named Sam Butler was killed in the fire along with Uncle Frank. Sam had worked for Daddy and Uncle Frank for as long as I could remember. The firemen found him lying dead at Uncle Frank's bedroom door, garden hose clutched in his hand. The water was still running.

Sam's mother was an old woman who still worked sometimes for Aunt Mary, and babysat for Bubba, Mercer, and me on those rare occasions when Mother and Daddy went out alone to the picture show. We called her Aunt Rossey, as we'd been taught to do. She had gnarled fingers; her hands were often twisted around the worn stick with which she stirred white people's laundry over the cauldron in her dirt yard, scraps of wood and coal burning under her large black wash pot. Her small, unpainted shack was perched on stacks of brick at its four corners. Her walls were papered with pages of old magazines discarded by her white employers, and calendars advertising the black funeral home, with a different picture of the fair-skinned, blue-eyed Jesus for each month of the year.

Aunt Rossey lived in the black neighborhood behind the houses of white people on North Broad Street. The black people's shanties were separated from the white people's houses by a narrow dirt alley and a tall fence, concealed on the white people's side by a wall of thick bamboo that was home to starlings and rattlesnakes.

Sam had died a hero, leaving Aunt Rossey alone to bring in the wood and coal for the fireplace in winter, with nobody to sit at the kitchen table with her, eating turnip greens, black-eyed peas, ham hocks, and corn bread dunked in buttermilk. Sam had died and Uncle Frank had died, but our two families were separated in their grieving by segregation that even then stood thick as the fence and bamboo wall that divided the two neighborhoods. I wondered if Sam would want any white angels to bring him up to heaven. Maybe he would have wanted only black angels. In my imagination I saw a group of black angels making a bed for Sam with intertwined hands and arms. I saw Sam's head resting on an angel's chest, his big bare feet dangling, drifting through the clouds.

Uncle Frank and Aunt Mary's house was so badly damaged from the fire that his body had to lie in the house of his older son, Ashton, for the calling hours. The open coffin stood against the blank north wall of the living room, wreaths and crosses of funeral flowers on wire frames at its head and foot. The room was dimly lit and simply furnished. It had none of the affluence of Uncle Frank's living room, with its baby grand piano, plush carpeting, heavy, floor-length drapes, and art deco lamps and end tables. I'd spent many agonized times in Uncle Frank's living room standing in the middle of the carpet while he commanded me to turn around and around so some relative or other could see how much I'd grown since their last visit. "Look at her!" he'd boom. "Just look at her!"

But Uncle Frank was dead.

His daughter Roberta came up from Florida for the funeral. She was wearing a slim black dress and spike-heeled black shoes. When she walked through the door her presence filled the room. The crowd shifted as she made her way to the open casket. Leaning over her father's corpse, her long hair falling around her face, she carefully drew the stem of a red rosebud through the buttonhole in his coat lapel. Then—with a piercing howl of grief—she threw herself over Uncle Frank's body and sobbed into his new blue serge suit.

IV
1945

I will never forget the first time I walked up the walkway to the barn-red house on South Hansell Street in Thomasville, Georgia, to see Gem Vaughn Forbes. Peyton had taken art lessons with her when he was a young boy. Now I was hoping that I, too, would become her student. My mother drove me to the nearby town and parked in front of the house while I walked up the front steps, rang the doorbell, and stood, waiting. I was ten years old, a serious child who wanted more than anything to become an artist.

A face appeared beyond the glass pane of the door. Then the door itself opened and a tall woman with white hair looked down at me. Her posture was upright, regal, her voice formal, restrained. "Yes?"

She waited.

"I'm here about painting lessons," I said.

"Then you want to talk with Mrs. Forbes. I'm Mrs. Clemons. Go around the side of the house by the porch and through the garden. You'll find Mrs. Forbes in the barn."

I thanked her and walked around the house. I walked through the garden, toward the barn, from which the sound of hammer on nail came ringing and ringing.

The barn door stood open.

"Mrs. Forbes?" I asked, looking at the old woman bent over a small bench. Mrs. Forbes looked up, a hammer in her hand, and smiled.

"My name is Margaret Richter," I said. "I'm here about taking painting lessons from you."

She laid the hammer on the ground beside the bench and walked to where I stood in the splash of sun that spilled through the trees. Like Mrs. Clemons, Mrs. Forbes had white hair. But where Mrs. Clemons was tall, Mrs. Forbes wasn't much taller than a large child. Smiling as she walked toward me, she was all effervescence and light. Her blue eyes were bright and welcoming. "I'm delighted to meet you. I was just repairing a bench. Come with me to the house."

Together we walked through the garden. A fat robin pecked in the coarse grass; a mockingbird called from an ancient oak. "I call my garden Merrie Garden," she said, the grass bouncing back after each brisk step she took. The name sounded like that of a storybook garden filled with elves and fairies. No one I'd ever known before would have given a garden such a name.

We climbed the steps to the porch. Wisteria vines twisted themselves around the columns supporting the porch roof. Among the light-filled leaves and heavy masses of lavender blossoms, bees droned and buzzed. "This is a wonderful place to live," she said with a tone of such deep satisfaction that she could have been the prime creator looking around at her creation and pronouncing it good.

Mrs. Forbes twisted the knob of one of the French doors. "Come in," she instructed, opening the door and standing beside it until I entered the room. Then she closed the door and followed me in. Early-afternoon light flooded the room.

She gestured toward a daybed in one corner. It was covered with a brown throw. Pillows of many different fabrics and colors were piled haphazardly along its back. I walked across the worn Oriental rug and sat down. The bed was so deep that my back didn't reach the pillows at all. I squirmed awkwardly. "Make yourself comfortable," she said, sitting in the straight chair at a small desk. "Pile the pillows behind you."

I did. Then I looked around the room. It was very long and narrow. The window at the far end faced Paradise Park. In front of the window stood a formal sofa in a faded rose color, and a table and lamp. In the corner beside the sofa stood an old upright piano. In front of the sofa, the carpet had been worn thin. A pathway separated the formal sofa and the piano from the more casual and larger portion of the room where several chairs, the daybed, and a desk clustered together. The window at that end of the room opened to Merrie Gardens. It was at a small desk beside this window that Mrs. Forbes sat, facing me.

While Mother waited in the car, Mrs. Forbes and I made arrangements for me to begin art lessons the following Saturday afternoon. I was impressed that her walls were hung with real paintings and not reproductions, like the branch of magnolia on brush-textured cardboard that hung in our living room. I was especially enchanted with a figurine on Mrs. Forbes's mantelpiece. It was a hand-painted china cart with blossoms on it in soft, warm colors pulled by a little boy with curly blond hair and pink cheeks, his head turned toward me and thrown back in a gesture of gentle and joyful abandon.

By the time I knew her, Mrs. Forbes had long since given up the kindergarten that she taught in her home for so many years. Now only a few older children came to her for art lessons, and I knew only a couple of those who occasionally joined me. Mostly I remember being there alone with Mrs. Forbes.

Every Saturday afternoon I sat at the small desk in her sitting room or at one of the tables on her porch and drew and painted a still life of fruits or vegetables that she'd set up for me, or, when she was teaching me about perspective, stacks of books, cups, and saucers. Or I laboriously copied one of the many pictures that she'd clipped from magazines for students to choose from.

I painted, and she talked. She talked about attending the Chicago Institute of Art, and how once her instructor in the figure-drawing class reprimanded her for working so long on the face of the model. "This is a figure-drawing class," he'd boomed loudly enough for everyone to hear. "Not portraiture!" I tried to imagine her as a young woman in a real art school, red-faced with embarrassment at being publicly chastised, but I couldn't see her as anything other than confident. Mrs. Forbes, I thought, would have held her ground wherever she was. And she went more places than I'd ever thought of going. She talked about her teaching at the Sac and Fox Agency of the United States Indian Service and about her trip to England to see the coronation of King George IV.

She had a drawer full of poems and stories she'd written in response to her experiences, and she would sometimes read stories to me about Byfleet Manor in England, about Wapemac, the Indian boy who didn't want his braid cut off, or Wishewah, the little Indian girl grieving for her mother. Or she would read "Frowsy Old Grumble" or another of her poems. I was especially intrigued by her poem "Fireplace Imps," with all of its crackling, sizzling, spitting, and spouting. It fed my own fascination with fire and my love of sitting in front of the fireplace in my parents' bedroom, imagining a world in the shapes and colors of the hot coals and flames. But the poems' references to "grown-ups to tea" and the use of words like "wee bit" and "'twas" made them feel like something left over from another century. For the duration of the listening, I could be a contented child in some fairy-tale world or a simple, happy child, and not the child I really was.

The child I really was was troubled, but I told no one what I perceived to be the source of my trouble. I felt too frightened of what I thought and too ashamed of the solution that had erupted unbidden in my mind. When I was eight years old, and hanging upside down from the trapeze on the swing set in our backyard, I first realized the problem consciously enough to put words to it.

The swing set stood near an old oak tree that was half-dead and covered by wisteria vines heavy with blossoms. From where I hung I could see the wisteria on my left, while in front of me and across the coarse grass stood a large clump of banana trees. I loved the long, broad banana leaves and the twisted vines of the wisteria. More than anything else in the yard they reminded me of the jungle.

I was thinking about the jungle that day I'd been to a Tarzan movie at the Zebulon picture show. For nearly an hour and a half I'd sat in the dark theater, eating a king-sized Baby Ruth candy bar and a bag of buttered popcorn, while watching Tarzan swing from vine to vine through the jungle from one adventure to another. After sitting in the dark for so long, I had to squint at the blaze of the late-afternoon sun when I left the theater. It often took me the two blocks of my walk home before my eyes forgot the dark and got used to daylight again. For those two blocks that day I thought about Tarzan.

Home, I opened the front screen door, calling, "Mama!"

For years I'd called my mother "Mother," except when I was upset and in need of comfort.

I called again: "Mama!"

No answer.

I walked across the living room, into the hall, and to my parents' bedroom, where I stood at the open doorway looking in. Mother was asleep on top of the bedspread. Her glasses had slipped halfway down her nose, and one of her women's magazines—*Good Housekeeping, Ladies' Home Journal,* or *Redbook*—lay open and spread across her belly.

The hall behind me was dark, and the house felt large and empty with her asleep. I wanted her to wake up. I watched her belly rise and fall with each breath. The electric fan at the foot of the bed ruffled the pages of the magazine a little, but my mother didn't stir. Not daring to wake her, I hoped that my steady stare would make her open her eyes and look at me, but it didn't.

After a while I turned away and walked down the hall. I wished Bubba was home, but his room was empty. I went to my room, kicked off my shoes, took my dress off, and put on a pair of shorts and a T-shirt. Then I went out the back door to the swing set, where for a long time I hung upside down from the trapeze, thinking of Tarzan.

In the movie, Johnny Weissmuller played Tarzan. I don't remember the name of the actress who played his mate, Jane. Jane didn't matter. Tarzan was the one who rode the elephant at the head of the herd; he was the one who wrestled alligators and protected Jane from the charging rhinoceros. I wanted to be like Tarzan, not like Jane, leaping helplessly from the tree limbs into his strong arms, or fixing the food and waiting for him to come back from another adventure.

It wasn't just Jane I didn't like. It was suddenly and painfully apparent that I didn't like being a girl who would grow into a woman. I thought of Mother struggling into her girdle on a hot day, sweat already trickling down between her breasts when she'd hardly dried herself from her bath. I'd watched her straining to pull the sides of the corset together over her flesh, fastening the hooks and eyes one by one, then tugging the zipper closed with short, hard jerks.

I began to swing back and forth on the trapeze. I let my arms hang limp from my shoulders, fingertips touching the dirt where the grass had worn away. *Tarzan, King of the Jungle.* To be at home in all that wildness; to not be bound by rules and expectations. A large grasshopper hopped through the grass just beyond my reach. Then I heard the rush of water running in the kitchen sink. Mother was up, cooking supper.

Some days Mother didn't change from her nightgown until afternoon. On those days she moved slowly and her mood felt heavy like the heavy breasts that hung loose under her nightgown. Mother's life felt like a chore to be completed, a burden to be endured. She was always stirring a pot of grits or frying bacon and eggs, and the trash can by the stove was always running over. There were tubs to be scrubbed clean of scum and stray hairs, beds to be made, floors to be swept. And all the while, despite her slow and labored efforts, dust settled on the tables again, floors lost their luster, clutter accumulated. It was as if the house, with its attendant chores and demands, conspired to keep her forever captive; as if the tasks multiplied and took over her whole life the way kudzu vines took over abandoned places in the country, climbing walls, roofs, outhouses, and tool sheds.

Swinging back and forth on the trapeze, I was flooded with images from my mother's life. Relentless as kudzu, insistent and intimate as blood, they flowed through me. To be a woman was to be dead. I thought I would just as soon sit down in an electric chair and have someone strap me in and pull the switch. I'd never felt more alone and lonely. And it didn't matter that Mother was awake now, because there was nothing she could do. There was nothing anyone could do. I was a girl, and being a girl, I had no choice except to grow up and be a woman. My face felt hot. I gripped the trapeze bar with both hands and swung down. I felt sick to my stomach, and a little dizzy. I walked over to the oak and sat on the grass behind it. My mind filled with the image of mother's large, pendulous breasts. After her bath I'd watched her lift them—first one, then the other— and pat Yardley's bath powder under them with a large puff, clouds of powder rising all around her. I felt my own chest, smooth and flat under my T-shirt. I thought of Tarzan's chest, smooth and muscular. And Jane's chest, too, with its breasts. Maybe the problem after all had to do with breasts. Maybe when I grew up, I could find a doctor who would slice mine off. But as I thought this, I felt a rush of guilt flood through me, threatening the fragile hope I held in my heart. How could I think about doing such a thing? The thought itself felt like a sin. What would Mother think of me if she knew I had such a thought?

I went inside. My father and brother were already seated at the kitchen table waiting for their supper. Mother was spooning grits onto Daddy's plate. I sat down and put my napkin in my lap. "I wondered where you were," Mother said, spooning grits onto my plate. "I thought that picture show should have been over by now."

"I was out back on the trapeze."

Mother went to the stove, got a platter of fried eggs and bacon, and set it on the table along with a stack of toast. Then she sat down. I scooped a large spoonful of grits onto my plate, slid an egg onto it, and took two slices of crisp bacon, crumbling them into my grits. I cut a large slice of butter and dropped it into my grits. For a few seconds I stared down, watching the butter melt to a yellow pool. Then I chopped my egg up, mixed it with the grits and bacon, spread grape jelly on a piece of toast, and propped the toast on the edge of my plate. Without looking up, I began to eat.

V

1947

Dear God, don't let my mother die, I prayed.

The ambulance had sped past as I was walking home from town where, at age twelve, I'd taken my little brothers while Mother gave birth to my sister, Harriet, at home. I thought the ambulance turned into our drive, not into the road past Miss Sadie's, where in fact it did turn.

The baby, not my mother, I prayed over and over, my heart thumping frantically in my chest.

Opening the front door that day, I'd opened the door to a world suddenly gone out of control and nightmarish. My sister's shrill screaming filled the house.

She'd been born blue, umbilical cord twisted like a noose around her neck. Old Dr. Rogers had stretched a piece of gauze over her mouth and blown his cigar-soured breath into her lungs, pronounced her healthy, and left the house. But the atmosphere in the room was charged with pain, and Mother was unreachable.

After a while the nurse began to time my sister's screams. She found that she stopped screaming for no more than two minutes in three hours. Then she screamed the whole night through. The nurse decided that she had pressure on her brain, which was true. My sister had cerebral palsy.

Those first days and weeks after her birth have dissolved into a blur of confusion, pain, and despair. Mostly I remember my sister's screams.

Often I paced back and forth across the polished oak floor of my parents' bedroom, holding her in my arms. I walked between the mirror and the closet door until she fell asleep. That she could relax enough in my arms to fall asleep gave me as much comfort as it gave her.

Chapter Four

"If there is a way to communicate with you after I'm dead, if there is a way to cross over that threshold, I will come back to you," Mrs. Clemons said to me.

My mother was late in picking me up, and the cold winter light had drained from the room. A warm yellow glow from her chairside lamp illuminated Mrs. Clemons's hands, long-fingered and arthritic, articulate and dramatic. She was as old as my grandmother. A silk scarf fell around her neck in elegant folds, concealing the goiter on her throat.

"When I die, dear, lean close to my dead body," she said, leaning toward me as she spoke. "Perhaps it will be easiest to speak with you just after I cross over."

I lowered my eyes for a few seconds, staring at her feet, side by side in their black satin slippers on a small needlepoint stool. Behind me on the mantelpiece and propped against a pair of cut-glass candlesticks stood announcements of her death, addressed in her own hand. The cards were bordered in black and said: "Dear Friend, Grace Clemons has passed away on this __ day of ____, 19__." On the other end of the mantelpiece stood a snapshot of her mustached nephew from whom she awaited a visit year after year. On the wall beside me hung a picture of Death rowing a young woman across the River Styx. I say it was Death because I always thought of the somber figure standing at the stern of the boat as Death itself, though it was in fact Charon, the ferryman who rowed the dead across the River Styx into the underworld.

"Cold lips and breast without breath," Mrs. Clemons had recited earlier from Sir Edwin Arnold's poem "She and He." "Is there no voice, no language of death?" She'd recited the poem to me many times over the three years since I'd begun to visit her after I'd started taking painting lessons from Mrs. Forbes, who owned the house in which both women lived, and who lived below Mrs. Clemons.

She recited the poem slowly and passionately. And, as always, when listening to her recite the poem, I saw in my imagination a vast room, high-ceilinged and windowless, and at its center, a beautiful young woman's dead body lying on a slab of marble, long hair streaming down the sides of her pillow, strewn with blossoms, as was the hair of the young woman Death was rowing and rowing across the River Styx.

Stillness. Gloom. Cold. These words from the poem filled my imagination, where the image grew so still that it became more like a tangible presence than the absence of sound or motion. That stillness had a weight to it, like the heavy cloak Death wore.

During the three years that I'd taken my midafternoon break from my Saturday painting lessons and sometimes—as now—waited with her for my mother to come for me afterward, Mrs. Clemons often talked about her death. Sometimes she would announce: "I hear the bells tolling midnight in the distance and they are coming closer," her deep voice anchoring the words in a place of sober acknowledgment and resignation. Sometimes she made reference to the funeral announcements. But until that winter evening she'd never talked about communicating with me after her death. She spoke carefully and thoughtfully. "If you aren't with me when I die," she said, "go to my grave. The soul has to have a place to come home to."

Whatever my eyes said must have been an adequate response for her. I had no words and she asked for none. I didn't look from Mrs. Clemons's gaze as we sat facing each other, the small room filled with the silence of a connection I'd never felt before. The fear that I'd experienced earlier at the idea of leaning close to her dead body was replaced by the feeling of wonder that I, a thirteen-year-old girl, mattered enough to her that she would try to communicate with me even after death. And I knew that she mattered enough to me for me to listen.

The blast of a car horn rose from the street below.

My mother had come for me. I hugged Mrs. Clemons goodbye. Then I rushed down the stairs and out the front door, her words playing themselves over in my mind—*a place to come home to.*

II

I no longer remember what threatened Mrs. Clemons's health so much that she invited me to spend a night with her to keep her company. Her fear was so upsetting, yet no serious illness developed and I'm left with memories of a few details that anchor me in the turbulent waters of that weekend.

Before then I'd barely noticed what she referred to as her guest room, nor had I ever known her to have an overnight guest. She'd shown me her entire apartment when I first began to visit her, but until that weekend, there'd been no reason to go anyplace except the room in which we visited, and the kitchen where we sometimes ate one of her special salads or a bowl of fruit. Now, carrying a small blue suitcase, I followed her past the kitchen, down the hall, and into the guest room that opened onto a balcony overlooking Merrie Gardens.

It was furnished simply with a narrow bed covered by a white bedspread, a bedside table with a lamp, a bureau, and a straight chair. Mrs. Clemons had placed a white towel and washcloth on the foot of the bed. I remember quite well the thinness of the bath towel, the clean, pure smell of the soap in the bathroom, and how cold the enamel of the tub felt on my skin when, taking a bath later, I leaned my naked back against it. I also remember the pale pink blanket that lay folded at the foot of the bed. I unfolded it to cover the spread before climbing into bed and curling up between the sheets. I loved the feeling of the cool pillowcase against my face, but the room felt strange to me and not altogether comfortable, a foreign place inside the familiar space of Mrs. Clemons's apartment.

I had spent hours before that weekend listening to her talk about her life. Though she spoke of many hurtful experiences, they had happened to her so long ago that they had shaped themselves into stories, edges smoothed like pieces of broken glass tumbled by the sea. She had a storyteller's gift, and the forms that she created for holding the stories of her life also enabled me to hold them. No matter how great the loss or deep the grief, her stories satisfied a need in me, and ignited my imagination more than they distressed me.

But that weekend was different; her fear about her present health was so great that it seeped into every story she told, weighing it down with an unspoken anxiety that I felt so acutely that I, too, became heavyhearted and anxious.

Mrs. Clemons was a Christian Scientist. I puzzled about the pairing of those two words. A scientist was someone, usually a man, who peered through a microscope at germs squiggling on a glass slide, or at bits of leaves, flowers, or animal tissue. I'd seen photographs of some of these in *National Geographic* and sometimes in *Life*, and I saw that they were truly mysterious, so maybe there was some way to put the words *Christian* and *scientist* together. I knew Christianity was supposed to be about mystery, but judging from the words of the preacher in the Baptist church, I guessed it to be much more about moral rules and laws. Mystery had to do with the way light shone through the colors of the stained-glass Jesus, holding a shepherd's staff in one hand and a little lamb in the other, or the way Maggie Roddenbery's contralto voice filled the whole church when she sang.

Healing from illness without a doctor or medicine from the drugstore seemed like a very large mystery. Though our preacher sometimes referred to Jesus causing the blind to see and the lame to walk, this information felt more like ancient history than present possibility. Of all the people I knew personally, only Mrs. Clemons talked in the present tense about healing through her religion.

I had heard of other people who mixed healing and religion, but they were people who went to tent revivals, where they talked in tongues, played drums, and danced and rolled in the aisles in what they called religious ecstasy. My mother, who looked with disdain at overt displays of emotion, told me of her friend who attended such a tent meeting with her crippled son. Her friend had told her how the people gathered around the boy moaning prayers while the shouting preacher laid his hand on the boy's head, commanding the evil spirits to leave his frail body. Mother felt embarrassed for what she called her friend's appalling lapse of judgment. I wanted to believe that it was possible for that boy to get up from his wheelchair and walk, but felt my desire meant that I, too, had poor taste and would risk my mother's harsh judgment if I admitted my true feelings.

The only other people I'd heard of who were involved with healing and religion were the Catholics who flooded to Lourdes with dreams of miracles rendered through the water from a special spring. Fascinated, I'd read that the young Bernadette Soubirous was directed to the spring by an apparition of the Virgin Mary. But the Virgin Mary had no place in the Baptist Church, and Catholics seemed like a different species altogether, as foreign as Yankees.

Christian Science felt foreign, too, but it was a part of who Mrs. Clemons was, so I'd begun to learn bits and pieces about it. She never talked about a church but referred to the Christian Science Reading Room, a concept that seemed strange to me and not at all like going to church. She didn't read *The Atlanta Journal* like my parents did but read *The Christian Science Monitor*, which she kept folded on the table beside her reading chair. Once, she told me, she tripped and broke her ankle when cutting through Paradise Park on her way home from the grocery store. Despite the urgings of friends, she said, she stood fast in her faith and refused to go to a doctor, waiting and watching as the broken bone knit itself together again.

She'd been most adamant in her claims, which added to my anxiety that weekend; her fear about her present health felt to me like a crisis of faith. I say I *felt* rather than *thought*, because my perceptions were nothing I could articulate. But I felt the threat with a chilling surety. Her crisis precipitated a crisis in me. Her faith in Christian Science, strange as it was to me, was something I needed her to hold on to. I needed Mrs. Clemons to be unbroken and predictable in my world.

The weekend itself, with all its blank spaces and its few clearly remembered details, was pivotal in the relationship between us. Young as I was, I was able to stand with her during the storm of her doubt. I felt I'd proven myself to her in some essential way. That she had asked me to be with her, difficult though it was, felt like a privilege.

Fortunately, my stay was balanced by time spent with Mrs. Forbes. I had my usual painting lesson on Saturday afternoon, while Mrs. Clemons was at a special meeting of a group of Christian Scientists until early evening. After I'd painted for a long time, Mrs. Forbes suggested I stop and let her fix us an early supper. She led me into her kitchen on the other side of the house, took a large onion and a jar of mayonnaise out of the refrigerator, and set both on the enameled table at which I sat, watching. She peeled the onion, put it on the chopping board, and cut two enormously thick, sharply fragrant slices. She opened a loaf of bread and took out four pieces, which she put on two small plates. Then she spread mayonnaise on the bread, and onto one piece on each plate she placed an onion slice.

I sat waiting for the other ingredients of the sandwich, but there were none. She plopped the remaining pieces of bread on their mates, poured two glasses of milk, and sat down. An onion sandwich. In our family, onions went with hamburgers. I'd never heard of a sandwich with nothing but onion on it. And this was nothing like the food Mrs. Clemons served. She made wonderful cakes and cookies. Sometimes she mixed exotic salads of grapes, walnuts, celery, lettuce, tomatoes, and cucumbers, covered with a creamy dressing totally unlike those my mother made.

"This is one of my very favorite treats," Mrs. Forbes said, taking a bite of her sandwich. I took a bite of mine and, to my surprise, liked it.

When the painting lesson ended, Mrs. Forbes went into the foyer and pulled the string that dangled from a small bell at the head of the stairs. "Yoo-hoo!" she called, ringing the bell. "Yoo-hoo!" Mrs. Clemons came down then and played "To a Wild Rose" on the piano before we went upstairs for the night.

That night Mrs. Clemons and I sat together on the balcony that opened from the guest room and overlooked Merrie Gardens. The evening was cool, and we both wore sweaters. I felt emotionally drained and was grateful for the quiet that we shared. I'd never sat on that balcony before, and it felt strange, but the whole weekend had felt strange. Daylight was gone, and summer too, and frost had claimed the garden just days before. The yard looked colorless and drab in the dim light of early dusk. A few dry leaves were scattered on the lawn. From someplace in the pecan grove behind the barn, a mockingbird pierced the silence with its call. My heart ached at the sound, ached with its own need to somehow answer. Again the mockingbird called out, and its familiar notes evoked in me a longing deeper than anything I'd ever felt. It felt like homesickness, but for someplace I'd never known before.

III

Every summer Mother filled a basket with vegetables for me to take to Mrs. Clemons and Mrs. Forbes. She filled it with the bounty from her garden in the backyard or from the hampers of vegetables that my father brought home from his produce warehouse: radishes, peppers, potatoes, tomatoes, string beans, field peas, okra, carrots, cucumbers. She arranged them with the same care with which she arranged tiger lilies and aspidistra leaves in the brass bowl on the living room mantelpiece or camellias in the low, white bowl on the dining table. While housework defeated her at every turn, Mother was a devoted and creative gardener. More than at any other time, she appeared at peace with herself and the world when she was pulling weeds from a flower bed, planting seeds in the vegetable garden, or pruning the roses. Arranging the vegetables in the basket was one of Mother's pleasures, and it never went unnoticed by either Mrs. Forbes or Mrs. Clemons.

I loved carrying the basket from the car into the house, anticipating the pleased looks in both women's eyes when they saw it. On those Saturdays when I brought the basket, Mrs. Forbes announced my arrival by ringing the bell and calling out "Yoo-hoo!" to Mrs. Clemons, who came down and stood with her, admiring the vegetables. This was such a Saturday, and the three of us stood in the foyer looking at Mother's creation.

"A feast for the eyes," Mrs. Forbes announced, smiling.

"Lovely," Mrs. Clemons said. "Just lovely." Then—being the cook for both of them—she took the basket from me, saying, "I'm baking a cake with chocolate sauce. It should be ready for your lesson break." I watched her climb the stairs to disappear into the kitchen.

Mrs. Forbes and I went into her workroom, where, for a long time, I worked on a watercolor I'd begun the week before. She sat in her reading chair near the daybed, telling me again about her dream of someday having a book of her own stories, poems, drawings, and watercolors. Then she recited from Emerson's poem "The Rhodora" from memory, ending with " . . . beauty is its own excuse for Being." Afterward she announced, as she usually did, that she intended to live to be a hundred years old before she left for her "scouting space" in the next world.

I sat bent over the little desk, pulling my full paintbrush across the paper, the blue of a summer sky pooling along the horizon line in my watercolor. "And this is another poem I myself wrote," she announced, smiling: "O Bumblebee Humble Bee / droning and buzzing," she began, loving the sounds of the words as she said them, as they vibrated against her teeth and out through her lips. "Droning and buzzing so close to me," she continued, not remembering that she'd said the poem to me more than once already. "I know you think you're in Paradise / In the wisteria bloom on my porch."

I laid my paintbrush on the desk. Mrs. Forbes dragged a straight chair over beside me and sat down. We looked at my painting together. Against the blue background sat a dog, a white terrier with a black spot on its shoulder. A gray-and-yellow kitten looked up at its face. It was a sentimental picture copied from one of the prints that Mrs. Forbes had collected for her students to paint from. I thought I'd give it to Mother to hang over the chest of drawers in my parents' bedroom where my sister, Harriet, slept. I thought it was something Mother would like, and it looked to me like something one might have for a baby.

I rarely talked about Harriet to Mrs. Forbes or Mrs. Clemons. I didn't talk to them about her screaming, or how often I paced the floor with her. I didn't tell them how happy it made me when my pacing soothed the pain and I felt her relaxing into sleep, her small body limp against me, sweat-soaked and spent.

I told no one how scared I'd been walking up and down the driveway with Mother the night before Harriet's birth. She was late being born, and Mother was afraid that something was wrong. Walking, she said, might help the baby come. I told no one how hard I prayed, "Please, God, let it be the baby, not Mama. Not my mama, please." I told no one that I lived, from that time on, afraid that God had answered my prayer and kept my mother safe for me while the baby was forever paralyzed. I told no one that I lay awake nights, tormented by the thought that maybe Harriet's crippled and tormented body and brain were my fault.

Though I liked the sky color, I didn't like my painting. It didn't make me feel much of anything. Some of the explosions of line and color I'd seen in art magazines evoked feelings from me—Picasso's *Guernica*, Modigliani's long-necked portraits, the work of Braque and Cézanne. Mostly I loved Van Gogh's cypresses twisting their way toward the swirling galaxies in their thick-pigmented glory, and his self-portraits, his intense face so filled with color it was as if himself was no more or less than paint and a burning vision.

It wouldn't have crossed my mind to bring a print of one of Van Gogh's paintings to Mrs. Forbes's to copy as I copied the dog and cat, scenes of woods and streams, pots of roses, or bunches of grapes. He and his paintings didn't belong in that Victorian house across from Paradise Park any more than much of me didn't belong there either.

After I grew into my midteens and no longer spent Saturday afternoons painting at Mrs. Forbes's, there was a brief period when I tried to enter into Van Gogh's vision and paint as closely as I could in his style. I painted two paintings during that time. One was of my Aunt Sarah's house. It was an old white wood house with a gabled roof and a cypress tree in front. It looked very much like a house Van Gogh might have chosen to paint had he painted in South Georgia. I began the painting with an almost feverish excitement, the high-pitched roof rising against the brilliant summer sky, the cypress twisting itself toward the heavens in memory of Van Gogh. I don't know that I'd ever felt more at home and content painting than I felt painting my aunt's house.

It was with pride and excitement that I took the barely dry painting across the street to show her. I was prepared to make a gift to her of the painting. I imagined her hanging it in a place of honor in the old, high-ceilinged house, with its antique furniture and cut glass. My aunt was painfully polite as she looked at my painting propped against her old-fashioned wallpaper of horse-drawn carriages, men in top hats, and women in hoopskirts. Her tight smile was locked securely in place. But it was clear not only that she didn't want to hang the painting in her house but that she felt insulted by such a rendition of it. Feeling apologetic, ashamed, and hurt, I took the painting home. Trying to console myself, I told myself that my aunt simply didn't understand real art, that the loss was hers, not mine. In time I believed it.

That summer I painted one last picture in the style of Van Gogh. It was a self-portrait. I worked hard on it, standing before my easel and staring into a mirror hour after hour, sweating in the summer heat, piling the thick paint on the face in yellows and greens that reflected the colors Van Gogh used in his self-portraits. The eyes were very green. I was so absorbed in my work that my entire body jumped when my father's voice startled me.

"Sister?"

"Yes?" I replied, regaining my composure and returning to the world of ordinary consciousness. He stood behind me staring at the painting. I turned to look at him, but he shifted his eyes from mine.

"Sister, I've never asked you to do anything like this before," he said apologetically. "But I'm asking you to destroy that painting."

"What?" I screamed at him, incredulous.

"I'm asking you to destroy that painting," he repeated. I could hear the pain under his words.

"But doesn't it look like me, Daddy?" My heart ached with confusion.

"Yes, Sister, it does look like you, and I can't live with those eyes."

I looked at the painting. More than any other painting, I'd felt a real measure of satisfaction with this one even though it was as much Van Gogh's as mine. And it was the first time I'd been able to do a self-portrait that actually looked like me. I felt a flood of self-hatred tear through me. I jerked the painting off the easel and thundered through the kitchen, down the back steps, and out to the trash can. With an unquestioned rage I banged the canvas stretcher frame against the edge of the can repeatedly until it came apart, the splintered wood poking through the limp canvas, the painting smeared and covered with garbage.

But looking at my watercolor of the dog and cat with Mrs.

Forbes, I was several years yet from the destruction of my self-portrait. This day I watched as she made a correction in the line of the dog's mouth with her pencil. I looked at the watercolor washes, the mottled fur of the cat, the precise pencil lines delineating the shape of a paw, the angle of an ear. Mrs. Forbes said something complimentary about the painting, but what I felt was numbness.

If Van Gogh was as mad as the books claimed, he also had life in every stroke his brush made. What I wanted was life.

IV

1949

Once, when I was fourteen, I overheard Mother talking to Daddy about me. Bubba and Mercer must have been outside playing, for the house was still and quiet. I was lying on my bed on my stomach, head hung over the edge so I could read the book spread open on the floor beneath me. It was Tennessee Williams's play *A Streetcar Named Desire* with its unforgettable "I have always depended on the kindness of strangers," spoken by the tragic Blanche DuBois as she is being taken off to the insane asylum by a questionable-looking doctor in a hat and his stern matron assistant.

Our high school drama coach, Diana Thomas, had taken a group of us to Albany, Georgia, to see a production of it performed by a road company. I was thrilled to see "real" theater. It was a highlight of my high school experiences. We had front-row seats and were delighted when Stanley shook a bottle of beer vigorously, then popped the cap, spewing beer on several of us.

My relationship with Miss Thomas was another highlight of my high school experience. She was a small, perky young woman with a head full of short blond curls and the body of a phys-ed teacher, with well-developed calves and biceps. She was funny, mischievous, bright, and creative. She kidded me about my serious nature yet accepted me warmly. Warmth was one of the largest things missing in my home life, and I was drawn to her warmth the way someone parched with thirst is drawn to water. I was in plays she directed and took private speech lessons from her. I found any excuse I could think of to visit her apartment after school. Though I can remember little of what we did or talked about aside from speech, drama, and her ongoing account of the practical jokes she played in college, what I do remember vividly is warmth and laughter. I saved my money to buy her a bright-red leather wallet for her birthday, an extravagant gesture given my lack of money, but I believe I would have given almost anything to please her. Being in her presence made me happy.

The house was deathly quiet as I read about Stanley Kowalski's crude and violent tyranny, the crash of the radio as he hurled it through the window, shattering glass as he cleared his plate and glass from the table with a swipe of his hand. But my attention was drawn away from New Orleans's French Quarter by the words Mother was saying to Daddy. She spoke in a stage whisper, her voice filled with fear. She was talking about her concern over how much time I spent with Diana and her roommate, Betty Miller, and how that didn't feel normal to her. She'd heard, she told Daddy, that one of the symptoms of sexual perversion in girls was attraction to older girls or women.

"I don't know how I could live if Margaret were like"—she named a cousin who'd moved away from Cairo, never to return, a cousin rumored to be a lesbian. Mother sighed one of her soul-deep sighs. "I just don't know if I would be able to *live* if Margaret was like that."

I sucked in my breath and slowly let it out, careful not to move on the bed or make any other sound that would tell Mother that I was awake and had heard her horrible fear about me. She didn't know if she could *live* if I was "like that." I looked down at the book, trying to read, trying to erase what I'd just heard. I focused on page after page but could take in nothing beyond Mother's words.

Then the play came alive in my mind as Blanche told Mitch about how she'd walked in on her young husband—"a boy," she called him—and an older man, and how the three of them acted as if nothing had happened as they all went to Moon Lake Casino together. Then, on the dance floor, dizzy with drinking and dancing, Blanche blurted out that she had seen, that she knew, that he, her young husband, was disgusting.

"Disgusting."

He broke away and ran out of the casino into the night. Then a shot rang out and the music stopped. Blanche and everyone else ran to the edge of the lake, the place from which the shot had come. Someone restrained Blanche. Someone else said it was Allan Grey and that he had stuck a revolver in his mouth and pulled the trigger.

I felt awful.

Could I be—I couldn't even think the word—even though I was attracted to boys? Boys. *And* girls.

I agonized over the possibility that I could be so terrible as to kill Mother with shame. I'd always heard that it was normal for little girls to have crushes on one another. When did it stop being normal and start being something else? I thought of how I always enjoyed being the boy when I'd played dolls as a child. I even sometimes fantasized about growing up to be a man with woman lovers. Could I, I asked myself, be a queer? I could hardly bear to think the word. No. Whatever it was, it was a phase and I would grow out of it.

In high school I overheard talk about queers. One time there was a paperback book circulating among the girls. From what I overheard, it had sections in which girls did sexual things to one another. Whether because my usual depression was interpreted as disinterest or because the girls thought me too naïve to share such things, the book never got passed along to me. I was much too self-conscious to ask about it, so I spent a lot of time trying to imagine the things the queers did.

The other thing I heard about queers was that they always wore green on Thursdays. Knowing that, I was very careful to never wear anything green on that day of the week. I became self-conscious about my pale green bedroom walls and my deep-green bedspread.

I felt sick with shame that my attraction to Diana Thomas might be a horrible perversion. I saw her no less than before I heard Mother's fear about me, but a shadow had been cast not only on my relationship with Diana but on the basic nature of who I was.

Whatever I was, I told myself, *I am not a queer.*

V

Bobby was the most handsome man I'd ever seen. He worked at the sawmill and was an ex–army sergeant who wore corduroy pants and work boots or loafers. I was fifteen years old. I was at a party at Fred Clark's house when he came over to where I sat feeling miserably alone and out of place. Looking back, I'd describe his behavior as compassionate, and perhaps curious, but at the time I didn't analyze anything, I was just thrilled by the attention.

I couldn't believe that Bobby Blake was interested in me. I was timid and insecure, which, a friend told me, often made me appear cold and unfriendly. In a magazine—I believe it was *The Saturday Evening Post*—I'd seen a cartoon in which a psychiatrist was telling his patient reclining on a couch: "But of course you have an inferiority complex. You *are* inferior." Reading the cartoon, I decided that an inferiority complex was exactly what I had, and I had it because, just like the man in the cartoon, I *was* inferior, though I didn't know exactly what made me that way. The only thing I knew about psychiatry was that one went to a doctor who listened while the patient talked. If I was inferior, what good would talking do? *Talk can't change who I am,* I thought.

When Bobby called and asked me for a date I was surprised and happy. And after the first date, another, and then another. We cruised up and down Broad Street, met friends at the Blue Gable Drive-In, where we ate French fries with catsup, drank Coca-Colas, and smoked cigarettes. Once we double-dated with Judy Matthews and Ben Williams and went to the drive-in movie. We sat in the backseat. I remember the loud crackling sound my paper taffeta dress made when Bobby put his arms around me and pulled me hard against him.

He taught me how to shoot a gun, took me swimming at the Sand Pit, to dinner at Dodson's or the Silver Slipper in Thomasville. I was drunk on love, on his handsome face and muscular body. At one point he talked about marriage. He was much older than I, and was getting ready to settle down. Suddenly my imagination was filled with the image of the trunk of Bobby's car crammed full of vacuum cleaners, dust mops, dishpans, bottles of Windex, and cans of Old Dutch Cleanser. I told him that I wasn't about to spend my life pushing a broom. I was in high school. I was expected to go to college. I never questioned my parents' expectations. Certainly I was too young to think of marriage. In my dreams I imagined being an artist and living in Greenwich Village painting pictures and talking with other artists who sat at sidewalk tables in front of coffeehouses, watching the stream of humanity passing by.

When Bobby and I finally broke up, he told me that he'd been moved by my sadness, that he'd only wanted to make me happy. But he was not in love with me. I went numb. We were parked at the Blue Gable Drive-In under a pecan tree near the back of the building. I remember the squat old woman standing at the window taking our order, and how she cocked her head to one side, listening.

I couldn't look at Bobby.

All the nights of necking in a parked car in the woods; all the nights at the Blue Gable when I'd traced his fingers with my own, loving the shapes of his fingers, his fingernails, the swirl of his thumbprints; all the nights I'd followed the muscles in his neck to run my fingers through his thick dark hair. Days on the beach at Alligator Point. And the night he parked in an old country churchyard where an owl kept hooting its mournful cry from someplace deep in the woods. "Do you hear, Bobby?" I'd asked. "Do you hear the owl?" But I was asking a larger question than I could comprehend. I was asking if he could hear what I was hearing; I was asking if he could touch that deep place inside me where I stood so very much alone.

"Yeah, I hear the owl," he'd said, lighting a cigarette. To him, the moment was ordinary, while to me it held poetry and mystery that went beyond my ability to articulate. It was night and nature and God all caught in the prolonged and haunting hooting of the owl.

If it was true that I had simply fallen in love with love, it was also true that the object of that love was Bobby Blake, with his soft brown eyes, his strong chin and jaw. I had fallen in love with his teasing grin, with his perfect ears flat against his fine skull. I had fallen in love with Bobby Blake, who had only taken pity on a quiet young girl with grief in her eyes. Now Bobby was discarding me with a condescendingly calm tone of voice, and I felt that I'd be brokenhearted forever.

Light from the open kitchen door spilled out onto the squat old woman who stretched her mouth in a broad grin at Bobby as she took our order. He had just told me that he didn't really love me, that he was breaking up with me forever, and what I took in, what I have forever held inside me, is the image of that old woman, gold fillings flashing in her grinning mouth. That, and the colored lights strung from pecan tree to pecan tree to mark the boundaries of the Blue Gable parking lot.

VI
1952

Margaret Rushin sat at her piano playing the song "I Get Along Without You Very Well" while I sat in the lounge chair next to her, listening. That had become my favorite song since Bobby had cut me off and—I felt—broken my heart forever. The lyrics were about heartbreak and loneliness, and I cherished every syllable.

Margaret was patient with my repeated requests for the song.

She and I had been friends since early childhood when she lived nearby with her family in the home of her Grandmother Wyche, my great-aunt. But not long after I'd grown accustomed to playing with Margaret at her grandmother's, her parents built a new house several blocks away beyond the elementary school we attended.

In their new house Margaret had her own room in which we spent the night together. We often lay awake for hours reciting the dialogue for plays that we made up. Sometimes we stayed at my house nights, but I preferred sleeping at Margaret's because we had more freedom there to do as we pleased. And later, when we were teenagers, I could smoke cigarettes at Margaret's long before I was permitted to smoke at home.

I was thrilled when her mother asked me to paint a Mexican mural on one of the kitchen walls. I cringe now to think of the quality of that painting. But as I painted the cactus-filled desert with its donkeys and Mexican men in their sombreros, I felt exceedingly proud of my accomplishment. Margaret's mother liked the mural and left it on the wall until she had the kitchen painted many years later. She always loved my painting and drawing. I was deeply moved when I went to see her after Margaret's father died and found her lying on her bed holding a pencil portrait I'd drawn of him years before.

Margaret was at home for her father's funeral. As close as we were as children and teenagers, once we graduated from high school and left Cairo, we rarely—if ever—wrote to each other. Margaret married a soldier and left for Germany with her new husband. I left for college. Neither of us returned to Cairo often, though we usually managed to end up visiting at the same time. And seeing each other, we always began to talk as if continuing our conversation from the day before. Ours was an enduring relationship that required no words to sustain it.

But the afternoon I sat beside her piano while Margaret played "I

Get Along Without You Very Well," I had no idea that we would be such good friends not only in childhood and adolescence but in old age as well. And I certainly couldn't have imagined the life that lay before me. It was enough to have Margaret comfort me with music while her mother made my favorite potato salad in the kitchen where we would soon be eating supper.

Chapter Five

I

1953

DURING MY FRESHMAN YEAR OF COLLEGE AT FLORIDA STATE UNIVERSITY
in Tallahassee, I had a crush on my housemother, Nina Lawrence,
who was retired from serving in the navy. She was a short woman
with prominent features, clear blue eyes, and prematurely snow-white
hair. I did an oil portrait of her, which gave me an excuse to spend
long hours in her apartment, looking at her, being with her. She had
a friend, a younger housemother in a nearby dorm, and the three of
us often walked downhill from FSU to downtown Tallahassee for
dinner. One evening, just before I knocked on Miss Lawrence's partially opened door, I paused, for the two women were talking about
me. Miss Lawrence was saying to her friend that she was concerned
that my being with her so often might cause someone on the university staff to think that we were having a lesbian relationship. She actually used the word *lesbian*. But there was nothing hysterical in her
tone, just a calm concern. I called her name, knocked, and opened
the door all at once. I didn't want to eavesdrop on her any more than
I already unintentionally had. Both women greeted me warmly, and
we set off for downtown together.

One night a group of us girls had a couple of drinks and someone reported us to the dean of women. Miss Lawrence didn't appear

especially upset about it; she knew me well enough to know that I was no serious drinker, but she was concerned about the state of crisis it threw me into. I was upset because the dean would notify my parents, as was customary with any serious infraction of the rules. They'd be told I'd been reported for drinking and that I'd be confined to the campus and would have my dating privileges taken away for two weeks.

My upset must have been evident as I sat across the desk from the dean. "Margaret," she said in a warm, accepting voice. "Don't make this larger than it is. You've not committed a crime, you've broken a college rule." I was grateful for her support, but she didn't know my mother and how hysterical she got about anything I did that went against her own rules. I often thought that she'd expressed the same upset when she found out that I'd smoked a cigarette that she would have expressed if I'd told her I was pregnant. And my drinking? To imagine her response made me feel frantic. I asked the dean when she was going to send the letter. I wanted to tell my parents myself before they got it. She assured me that she'd wait for a week before sending it.

Relieved, I went back to the dormitory to begin to think about what I'd write to my parents. "Don't make a mountain out of a molehill," Miss Lawrence had advised, and invited me and her fellow housemother for dinner in town that night.

For two days I thought of the letter, then finally sat down at my typewriter and wrote it. "Dear Mother and Daddy," I wrote. "I am very tired of living on the pedestal on which you've placed me ever since I was a little girl. It's very lonely up here." Then I told them about the night that I had something to drink and how I was now confined to the campus for two weeks. The only male I was permitted to see was my father. I also told them that they would soon be getting a letter from the dean of women telling them this. "All my life," I continued, "I've been searching, longing for unconditional love. I need that unconditional love from you. I need it now. As of this letter I've climbed down from your pedestal. I love you both deeply, but I can no longer live the life you have demanded of me."

Without taking the letter from my typewriter, I reread it. I felt good about it, but I wanted to let my emotions cool a little before signing and mailing it. I walked to a coffee shop across the street from the campus and had my usual cream-cheese-and-olive sandwich and a Coke. Then I smoked a cigarette before walking back to my room.

The door stood open. Mother was sitting at my desk. She'd taken the letter from the typewriter and was reading it and crying. In all the months I'd been at FSU, Mother had never once come to see me unannounced. My safe place was no longer safe. Here, I'd thought, I could write anything I wanted to write without worrying about Mother reading it and getting upset. Here I could be myself without Mother's judgment. Now here she was in my room, reading and sobbing.

"I saw that the letter was addressed to me," she said in an almost apologetic way. "I had some errands in Tallahassee. I'd thought . . ." Her voice trailed off. Then she sniffled, wiped her nose with a Kleenex from her purse, and dropped it into my wastebasket. "I need to be going now," she said, then folded the letter and put it into her bag. I followed her out the door and down the stairs.

After a few steps she stopped and turned around. Her eyes were very red, but their glare was so intense that I felt I could almost lose my balance under the impact. I leaned against the wall. "How could you do this to me?" she wailed. "I've tried and I've tried, and this is what I get from you. What have I done to deserve this?"

Her chest heaved with sobs. "I will never tell your father. I just don't think he could bear it. No, he must never know."

I turned and went to my room, closing the door behind me.

The next communication I received from home was a call from Daddy. He'd been to Atlanta on a shopping trip for the new dry-goods store that he was struggling to make successful. He said he had some gifts for me. He wanted to take me out to dinner. I knew Mother had told him about my being confined to the campus for drinking, though he said nothing about it.

Our time together was festive. Even though he bought the clothes for me wholesale, I knew he'd spent far more than he could comfortably afford. First there was a beautifully cut black crêpe dress with a white collar exquisitely embroidered with white silk and tiny seed pearls. Then there was a pair of black leather Capezio pumps with wooden stacked heels. Last was a rust-colored suede sports jacket. It was the most extravagant thing he'd ever done for me.

Daddy and I had a wonderfully good time together. I felt an unspoken bond between us. I didn't want him to drink any more than I myself wanted to drink seriously. I'd seen the destructive effects of drinking firsthand in Uncle Frank. But ever since Mother had told me how she'd kept Daddy from having a beer by threatening to make me, a baby, drink whatever he drank, I'd resented her using me to manipulate him. That night I felt he was celebrating the fact that I had broken one of Mother's rules, something he'd been unable to do because she'd made the stakes higher than he was willing to pay. I felt that we were co-conspirators. While Mother punitively withdrew from me in silence, Daddy moved closer and accepted my humanity.

II

My freshman year at FSU was my first and last. Edmund Lewandowski, the painting teacher I'd gone to FSU to study with, accepted the position as head of the Layton School of Art in Milwaukee. I wanted to go with him, but Mother had no respect for art schools. She intended for me to have a college education. It didn't occur to me that I had any right to oppose her. I applied for and got an art scholarship to the University of Georgia.

Miss Lawrence was going to leave FSU also, but before leaving Tallahassee she took me on a vacation with her to Pensacola, then

Saint Augustine, Florida. A week alone with Miss Lawrence: I was in heaven. In Pensacola, she pulled up to a coral-colored motel on the beach and rented a room with twin beds. Sleeping within feet of her and being with her all day and evening was more than I could ever have hoped for. It was a week of burning emotions and blazing sun, of long days on the beach, intense blue and turquoise water, and miles and miles of sand. I don't remember a single meal. Why would I remember food when there was Miss Lawrence's company to focus on hour after hour? Once, in Saint Augustine, I walked along a crumbling ruin of a stone wall by the water, and she reached up and took my hand in hers. Feeling her firm grip with my own, I could have walked for miles, my whole body trembling with the thrill of her touch.

After our vacation, Miss Lawrence took me home to Cairo. Then she moved to Saint Augustine. She wrote me notes from time to time. From the University of Georgia I wrote to her that I was seriously involved with a boy and had plans for marriage. She wrote back that she was happy for me. I've no memory of hearing from her after that. At some point she moved from Saint Augustine and I lost track of her altogether. In later years, I felt a longing to reunite with her, to tell her how much her love mattered to the love-starved girl I was, but I was never able to locate her.

PART TWO

The Beginning of Us

Chapter Six

JOHN ROBISON AND I WERE SEATED NEXT TO EACH OTHER, IN ALPHABET-ical order, in among the two hundred students enrolled in Human Biology 101 at the University of Georgia in Athens. My first response to him was that he looked very young. That, and that he had beautiful hands and fine features. He told me later that he'd thought I had capable-looking hands, that he'd loved watching them as I took notes. He also said that he'd loved my face. The man seated to my left was a short, dark-haired veteran of the Korean War with a wedding band on his finger. The three of us introduced ourselves to one another before class began.

The professor walked up the steps to the platform at the front of the room. He was a short, stocky man with clipped black hair that stood straight up. As he talked, he paced, or rocked back and forth on his heels, and waved his arms wildly, making me think of a frisky Scottie dog. Standing before the blackboard, he told us his name, a long name almost impossible to pronounce. After saying it, he told us that many of his students simply spelled his name this way—turning the piece of chalk sideways in his hands, he wrote in large, wide letters: S.O.B.

Then he began his first lecture.

John and I left the class together, talking about our wild and witty professor. When we came to the parking lot, he asked if he could drive me back to my dorm. He opened the door of his car for me, and I climbed in. On the way to the dorm he invited me to go with him to a local drive-in for a glass of iced tea.

We sat in the car and talked for hours about philosophy and religion. I'd taken an introductory philosophy course my freshman year at FSU and had spent much of that year discussing philosophical issues with other students from the class. While John had taken no philosophy courses, his intention was to be a Presbyterian minister, and many of the philosophical and theological issues that we were interested in were closely related. I liked his quick mind and articulate speech. And I'd never met a boy with whom conversation came so easily.

After that first meeting, both of us broke our prearranged dates for the following weekend, and neither of us ever dated anyone else. What if John had taken out Nancy Larkin with her long blond hair? What if I'd gone out with Tom Watson? Futile questions. The first letter of our last names, and the fact that we were seated next to each other in Human Biology 101, decided the course of both our lives.

John and I spent every available minute together. Mornings we ate at a university coffee shop, while "Sixteen Tons" or "Rock Around the Clock" blared from the jukebox. In the small room filled with cigarette smoke thick as fog, we ate glazed donuts, drank coffee, and talked. Then we were off to classes, he to Greek or comparative religion, I to French or a class called Art in the Dark, where we sat at long tables in the dark, drawing from slides of large, simple, black shapes on a white background that flashed for seconds on the enormous screen in front of us.

In the evenings John and I ate at Tony's, a small restaurant in downtown Athens. We ate lots of spaghetti and meatballs and told each other about our families. He told me about how his parents had run off together and gotten married when his mother was sixteen and his father seventeen. With a profound sense of nostalgia he told me how much he loved summers spent with his grandparents in Chickamauga, Georgia. He told me about going with his grandfather to his drugstore, or out to his farm, where he raised racehorses, and how sad he felt to leave his grandparents in the fall to go back to his parents in Athens, where his father was a student at the same university we ourselves now attended.

I told him I was from Cairo, a dusty little town in South Georgia—two blocks of stores, a movie theater, post office, courthouse, cotton gin, and jail, the kind of town you'd never stop in unless you needed to go to the filling station or—like me—grew up in and had to go home to visit. I told him about my father's failed business and his failing health. I told him about my sister, Harriet, and about how my mother's life was almost totally devoted to taking care of her. I told him about my sister's spastic clenched fists and her seizures.

One night, John nervously announced that he had something to tell me and asked me to go with him to a more private place. I couldn't imagine what dreaded secret he was about to disclose. We were silent as he drove to the outskirts of town, pulled off the road, and parked in the dark under a bridge. Then, his voice thick with shame, he told me that his father was a heavy drinker and had been a heavy drinker since John could remember. He told me about the many times his father was late picking him up at his military school in Atlanta. As a young boy, he'd waited alone until almost dark before his father would finally arrive, often drunk, to drive him home. He also described how his father had kicked him in the ribs when he was a little boy trying to protect his mother from his father's violence.

After telling me these things, John turned his face from me and looked rigidly ahead into the night as if he was afraid that I might reject him, as if I might find him unworthy because of his father.

It was very dark; there was just a sliver of a moon overhead. I looked at him. "Oh, John," I said. "I'm so sorry."

Then we were in each other's arms, John feeling the relief of acceptance, me imagining the vulnerable little boy trying to protect himself from blow after blow of his father's terrible shoes.

One evening shortly before Thanksgiving I sat on a couch in the dorm lounge, listening to a new song on the TV: "Teach Me Tonight." I was waiting for John to pick me up for a date but was completely absorbed in listening to every word of the song when John arrived.

"I'm listening to this new song, 'Teach Me Tonight,'" I said when he arrived. "I love it."

John ignored my statement. "Let's go now," he said impatiently.

"After this one song."

"I have something to tell you," he insisted.

"In a minute, John. Just a minute."

Teach me tonight.

It was raining as we ran to his car. I expected him to drive us someplace, but the key dangled from the ignition while he took something from his pants pocket. Nervously, he cleared his throat as he fumbled with it.

The rain grew harder, beating down on the roof.

"I'd like you to wear my fraternity pin," he said. He'd just gotten it that day. In college at that time, being pinned was the first step toward becoming engaged.

"I'd love to wear your fraternity pin, John," I said softly.

John leaned over and pinned it on my sweater. His hands trembled as he struggled with the tiny clasp while trying to not touch my breast.

"I love you, John," I whispered. But for some reason I couldn't understand, I cried as I said it, the hard rain plastering fall leaves all over the windshield.

II

I still have the photograph that I took one day of our shadows side by side and stretched out long before us on an asphalt highway near Athens. Though I didn't realize it consciously then, that picture captured the fact that the relationship would bring out the shadow sides of both our personalities. The road in the photograph stretched out as far as we could see, disappearing in the distance where the hills of North Georgia rose.

Our conversations were often about our families. John said that I was the first person he'd been able to really talk to since his Grandfather Elder died of a heart attack when he was twelve. Since that time he'd been lonely for a real emotional connection. When he kept telling me that he didn't know how he could live without me, I felt both flattered and uncomfortable. Something about him felt immature, even though he was a few months older than I was, had held summer jobs for many years, had had his fling with drinking in high school, had dated several girls before meeting me, and was already student minister to two small rural churches near Athens.

A minister. I was pinned to a ministerial student. As an adolescent girl in the Southern Baptist Church, I'd often fantasized about becoming a missionary myself. Girls could be missionaries, not ministers. But I had to dismiss my fantasy because I was already as addicted to cigarettes as my father was. As long as I continued to smoke, I felt unworthy of being a missionary. I'd tried to give it up many times. Then I'd give in and reach for another cigarette, sucking the smoke deep into my lungs and exhaling with a sense of great relief and miserable failure.

I was not good enough to be a missionary.

Now there was John, who didn't smoke or drink, and who didn't even say the word *damn*. John, who stood in the pulpit Sundays preaching like he was a young Billy Graham. John, who would soon begin to insist that I stop smoking. Aside from the fact that I was strongly addicted to nicotine, my smoking became a focus for the power struggle beginning between us.

John was intensely jealous of my absorption in painting and drawing. His jealousy came at a time when my confidence in my art had been greatly diminished. At FSU my freshman year, Edmund Lewandowski, the head of the art department, had expressed great faith in my work. "Margaret," he'd said. "You and I are both reaching for the highest star, and we'll both get there."

Unlike Professor Lewandowski, who had been my consistent inspiration, I saw Lamar Dodd, head of Georgia's art department, only once. That was when I showed him a portfolio of my paintings and he gave me a scholarship. I didn't talk with him again after that interview. At Georgia I got no special attention. While Art in the Dark trained both my eyes and my hand, it gave nothing to my spirit. And I didn't know a single other art student well enough to go out for coffee with and talk about art. I ached for FSU, but everyone who'd really mattered to me had also left.

Given the lack of support and my loss of confidence, it didn't feel like a huge sacrifice when I gave in to John's insistence that I change my major from painting to education, so that I could teach while he got his degree in theology. I agreed to do as he wished and pushed thoughts of being a painter from my conscious mind.

I continued to talk with John about philosophy and theology, but he became angry when I didn't accept some of his theological beliefs as my own. During one heated discussion about predestination and free will, he slapped me hard across the face because I disagreed with him. Stunned and frightened, I asked him to take me back to my dormitory. As soon as he parked his car, I opened the door and walked quickly to the safety of the building. John came rushing behind me, apologizing, begging me to stop and talk with him. I walked hurriedly through the lounge and up the stairs to my room.

Later that night John called and asked me to talk with him.

I said no.

The next evening he came over to the dorm and called me on the house phone, begging me to come down and talk with him for just a few minutes. He told me that he was horribly sorry about slapping me and needed my forgiveness. If I would only come down to the lounge for a few minutes. Please.

"For a few minutes," I agreed, "but I'm not going out with you again."

We sat across from each other near the housemother's office.

Of course he said he was sorry. He didn't know what had gotten into him. Of course he said he would never do it again. Then he begged me to go out with him one more time.

"No." I was afraid to go out with him.

"Only to talk," he pleaded.

"No." I was afraid I would give in to him.

"I love you. At least do this one thing for me."

"No."

"Please, Margaret."

He drove us to Posse's Barbecue Drive-In several miles from town. We sat in the parked car and talked. He wanted me to come back to him. He reminded me of how he had talked to no one but me since his Grandfather Elder died when he was just a twelve-year-old boy. He couldn't live without me. He would kill himself if I left him.

I steeled myself against his pleas. "No," I said, "I can't continue this relationship." I was not going to give in to pity. Or to guilt. I had to get away.

"I'm not going to come back to you. I can't."

He grew quiet. Then he began to mutter nonsensical sentences. "The old yellow dog jumped over the stile," he said. And "Catsup is spilling out of the airplane." Then he stared out the front windshield, saying nothing. I felt afraid and puzzled.

He started the car and headed back to town but took the long way. The dirt road was desolate. Fields of corn spread on either side, and there was an occasional shack, dimly lit and set back from the road. As soon as we were at some distance from the restaurant and traffic, and alone on the road, he began to mutter other nonsensical phrases, so nonsensical that I couldn't even then hold them in my mind.

Again he grew quiet.

After a few miles of silence, he suddenly slumped over the steering wheel as if unconscious. I struggled to get control of the wheel, then pressed my body close against his so that I could reach the gas pedal and brake. I drove the rest of the way back to town with him stone silent beside me, his head knocking against the glass of the closed window every time I went over a bump.

When we arrived at the house in which he had rented a room, I was able to rouse him and walk him to the door. He swayed from side to side as he walked and had a strange dazed look in his eyes. I drove his car back to my dormitory.

The next day he claimed to remember nothing of his behavior the night before. But he still insisted he would kill himself if I left him.

I stayed. I stayed because I didn't know how to leave. I stayed because I cared about him. I stayed because I was terrified that he really would kill himself. I stayed, hoping that come summer, I could persuade Mother and Daddy to let me drop out of college and go to art school like I'd wanted to do from the beginning.

III
1956

My sister, Harriet, died of pneumonia in late February. She was only nine years old.

"It's a blessing," Aunt Bama said when she and Uncle Earnest came to Athens to drive me home for the funeral. I didn't smoke cigarettes in front of them, so I was glad when we stopped at a filling station. I squatted over the toilet and peed, then stood and lit a cigarette, sucking the smoke into my lungs and expelling it into the small airless room with its dirty sink and stench, while Uncle Earnest and Aunt Bama waited in the car, the attendant pumping gasoline and cleaning the windshield of smashed bugs and bird droppings.

"A blessing," my aunt had said almost as soon as they had picked me up at the dormitory. I took another drag from the cigarette and threw it into the toilet. My sister's death a blessing? A relief, she meant, like peeing. Now Mother could go back to teaching. My aunt talked constantly as my uncle drove in silence. "A blessing," she repeated until the drive was finally over and I was standing in my front yard in my mother's arms.

"It was either her or me," Mother said, her face colorless and drawn. "I'd reached the end of my endurance."

When I went into the house, I walked through the living room and stood at the door to the dining room looking across at my sister's bent arms and clenched fists rising from the coffin. When I walked closer and looked down at Harriet's body, I saw that her hair had been brushed away from her head and arranged around her face like a halo. It looked grotesque.

"Please brush her hair down like she wore it," I said hoarsely to the undertaker and turned away quickly, smelling the scent of the funeral wreaths that didn't mask the odor of formaldehyde. I felt like I might vomit.

The undertaker, a kind man with large blue eyes, a man I'd known since we were in high school, did as I asked. Then he apologized for Harriet's bent arms. He explained that he would have had to break her bones to get her arms to lie down in the coffin.

I don't remember what the preacher said to those of us gathered in the living room that day. I only remember hearing a high school friend—dead for many years now—singing "Jesus Loves the Little Children," her beautiful soprano voice filling the house while I stood, silent, dry-eyed, and numb. Nor do I remember the drive on the Thomasville highway to the new cemetery, where my sister's coffin was lowered into the earth on the barren hill that rose across the road from where the slaughterhouse once stood.

I flew to Atlanta, where John met my plane and then drove me back to Athens. I told him about Harriet's bent arms and clenched fists, an image that I would carry inside me for the rest of my life. Then, for the first time since I'd seen my sister's dead body, I cried.

IV

Harriet was dead. Depression gnawed at Daddy's days. His heart disease was getting worse. He was no longer able to bring in enough money to pay the utilities bills. Aunt Bama often paid them while wringing the last drop of self-respect from him by not giving him the money but writing checks to the utilities companies herself.

"I'm only a shell of a man," Daddy would groan. "Only a shell of a man."

He talked of suicide. But as sick and miserable as he was in his life, he was more afraid of death. Often he stretched out on his bed and talked about his fear of dying. I lay on Mother's bed, watching the play of late-afternoon light on the walls. I no longer screamed at him like I'd done when I was younger—"Daddy, you're too afraid to live!"—but listened to him with an intense sorrow I couldn't touch with words.

In her forties, Mother was attending college again. She went to Valdosta State to renew her teaching certificate. Some weekends we drove over to visit her. More often than not, she stayed in her dormitory and studied.

My memories of that summer are a blur of Daddy's talk about death, mounds of dirty dishes, burnt food, line after line of laundry, wet fabric clinging to my arms. By that time I smoked in front of my parents. Nicotine dulled my feeling of despair. The next cigarette became one of my major reasons to live through the days. Daddy, a heavy smoker most of his life, seemed happy to have the company. It was the thing we did together. That, and talking about death.

I'd done little of the housework or cooking in the past. "You'll have the rest of your life to do such things," Mother had always said to me with a sigh. "The whole rest of your life." That summer I learned by trial and error what it was to run a house for two adolescent boys and a depressed man. At nineteen, I was initiated, taken through my rite of passage to being a Southern housewife in the 1950s.

It was a long summer, with its hot and humid days, the air outside filled with gnats and mosquitoes, and inside the faithful drone of electric fans. Nights, our dog, Trixie, sat in the driveway howling at the moon.

When Mother came home for a weekend, I pleaded with her not to send me back to the university. I had to get away from John, I said. He frightened me. And I told her about his slapping me, and about his bizarre behavior at Posse's that night.

Didn't she hear what I was telling her? Didn't she believe me? Certainly she didn't want to believe me. How could the refined, soft-spoken John that she had met possibly do those things? Perhaps she thought I was being dramatic about nothing. "Such a flair for the dramatic you have," Mother had exclaimed much of my life. "Such a flair!"

Whatever her reasons, after listening to my story she said in her usual controlled tone: "Margaret, if you don't want to go with John, just tell him."

Just tell him. But I knew she didn't mean it. And I wished it had been that simple. I wished I had the self-confidence, wished I didn't have the guilt and feeling of responsibility that kept me with him. I wished I didn't love him. And did I have a right to do other than what I knew Mother really wanted? I was her daughter. And Daddy's daughter too. Someplace deep inside me I felt I was more their property than my own person.

I knew Mother wanted me to marry John. Then I would not go off to New York City to be a painter and live the life of a bohemian artist in Greenwich Village. "My daughter, Margaret," she could say. "The minister's wife." I would be like the wooden bride doll that she had given me, the only doll of mine that she never gave away.

Now I stood ironing Bubba's summer shirts, two each day—one

for work and another for going out in the evening. He kept bringing them back to me—a wrinkle in a collar, a puckered hem. That summer something took my dreams away. I learned to iron a shirt without a single wrinkle. In my mind my sister's clenched fists were always rising from the coffin.

I made plans to marry John, who said he needed me, who said he'd take his own life if I didn't give him mine. But now so little about that summer stands out—ironing mostly, and my embarrassment when my father asked me to cook his hamburger again because blood kept leaking onto his plate.

Chapter Seven

JOHN AND I WERE MARRIED ON SEPTEMBER 15, 1956. BY THE TIME WE finished college I was several months pregnant. The day of our graduation ceremony I felt nauseated and didn't want to face the crowd and the heat. I couldn't have cared less about receiving a diploma for a degree in education. If anything, it embarrassed me, since I had little respect for the course requirements for that degree. Mother was pleased though. She and Daddy attended along with John's parents. I stayed home and cooked dinner for all of us. I was upset when I burned the carrots, but John's father said he was glad I burned them because he hated carrots more than anything. When I remember that day, the first thing that always comes to mind is the image of those carrots at the bottom of the burnt pot.

After graduation we moved to Ila, a small town near Athens in which John had served for the past year as student minister in the Presbyterian church. A perceptive member of the congregation told me that she believed he would end up being a teacher rather than a minister, which is what happened. While John enjoyed preaching, he found visiting members of the congregation at home and relating to them burdensome and uncomfortable. By the time we moved into the manse (the house supplied by the church for its pastor), John had already received a Danforth Fellowship to do graduate work in philosophy. He agreed to preach Sundays until he finished his master's at Emory University on the outskirts of Atlanta. In the meantime, he continued his study of logic with Rubin Gotesky, one of his professors at the University of Georgia. They spent an evening each week together.

Our son John Elder was born August 13, 1957. He was named after the grandfather John had loved so dearly. There were no tests then to determine the sex of a baby before it was born, but almost from the beginning I felt certain our baby was a boy, and we named him before seeing him.

Waking the morning of the twelfth, I knew he was coming soon. I packed my bag, including an outfit for him to come home in. Then I spent much of the day washing clothes, cleaning the house, and packing maternity outfits away in boxes. After dinner I took a shower and changed clothes for the trip to Athens.

John left me with friends for several hours while he had his weekly meeting with Professor Gotesky. I remember nothing about my time spent waiting for John except that I was having contractions. When he picked me up, we immediately went to Saint Mary's Hospital.

The contractions had grown intense and my doctor insisted on giving me "twilight sleep," a combination of morphine and scopolamine that was supposed to give me amnesia so that I wouldn't feel or remember the pain of childbirth. I was in extreme pain and still remember most things about the labor and my baby's birth. I also remember the doctor telling John that I would remember nothing and that he should go home to bed. Which he did.

It was a long, lonely, and torturous night. Shortly before breakfasttime I was taken to the delivery room. My feet were fastened in stirrups and my hands were strapped down. I felt frantic with claustrophobia. After struggling unsuccessfully to free myself of the constraints, I calmed myself as I watched the doctor lift the baby by his feet and smack him hard on his bottom, eliciting a piercing howl. I flinched at what felt like a violent act.

"Is he all right?" I asked.

He was born two weeks late, just as my sister had been, and I'd spent those long two weeks praying that he wouldn't be brain-damaged.

"He's fine," the doctor replied, and a nurse whisked him out of my sight.

It was much later before a nurse brought him to me and I saw the deep forceps marks on both sides of his extremely elongated head. His experience of his birth had to have been at least as difficult as mine, probably more so. The thought haunted me. But more than anything, I clung to the doctor's words that he was "fine."

After our first night in the hospital, the nurse who brought him to me told me he'd screamed all night. She had never heard a newborn scream as much and as loudly as he did; it was the topic of talk among the nurses that night. She didn't mention anyone holding him, and certainly no one brought him to me. It hurt to know how much he'd suffered. When I finally saw him he was exhausted. He didn't have the energy to nurse but fell asleep in my arms.

II

Mother came to help me for a few days when we went home to Ila. John Elder screamed or cried much of the time. I was breast-feeding him, and Mother was convinced that he was crying so much because my breast milk was inadequate. Desperate, I came to believe her, stopped breast-feeding him, and gave him a bottle. Mother went home to Daddy, and I finished packing our belongings for our move into an apartment in Mudville, a group of old army barracks that had been made into apartments for graduate students at Emory University.

When John Elder was two weeks old we moved. We had a small bedroom, a small living room, and a breakfast bar separating it from the kitchen, where my old wringer washing machine stood next to the sink.

John Elder continued to cry and scream.

I was puzzled, frustrated, and exhausted. When he was six weeks old, I took him to a pediatrician. I told the doctor that he screamed or cried much of the time and I didn't know what to do. He responded: "Just get used to it. He was born this way."

I had no other place to turn for help.

I thought of Harriet, who spent the early weeks of her life screaming because of pressure on her brain. By walking back and forth in my parents' bedroom I had been able to calm her so that she fell asleep in my arms. Now I held my own baby in my arms and walked back and forth in our Mudville apartment. My baby screamed. I sat down and rocked him. He screamed. I got up and walked him. He screamed. I walked him some more. He screamed. He must have given up and fallen asleep eventually, but what I remember now is the screaming. That, and my despair.

John couldn't tolerate our son's screaming. By this time he had begun to drink, and he stayed out late nights, talking with his fellow philosophy students and drinking in a local tavern. Once he came home late, hit me, and threw me to the floor. When I tried to talk to him about what he'd done, he went to bed and uttered nonsensical phrases the way he'd begun to do when, according to his mother, he was a child wanting to escape his alcoholic father, who physically abused both of them. There was no way to get through to John. After sitting in the living room for a while, smoking a cigarette to calm myself, I too went to bed, and eventually to sleep.

That year at Emory, John's anger intensified as my sense of resignation settled in. I wouldn't have called myself depressed at the time; I was too busy to know how I felt. But looking back, my depression is evident. When I got up in the night to feed John Elder, I began to feed myself as well. I ate cookie after cookie, as if cookies could comfort my lost, lonely feeling.

III
1958

When John Elder was old enough to stay awake and crawl around the floor and play with his toys, he finally stopped screaming during the day, but he still screamed every time I put him to bed, either for a nap or for the night. The pediatrician told me to let him cry himself to sleep; otherwise, he warned, I would spoil him. I tried to let him cry for fifteen agonizing minutes before I went into the bedroom to find him sweaty and exhausted. He and I were both so upset that I never did that again. Clearly he was too distressed to be left alone—this had nothing to do with spoiling or not spoiling him. For some reason my son had an intense discomfort that I could not understand, but I wasn't going to make it worse by abandoning him.

Mother spent her entire life suffering guilt and remorse because, when I was a baby, she left me closed up in my room, crying for hours until I fell asleep from exhaustion. She treated me the way she was taught, never picking me up except to feed me, and feeding me on a prescribed schedule that had nothing to do with my hunger. Whether I remember my suffering or think I do because of Mother's recounting it to me, I was as haunted by those experiences as she was. When, in middle age, I went to a hypnotherapist, I remembered—or thought I remembered—how cold Mother's touch was, and how hungry, lost, and frantic I felt when closed in that room. I didn't want to give my own baby such memories.

Early one morning John Elder woke crying. I did everything I could to get him back to sleep, but he continued to cry. Finally, he began to mutter what sounded like the word *car*. He was much too young to talk, so I thought I must have misinterpreted his sound. But after he repeated it several times, I wrapped him up in a blanket and took him out to the car. As soon as I put him inside he stopped crying.

Had he really said *car?*

He was only eight months old; the idea seemed ridiculous.

I took him into the apartment again.

He immediately began to cry. "Car car car," he repeated.

I put him in the car again. Again he stopped crying.

But he was too young to be able to talk! I still couldn't believe he was actually saying a word and knew what it meant. Once more I took him inside. He began to cry.

"Car," he said with frantic determination. "Car."

With equal determination, I picked up the car keys. This time I put him in, started the car, and began to drive. He fell asleep almost immediately, but I drove for a long time, wanting to be certain he was deeply asleep before I risked parking the car and taking him out. He was sleeping so soundly that I was able to put him into his crib and go back to bed myself.

John Elder had said his first word.

It wasn't the expected *Mama* or *Dada.* He had said the word *car,* and meant it. He had finally told me exactly what he needed to comfort and calm him, and it wasn't me—it was the car. So be it. At last I knew something I could do to ease his distress. At least sometimes. I don't know how many miles I put on the car driving over the dirt and often muddy roads of Mudville, but drive I did. In a year of extreme struggle and frustration, and what often felt like failure on my part, there was this one shining moment of success—my son had spoken to me and I had understood.

IV

When John Elder was a year old, we moved to Philadelphia so John could study for his doctorate in philosophy at the University of

Pennsylvania. Lucille Jones, a longtime friend of my Aunt Curtis, found us an inexpensive apartment in West Philadelphia. It was in an old red-brick row house on Spruce Street that had originally been a one-family home. Our apartment was on the first floor and was divided by the common entryway and the stairs to the apartments on the second and third floors. Our living room, to the left of the entryway and just before the stairs, was long and narrow. Our bedroom—what must have originally been the dining room—had enormous double sliding doors. Every time someone closed the front door, our bedroom doors glided open.

The only room that felt private was the kitchen, with its heavy oak table and sideboard and a marvelous old wooden wall clock that ticked loudly as its pendulum swung back and forth, marking the seconds, minutes, and hours of our new lives in that peculiar apartment.

Mrs. O'Donnell, an old woman with henna-dyed hair and a limp, lived on the second floor. Her only friend, our landlady, lived on the third floor but was rarely at home except nights, as she spent her days cleaning houses.

Mrs. O'Donnell kept her brandy hidden in the cabinet of her grandfather clock—a secret she shared with me—because the landlady didn't approve of drinking. From what I could see, Mrs. O'Donnell had little else besides those stolen sips of brandy and an apartment with knickknacks on every available surface.

She was lonely.

Most mornings she knocked on my door shortly after she heard John leave for the university.

I don't remember much about the monologues she delivered during those visits. I felt compassion for her in her loneliness, but I felt trapped as she talked on and on. Some days I was able to get John Elder and myself dressed so we could slip out of the house before she came down. Then we'd spend the morning in the public park several blocks down on Spruce and across Baltimore Avenue.

John Elder contented himself digging in the sand with a large cooking spoon, or playing with one or another of the little cars or trucks I had brought with us. I sat on a bench and read, or simply watched him and the many other people in the park. John Elder never played with any of the other children, and though I must have at least occasionally talked with another mother, time has erased memories of those encounters. What I do remember vividly are fall's brightly colored leaves on the trees and winter's bitter cold that Georgia's mild climate had not prepared me for.

Sometimes Mrs. O'Donnell came downstairs to visit when she heard us return from the park, but it was usually time for lunch and John Elder's nap, so her visits then were brief. Visits with the landlady were even briefer. I saw her when I paid the rent, and once when she chastised me for not cleaning John Elder's handprints off the glass pane of the front door. I'd not noticed that he had sometimes touched the glass when I held him up so that we could watch John arriving home from his day at the university.

John Elder was walking quite well, and saying many other words in addition to *car* by the time we lived in that apartment on Spruce Street. Though he had no idea what it meant, he loved saying the words "My father studies philosophy at the university." His pronunciation was as clear as mine.

He still cried at nap- and bedtimes, but I'd discovered something that soothed him to sleep almost as easily as the car. It was a small canvas swing that I hung from the top molding of the doorway to the kitchen. He sat in it while I gave it an occasional push to keep it in motion until he tired of playing with its string of colored beads, closed his eyes, and dropped his head in sleep. I kept the swing swinging until I was certain he was sound asleep before taking him out and putting him to bed. Otherwise, he awoke screaming and I had to begin the entire process again.

Sometime during those early months in Philadelphia he gave up the swing in favor of my reading him to sleep. I'd read nursery rhymes to him since he was a baby, but until then he'd never gone to sleep while I was reading.

At the same time that he began to listen to me reading to him, he began to insist on keeping his shoes on with his pajamas. I had to wait until he was sleeping soundly in his crib before carefully removing them.

John Elder was already firmly entrenched in certain habits and preferences. For the entire second year of his life, he wanted me to read one book and one book only: *The Little Engine That Could*, the classic story of the little blue engine that accepted the almost impossible task of pulling a long train up a steep hill, when larger and stronger engines refused to undertake the task. It was the story of optimism, of faith in oneself to triumph over challenges. "I think I can—I think I can," the little engine repeated as it chugged its way up the hill. "I thought I could!" it said after it had reached the top and started down the other side. I read the book over and over until John Elder fell asleep. And though he never repeated the words aloud as I read, I feel certain that that chant, "I—think—I—can, I—think—I—can," burned itself as deeply into his brain as it did into mine.

V

The first time John Elder and I visited Lucille Jones in her tall, thin row house, both of us were utterly fascinated. Its rooms were crammed full of more furniture, knickknacks, teacups, cut-glass bowls and vases, candlesticks, candy dishes, and decanters than any other house I'd ever seen. Most if not all of the furniture had been purchased at antiques shops or secondhand stores, each piece holding its stories silent forever in its old wood and upholstery. On the walls were the many oil paintings Mrs. Jones painted before she developed an allergy to turpentine.

Mrs. Jones was one of the most important people in my young life, and I adored her. I loved the imagination she had put into furnishing and decorating her house, and the fact that she valued the comfort of family and friends. "I would never have a coffee table people couldn't prop their feet on if they wanted to," she said. It mattered to me that she had been a painter and still played the piano.

She filled her life with art and music. And she filled mine. She introduced me to the Philadelphia Museum of Art, took me with her to exhibits at the Philadelphia Art Alliance and to concerts by the Philadelphia Orchestra, led by Eugene Ormandy. And it was to her that I also talked most about my feelings and my marriage. With her I could express emotions that I was never permitted to express in my mother's home, or at home with John. With her I felt free. As soon as I sat down on the living room sofa and began to talk with her, John Elder began to rush from one thing to another. He wanted to touch everything.

"Don't touch!" I screamed as he reached out to feel the face of a plaster angel standing on a tall wooden pedestal. What if the angel were to come crashing to the floor, breaking its spread wings in the fall? "Don't touch!"

Mrs. Jones leaned toward me and smiled. "If anything gets broken, it will be my fault, not yours." Then she looked at John Elder touching the angel's foot. "John Elder is more important to me than these old things," she said.

I knew she meant it.

I never again told John Elder "Don't touch!" or "Be careful!" when we were at Mrs. Jones's house. And in all the years that we visited her, he never broke a single thing. But he touched everything he could reach and looked at everything he couldn't. He touched vases, cups, and candy dishes. He ran his fingers across the bumpy cut glass of the decanter that Professor Jones poured his sherry from when he was downstairs rather than upstairs in his study preparing lectures for his classes or working on his book about Shelley.

Rows of colored glass bottles stood on shelves in the bay window in what had once been the dining room but now held a grand piano. Sunlight streaming through the window made it glow like stained glass. This was John Elder's favorite room. His reason lay in the chest of drawers under the window. The bottom drawer was filled with a train engine, train cars and tracks, trucks, blocks, soldiers, and other toys left over from the childhoods of her two grown sons. "This," Mrs. Jones announced, "will be John Elder's special drawer."

The drawer was heavy, with leaf-covered vines carved on its front, and large metal handles that John Elder tugged and tugged at until it slid open. Then he spent a long time simply holding the large Lionel engine and looking at it with awe. Sometimes he pushed the cars and trucks. Sometimes he lined the little soldiers up on the Oriental rug, worn thin from all the foot traffic to the kitchen through the years.

John Elder loved Mrs. Jones's kitchen. He loved to sit at the old oak table and push its huge lazy Susan around, rattling the teaspoons standing in a mug on it. The table was round and had clawed feet. I sat at it and drank coffee with Mrs. Jones while John Elder ate cookies or ice cream and then went to the dining room where he played with the toys from the toy drawer.

When I was ready to leave, I would call to John Elder: "Come here, it's time to go." I would pick up my pocketbook and walk through the kitchen, dining room, and living room to the front door. "John Elder!" I would call.

"Just a minute, Mama."

"Hurry!" I always responded. But my heart wasn't in the word. I loved being at Mrs. Jones's house as much as he did. And I must have often stood at the front door a full ten minutes more, talking with her before John Elder came to go home with me.

VI

One afternoon our upstairs neighbor Mrs. O'Donnell asked me to pin the hem of a dress she had sewn for herself. John Elder had never seen her apartment and, standing next to me, looked around with great interest as I knelt before Mrs. O'Donnell and began to pin the hem.

Suddenly something captured his attention and he started to walk across the room.

Just as suddenly Mrs. O'Donnell grabbed him and held him against her with a firm grip. Startled and frightened, John Elder bit her arm. She let out a little cry and dropped him to the floor. Picking him up, I mumbled a halfhearted apology and told her that I guessed I wouldn't be able to pin her hem that day. I felt embarrassed that John Elder had bitten her—the skin wasn't broken—but I couldn't blame him.

After dinner that night, our landlady called for me to come up to Mrs. O'Donnell's apartment. I left John Elder with John and climbed the stairs reluctantly. I found the two women in the kitchen. Mrs. O'Donnell was seated silently at the table. The landlady was standing by the stove with her feet far apart and her arms crossed over her chest. As I entered the room, she began to scream at me. "How dare you let that son of yours bite my friend! What kind of mother are you?"

Before I could respond to her accusations, she picked up a large iron skillet from the stove and began to chase me around the table with fierce determination. "How dare you!" she screamed as she chased me. "How dare you!"

We circled the table several times before I was able to run out the door and down the stairs to my apartment.

John and John Elder were in the kitchen.

"We're moving, John," I announced. After John Elder was asleep I told John the whole story. He supported my decision, as I knew he would.

I spent most of the night packing.

The next day I called a real estate agent and told him what we were looking for. There was a vacant apartment in a building on the corner of Forty-fifth and Pine. After looking at it, I signed a year's lease.

We moved the next day. John left a check for the rent on a table in the entryway. I never heard from or saw the landlady or Mrs.

O'Donnell again, though I sometimes thought of Mrs. O'Donnell alone with her things and her brandy.

VII
1961

John Elder was almost four and Doug was three when they first met in the park. Doug was John Elder's first friend. They played in the dirt while Doug's mother, Jean, and I talked. Sometimes playing with each other was difficult for the boys.

I never watched daytime TV and only let John Elder watch *Happy the Clown* in the morning. But somehow one day he watched *The Three Stooges.* After seeing the way the men hit one another, he began hitting Doug. He ignored all my attempts to make him stop. I never understood why he hit Doug, but Doug remained his friend no matter what John Elder did. The friendship only ended when Doug's father finished the courses he'd been taking at the university and moved the family back to Billings, Montana.

John Elder never mentioned Doug to me again.

I had no address for Jean, and it was a very long time before I heard from her. When I finally received a letter from her over a year later she told me she'd given birth to a baby girl. But the news about Doug was shocking—he had drowned in an irrigation ditch near their home.

I felt devastated. What could I possibly write in response? Again and again I began letters to Jean only to tear each up and begin another. Days became weeks, weeks became months, and months became years. Still I mailed no letter to Jean. But I thought about Doug and his death a great deal. I wrote nothing to Jean and heard nothing from her.

What remained for me was a painful, guilt-filled silence.

John Elder began attending nursery school, where he hit other children until he finally realized that hitting wasn't conducive to keeping them as friends. He no longer talked about *The Three Stooges* and continued to say nothing about Doug.

VIII

I was feeling as bad as I'd ever felt. John was having an affair with a secretary in the German department at the university. I don't know what made him go to the German department the first time, but he came home that day talking excitedly about a secretary who sat at her desk holding one of her breasts in her hand. He was fascinated by her. Shortly after meeting her, he took his wedding ring off, saying that it was no longer comfortable to wear. He also began to come home later than usual. He wouldn't admit that he was having an affair, but the fact was undeniable and I'd reached the limits of my endurance. I'd begun to vomit much of the food I tried to eat, and my weight dropped rapidly from 145 pounds to 118.

Whenever I tried to talk with John about my feelings, he'd collapse in the bed and mumble nonsensical phrases. I would struggle to make him communicate with me, then finally give up. Either he was split down the middle in a terribly frightening way, or he was a hell of a good actor. In the twenty-five years I was with him, I was never able to say for certain which he was. Perhaps he was both.

"I'm going to Georgia," I finally told him. "You can make up your mind whether you want your marriage or your girlfriend, but I can't take this."

"If you go south, you'll be abandoning me. If you leave, I *will* have an affair," he yelled.

"You're already having an affair, John."

I packed John Elder's and my suitcases and arranged for our flight.

My mother-in-law, Carolyn, met us at the Atlanta airport. I planned on staying for a while in Lawrenceville, about two hundred miles from my parents in Cairo.

Carolyn and I sat on her front porch and rocked in their old-fashioned high-backed rocking chairs with wicker seats. John Elder played with his cars, pushing them between the chairs and mumbling to himself. The porch ran the full length of the house and had a two-story ceiling, the portico supported by enormous columns that came from an old mansion on Peachtree Street in Atlanta. Carolyn and Jack's house didn't look unlike those old plantation houses in *Gone with the Wind*. But Jack and Carolyn didn't have a well-kept lawn where friends gathered and drank mint juleps while servants waited on them hand and foot.

Jack and Carolyn didn't have any servants or friends. At least not mutual friends. They related to people at work during the week, but many weekends were spent with Jack drunk and sometimes violent toward Carolyn. Once, while drunk, he'd blasted holes in his bedroom ceiling with a shotgun. Another time he hurled a heavy antique baby cradle down the stairs after Carolyn. She spent the weekends doing laundry, ironing, smoking one cigarette after another, and cooking huge meals. There was no time for friends on weekends.

One day when I was there, Carolyn came home with an enormous cut-glass punch bowl and about fifty cups. She already had so many sets of china that the two huge mahogany china cabinets couldn't contain them. Some sets were still packed in boxes stacked in a corner of the dining room, which was where the new punch bowl and cups went.

"You all can use these for our funeral," she said to me. "They were just so pretty I couldn't resist them." Carolyn was always buying things. "My pretties," she'd call them affectionately. "All my pretties." But as much as she loved her "pretties," except for holidays and special occasions, she served all our meals on cracked and chipped odds and ends of bargain buys. Hardly anything matched anything else.

The house stood in woods so thick that what grass grew in the front yard was sparse and struggling for life. In front of the porch Carolyn had planted a few scraggly shrubs that managed to survive, but mostly there were the woods through which a long winding dirt road led from the highway to the house.

That afternoon we sat on the porch waiting for Jack to come home from his four days on the road as a traveling salesman for the division of Vicks that sold veterinary medical supplies. If the tires spat gravel or the car moved in any inconsistent way, then we knew Jack was drunk and braced ourselves for his arrival. If the sound of the car was perfectly normal, then we knew that Jack was so drunk he had had to pick up a hitchhiker to drive him home. We braced ourselves even more firmly.

Jack's father, John's Grandfather Dandy, who'd built much of the house himself, came out the front door wearing a pair of pants from one of John's old high school military uniforms, gray with a wide black stripe down the outside of each leg, making me think of a Georgia convict. He turned his back to us, unzipped his fly, and peed in the bushes.

Then Carolyn and I heard the car, smooth and steady on the driveway.

After the hitchhiker parked the car, Jack opened the door and came reeling across the yard and stumbled up the steps, his eyes lit with fury. "You come in the house!" he yelled at Carolyn as he opened the door.

The hitchhiker—a nice-looking young man—stood awkwardly by the car. Jack yelled for him to come in and meet the family. He did as he was told.

I don't believe Carolyn did a thing before Jack turned on her, cursing at her while he slammed her up against a wall in the kitchen and began choking her, her head knocking against the plaster. I'd followed the hitchhiker into the house.

"Hey, big boy," the hitchhiker said to Jack. "Enough of that, old buddy."

He wrestled Jack's big hands from around Carolyn's throat. Jack was too drunk to put up a fight. In the face of opposition he turned and left the room. I could hear him stomp up the stairs, then collapse onto the cherry four-poster bed he shared with Carolyn. He'd be passed out for hours before he'd rouse himself enough to bellow for Carolyn to come to bed with him. Then he'd go back to sleep for the night.

Carolyn leaned against the wall coughing.

"Think you ought to go to a doctor?" I asked.

"No. I'll be all right now." Her face was alternately red from coughing, then white.

"We need to drive this young man to a main highway so he can get to where he's going."

Carolyn picked up her purse and car keys, walked to her Cadillac, which was the color of dried blood, and slid into the driver's seat. John Elder, who loved cars more than almost anything, came running, and got into the backseat with the hitchhiker. I got into the front seat next to Carolyn. I really wanted her to go to a doctor, not so much because I thought she was injured badly that time but because I wanted someone to know what was going on in the Robison house in the woods. But she let the hitchhiker off, went to a drive-in for a cone of soft ice cream for John Elder, and drove back to the house.

Jack was out cold for the night.

The next morning he began to drink before breakfast. He drank all day long. That night, just after I tucked John Elder into bed, Jack yelled for me. I clenched my teeth. He'd used the same tone he'd used with Carolyn so many times. I kissed John Elder good night. Then I walked into the master bedroom with its Oriental rug and cherry highboy over which hung a print of a couple of young ballerinas bending to lace their slippers. There was Carolyn's dressing table with little lights around the mirror. An enormous TV faced Jack's easy chair. In the ceiling above the chair, the unrepaired shotgun holes gaped.

Carolyn was packing her cosmetic case when I entered their bedroom. Tubes of lipstick, mascara, bottles of makeup, face creams and hand creams, perfumes and powders, nail polish, hair rollers, and hairspray were strewn around the open case on the bed. Jack was sitting in his chair, hair uncombed, his bathrobe old and ragged. "Margaret," he moaned, "come here." He looked at me with a hangdog expression. "Carolyn's leaving me, Margaret. She's really going to leave me this time."

"I think that's the smartest thing she's ever done," I snapped before thinking.

Almost as soon as the words left my mouth, Jack was up and coming at me. I ran into the room that I shared with John Elder, who was in bed but not yet asleep. The closet had been built out into the room, creating a wall that faced the door. I put one foot against the closet wall and the other foot against the door. Then I locked myself hard in that position while Jack pushed against the door, cursing me and demanding to be let in.

Dandy heard the commotion and came upstairs and talked to Jack, persuading him to come back to his room and cool down. As soon as he was in his room with Dandy, Carolyn, John Elder, and I raced down the stairs, out the front door, through the woods to her car. It was parked in a little cleared space halfway between the house and the highway. She usually parked it there facing the highway because she knew that if Jack was drunk and running after her, he'd fall in the woods before he could get to the car. We got in, Carolyn turned on the ignition, pulled out into the dirt drive, and, on reaching the highway, turned right. It didn't matter which direction she chose. I thought she was going to a motel, but she just drove aimlessly over half the roads in the county.

"Aren't we going to a motel?" I asked finally, exhausted. John Elder lay asleep on the backseat.

"I just want to go back home and check on things," Carolyn responded. "I'll park in the woods and keep the engine running. If I'm not back in fifteen minutes, you take John Elder and go to a motel."

When we arrived back at the house, she took off walking down the dark road without even a sliver of moon to light her way.

John Elder slept, while I sat there smoking a cigarette.

It was no time before Carolyn was back and climbing into the driver's seat.

"It's all right. We can go back to the house and go to sleep. Mr. Robison called the police and had Jack locked up in the county jail overnight."

When we got to the house, Carolyn called the sheriff's office and asked if they'd taken Jack's tie and belt and anything else that he might hurt himself with. The sheriff assured her that he had. Then, without another word, and as calmly as if we'd all spent a quiet evening watching TV together, she crawled into bed and went to sleep.

I packed our suitcases. Then I lay awake for a long time, thinking. Come morning, I'd catch the first bus to South Georgia. I didn't want to see Jack's shame or rage-filled face again. But Dandy had picked Jack up at the jail and brought him home by the time I got up the next morning. Jack was quiet, saying nothing as I got John Elder and myself ready for our bus trip. He offered no apology but, without looking me in the eyes as I passed, said goodbye in a subdued, sober voice.

"Goodbye," I responded in a flat voice as I followed John Elder into Carolyn's car and slammed the door. I didn't look back. Carolyn drove us to the bus station, where, heavyhearted, I hugged her goodbye, took John Elder by the hand, and boarded a bus to see my parents in Cairo.

IX

The motion of the bus quickly put John Elder to sleep. I leaned back in my seat, lit a cigarette, and looked out at the familiar landscape. Miles and miles of pine trees, farmland, and muddy streams and rivers flashed past the window. I put my cigarette out in the ashtray on the armrest and closed my eyes.

I loved Jack, but I could hardly bear being around him when he was drinking. When he was sober, I used to tell him he was like the little girl in the nursery rhyme: When he was good, he was very, very good. When he was bad, he was horrid.

There were many good times with him. I remember him taking John Elder and me on trips to Atlanta, twenty or so miles from Lawrenceville. I especially remember the time he took us to a factory that made stuffed animals. The owner and designer of many of the animals was Jack's friend, and she allowed him to fill the car and its trunk with stuffed animals. Our little apartment in Mudville was crowded with these creatures until I'd given most of them away to Mudville's eager children. Still, John Elder had so many that their funny faces stared back at me almost everyplace I looked. Another time, Jack took us to an ice cream factory owned by another of his friends. That day he filled up the car's trunk with ice cream and dry ice.

Jack was often extravagant. Despite his heavy weekend drinking, he was his company's most successful salesman and made a good living. He bought Carolyn more diamonds than she had fingers on which to wear them, and once bought her a necklace said to have been made for one of Napoléon's mistresses. Even after all these years, I remember sitting on the front steps of the house with Carolyn while we hulled strawberries together, the plump red berries in a pink dishpan full of well water, sunlight finding its way through the forest to warm our faces. Or the time we walked through the grasses and bushes across the highway, searching for wildflowers to dry and make into bouquets. And it was Carolyn who taught me how to fry chicken and bake corn bread the way John liked them.

I remember all the Christmases we spent in Lawrenceville, wrapping paper strewn over the Oriental rug, and John Elder playing with all his toys. And I won't forget the Christmas Carolyn nailed the stump of the tree to the polished oak floor because it kept falling over in its stand.

Sometimes she and I just sat on the porch in the rocking chairs and watched John Elder play with his cars and trucks while we drank coffee, smoked cigarettes, and talked about nothing special at all.

X

While I was in Cairo, Mother was away from early morning until around four in the afternoon teaching fifth grade. My brother Mercer was at school during the day, then out mowing lawns until suppertime. He was no longer the laughing baby or happy child everyone had praised. Instead, he conveyed a deep sadness that made me want desperately to help him. But I couldn't even help myself, and Bubba was at Georgia Tech.

Daddy's depression had grown more intense over the years, and his angina had worsened. His doctor didn't even suggest that he stop smoking. Instead, he said Daddy's heart had been in such bad shape for so many years that it was a miracle he was alive at all, and he didn't want to take away one of the few pleasures left in Daddy's life. Mother had written me that she had come home from school one winter day to find him asleep in a chair by the gas heater in their bedroom, cigarette burned down to his knuckles. She'd also written me about Daddy's trying to persuade her to commit suicide with him.

Daddy said nothing to me about suicide. He was relieved to have me with him during the day. One afternoon, when Mother was especially late coming home, I lay on her bed while Daddy lay on his bed, talking. Light from the setting sun sifted through the pines and gave the room a warm, melancholy glow. Daddy spoke softly about his terror of death. "What do you think happens after we die, sister?" he asked. I had no answer to his question, but by then I too had suffered severe depression and had thought about suicide.

I didn't talk at all with him about the difficulties in my marriage. Daddy was almost totally unable to listen to anyone about anything for long. At sixty-one he was already an old man, frail and defeated.

His anxiety was so great and so constant that he was driven to talk incessantly to keep his demons at bay. "I'm only a shell of a man," he'd say, repeating that familiar phrase over the years of his slow decline.

One day he gave an agonized confession. Harriet had been extremely difficult to feed and always ate baby food. As soon as one gave her a mouthful of pablum, or something else, it immediately came rolling from her mouth and had to be scooped up and put in again. Mother usually fed her, each meal taking an hour or more, while a soap opera played on the radio. More often than not, Harriet threw up her entire meal after Mother had finally managed to get it into her. Then Mother had to start all over again. Daddy told me that once, on a rare occasion when he'd been feeding Harriet, he'd grown so frustrated that he'd slapped her face. Tears streaming from his eyes, he said his life was haunted by what he'd done, and he could never forgive himself.

Daddy also obsessed about what he imagined were Mother's attractions to everyone from the school principal to the janitor, the salesman in the shoe shop to the grocer or the butcher. Anytime she was late coming home, he accused her of spending the time with another man. "Wyman," Mother snapped one day. "You have long since killed any interest I might have had in men."

Life had tired Mother out long before she began teaching again. But to teach all day only to come home to his accusations, threats of suicide, and anxiety-riddled talk tested the limits of her endurance. She often wondered if Daddy had over the years suffered ministrokes that had affected his personality. His anger had intensified, and he'd begun to throw things. Once, Mother told me, he'd thrown his shoes at Mercer, whom he suspected had been fathered by someone else altogether.

"Just look at that curly blond hair!" he'd scream at Mother. "Just look at it!"

Yet, despite their anger toward each other, the image that persists in my mind is still of my parents walking together through the yard in late afternoon, holding hands, flowers blooming everywhere.

One morning Daddy and I sat in the wicker chairs in the break-fast room, drinking coffee and smoking cigarettes. Daddy faced the glass door beyond which stood the birdbath and the bird feeder that he filled every day of his life. I faced him. He began complaining to me about Mother and the many things she did or failed to do. Then he talked about how lonely he was.

I listened as long as I could bear it, then picked up my cigarettes and went out and sat on the back steps. I lit one and inhaled deeply. I looked at the maple tree. I remembered the day in my early teens that I'd stood at the back door after a heavy rain, looking at that maple and the water pooled in the grass beside it. The maple, the grass, the rain, and the sky were everything, and I was a part of every-thing and everything was a part of me. But that day I couldn't bring the moment back vividly enough to comfort me.

I ached for Mother, for Daddy, for Mercer. I ached for myself. There was no comfort to be had with my family, no wise words of direction, no relief from pain. What I felt was the draining away of the little energy I had. Certainly there was no support for me to leave John.

It was time for me to go home.

Years after Mother's death, Mercer told me that Mother had been afraid I would leave John and bring John Elder with me to live with her, with them. She hadn't realized that even going back to John with his lover was more tolerable to me than staying in Cairo. There was nothing there for me except sadness.

Heartsick, I packed our bags and made arrangements to fly home to Philadelphia. Mother and Daddy drove us to the Albany airport, where we took a small propeller plane to Atlanta, then a jet to Philadelphia. Home to a husband who was having an affair with an-other woman.

Nevertheless, after three or four weeks in Georgia, I was going back to the only home I had.

Chapter Eight

I CAME BACK TO PHILADELPHIA AND IMMEDIATELY FACED MOVING OUT OF our apartment and into the former house of one of John's professors. A whole block of row houses near the university, including the house of John's professor Betty Flower, was to be torn down to make a parking lot. Professor Flower had bought another house and had agreed to let us live in the old one rent-free until it was torn down. In exchange for this, I reupholstered her couch, while John did odd jobs around her new house.

By the time we'd moved into the three-story house on DeKalb Street, John said he had ended his affair but felt a need to tell me about it. We were in bed one night as he began to describe their lovemaking. I couldn't bear to hear such graphic details. "Please, John," I cried out, "don't tell me these things!" I broke into hard sobbing.

John Elder woke and called from his room: "Daddy, please be good to Mama."

I composed myself and rushed to him. I sat on the edge of his bed, stroking his head and assuring him that I was all right. In seconds he was asleep again. When I went back to bed John was no longer there. I went downstairs, but he wasn't there either. Then I went up to the third floor, which was used for storage and little else.

John was sitting on a packing box, head in his hands.

"John, come back to bed. He won't remember in the morning."

John looked up at me, tears streaming down his face.

Seeing his pain, I forgot about my own.

"No, Margaret, he'll remember when he's forty, and it'll hurt more then."

But he got up from the box and together we went back to bed. Our backs to each other, we went to sleep. Or pretended to sleep.

Even though John was no longer seeing the secretary—or so he said—I needed to talk, to express my own feelings about their relationship as well as ours. But he refused to listen. I told him that I had to leave unless he went to a therapist. He stiffened at my ultimatum.

"Both of us," I said. "I'll go to the therapist too. I'm going to take John Elder to Al and Judy's while you make up your mind." Al was one of John's best friends in the philosophy department, and Judy was one of my best friends. "Think about it, John, if our marriage matters to you at all. I can't go on living like this. I'll leave you for good this time."

John stood at the top of the stairs. I stood by the front door and called John Elder. I wanted to get our son to a safe place before I came back to deal with his father's response.

After leaving John Elder with Al and Judy, I stopped to tell Mrs. Jones what was happening. I was enough afraid to want her to know.

"I'll go home with you," she said, picking up her purse.

"No, I want to go alone," I said. Which wasn't true, but I was afraid she might get hurt.

"Once Lucille has made up her mind to do something, you can't change it," Professor Jones said, lighting his pipe. "You're wasting time arguing with her."

I was grateful to have her support.

We found John unconscious, sprawled spread-eagle on the kitchen floor.

He'd cut his wrist with a black, bone-handled carving knife, the blade too dull to slice a chicken breast. Pages of a letter lay scattered around him on the floor, and a half-empty bottle of scotch stood on the kitchen counter.

It was immediately apparent to me that the wound was superficial. I ran upstairs to see if he'd taken an overdose of anything in the bathroom medicine cabinet but could see nothing missing.

When I got back to the kitchen, Mrs. Jones was kneeling over him. He was mumbling incoherently while reaching for her breast. She stopped his hand and stood. I collapsed onto the couch, sobbing.

"He's going to be all right," she said comfortingly. "He's not dead."

I'm not crying because he's dead, I thought. *I'm crying because he's pulled one more trick to try to keep me.*

Mrs. Jones went to the phone and called the police. They came immediately. Suddenly conscious but with a blank face, John got up and walked out of the house between the two policemen to their waiting car. They put him into the backseat with one of them. Mrs. Jones and I rode in the front seat with the other.

We rode to the hospital in silence.

In the waiting room John sat across from us in between the policemen. Mrs. Jones and I sat trying to put the pages of the letter he'd scattered on the floor into some order that made sense, which was difficult, as the pages were unnumbered and the contents weren't coherent. In the letter John referred to himself in the third person and asked for help.

A receptionist came out of an office and called John's name. "He'll talk his way out of there in no time," I said to Mrs. Jones. "I know John and his tricks and manipulations. He's so damned bright. He'll have that doctor wrapped around his little finger."

In moments the doctor came out into the waiting room, John following.

"Mrs. Robison," he said, shaking my hand. "Your husband has had an emotional shock. Just take him home, fix him a cup of tea, and put him to bed. He'll be all right in the morning."

As always, I ended up feeling trapped.

Mrs. Jones broke through my despair, announcing with authority: "There is no way Margaret is going home with that man to fix him a cup of tea or anything else."

Startled, the doctor looked at her, then looked again.

"Are you Freddy Jones's mother?" he asked with amazement.

"I certainly am, and I would like to talk with you in your office," Mrs. Jones said.

"Yes. Yes, of course" he said, leading the way. "I went to medical school with Freddy. Freddy Jones's mother! Well, you never know."

"There's no way Margaret's going to take John home with her," Mrs. Jones said firmly as he opened the door to his office. She held John's letter in her hand. By the time she came out of his office, it was clear that the doctor had other plans for John.

He was taken to a psychiatric hospital on the outskirts of Philadelphia, a posh place where Judy Garland and various other celebrities had spent time. John signed himself in, agreeing to stay for six weeks.

I drove Mrs. Jones home, picked John Elder up from Al and Judy's, and drove home. Nothing was solved, but at least there was now time to think. But how far had thinking gotten me before? At least I didn't feel so alone. Mrs. Jones was supporting me. And John hadn't gotten away with another melodramatic trick.

John called his mother, who came up from Georgia and stayed in the house with me. One day she lied, telling me she was going to downtown Philadelphia when in fact she went to John's department at the university. I don't know what she thought she could do or find out, but Betty Flower called me in hysterics. "What in the world made John's mother come poking around the department? I asked her not to come back. I've worked damn hard to conceal John's affair and hospitalization from Nelson. You know how conservative he is. I don't think that he'd work with John on his thesis if he knew all this mess." John was one of the few graduate students to write his thesis under the direction of Nelson Goodman, a prominent philosopher who was already included in history books. To threaten that relationship would threaten John's entire career.

My mother-in-law came home that day with a sketchy report of her trip to the city. I asked her no questions. It was evident that she'd mistrusted me. She was John's mother after all, not mine. "I'm glad you enjoyed your day," I said, and let the issue drop. I was grateful to have her keep John Elder when I visited John and his doctor at the hospital.

During one visit the psychiatrist said that John was extremely bright and used that intelligence to avoid dealing with his emotions. "And he can talk circles around me," he said. "Ideally, he needs a much older doctor who could command his respect."

"If I were your therapist," he said, "I'd tell you to run like hell. But I'm his therapist, and I say to you that his life depends on your staying."

And my life?

His life depended on my staying.

But now he was in a mental hospital.

I no longer knew how to live my life. I had to get away. To think. To talk. John told his mother that if she really wanted to help, she could keep John Elder for a couple of days so I could go to New York City for the weekend to visit my old college friend Ilse. She agreed.

At the train station, before I got onto the train to New York, I called my Aunt Curtis. I told her that I might have to leave John. Just weeks before the phone call, I'd sat with her on the grass on the university campus and poured out my heart, telling her painful things that I'd told no one else. Now I needed her support. Instead, she gave me a lecture about how John was "Ivy League" and life would be better once he finished graduate school. Heartsick, I hung up the phone. In New York I talked to Ilse. She listened until very late that night. Then she rubbed my back until I fell asleep.

She left for work before I woke the next morning. Beside my bed she'd propped a large sign with her psychiatrist's phone number and her own office number printed on it.

Clearly I couldn't call him. He'd give me medication. I imagined being put to sleep by the heavy dose of something. *No. If I'm tranquilized to sleep*, I thought, *I'll never wake sane.*

Sane, I thought. Somehow it was a matter of keeping my sanity, and to remain sane meant to remain conscious and free of drugs.

Then this flat, declarative sentence came to my mind: *I'm going to kill myself.*

I'm going to kill myself with a razor blade from Ilse's medicine cabinet.

In my mind's eye I saw the package lying on the right side of the bottom shelf of her medicine cabinet. But how did I know exactly where Ilse kept her razor blades? I'd never look into someone else's medicine chest. But a part of me must have looked, and kept the looking secret from the rest of me. Where would my conscious mind have been?

I'm going to kill myself.

No. I'm not going to kill myself.

Yes. I have to kill myself.

A calm, observing self escaped my body and floated above me. It watched as two other aspects of me, two personalities, broke off from the core of who I was and faced each other in a struggle: one fighting to take my life, the other to save it.

My body was paralyzed.

The life-taking personality was without hope. It saw no other course of action except to commit suicide.

The lifesaving personality argued. It talked about my responsibility to care for my son.

But there are other people who could take better care of him than you, my hopeless self told my lifesaving self. *You're not a good mother anyway.*

You wouldn't really mess up Ilse's apartment like that, would you? All that blood. Hell of a way to treat a friend, the lifesaving self said with forced humor.

The hopeless self found nothing amusing. It was determined that I kill myself. It could see no other solution.

For hours the debate continued while I lay paralyzed. Then the lifesaving self spoke strongly: *Stay with him. Stay until you find a safe way out.*

This is no solution. You're only saying this to save my life, the hopeless self responded.

It doesn't matter if I am. The important thing is to save your life.

To save my life. Yes.

To save my life.

The two aspects of myself moved to a place of agreement. They merged, then slipped back into the whole as if they were pages temporarily fallen from a book. Now all of me was once again inside my body.

And I was no longer paralyzed.

Terrified that I would lose my tenuous hold on life, I got up quickly.

My body and hair were drenched with sweat.

Shower. I have to take a shower, I thought. *Then get outside as quickly as possible.*

But did I dare go into the bathroom with its razor blades waiting?

I rushed in and turned the shower on.

Get out in a hurry. Just get in and out in a hurry.

Outside the day was bright and clear. It was hours until Ilse got off from work. What if I would again split apart, perhaps killing myself this time?

Don't stay alone. For God's sake don't stay alone.

I walked up and down the streets of the city. Terrified, I walked a long time, until my attention was caught by a solitary wall standing in the rubble of a wrecked building. I stood behind a chain-link fence watching the demolition crew at work, watching the huge iron ball swing into the wall again and again until there was nothing left standing at all.

Next door to the ruined building, a movie theater marquee advertised *The Guns of Navarone.* I was exhausted. Would the movie take my mind off myself? "Compelling and suspense-filled," the ads claimed. Surrounded by a theater full of people, perhaps I'd be safe from my mind. Perhaps I'd be able to rest a little. I bought a ticket and went in.

I sat there in the dark, still absorbed in my terrors. Then, on the screen, the side of a mountain slowly opened, revealing an enormous gun pointing straight at the audience. The camera moved in close, filling the screen with the image. For the rest of my life I would carry with me the image of that gun, at close range, pointed directly at my face.

When I got out of the movie, I met Ilse in front of her office building. We went to a little Chinese restaurant for dinner. I couldn't eat but sat trying to put words to the experience I'd had in her apartment that morning. She listened quietly. Then she told me that she wanted us to take a ride on the Staten Island ferry to see the Statue of Liberty.

We took the subway to the ferry. I was disappointed that the statue was so far from the boat. Memory has pushed it even farther away. Liberty. Maybe that's why Ilse took me there. What did liberty mean? I had no idea. I looked out across the choppy water to the figure flooded with light, while my head began to throb. My headache increased in intensity as we rode the subway back to Ilse's apartment. After taking two aspirin, I finally fell asleep, exhausted.

The next morning I took the train back to Philadelphia. The train car was filled with actors on their way to give a performance there. The energy level was high, the conversation constant. I closed my eyes, blocking out the animated chatter, aware now of the sound of the wheels of the train, their rhythm and click, and how they seemed to echo the words "A safe way out, a safe way out, a safe way out, a safe way out . . ." *Stay with him until you find a safe way out.*

Once I was home, my mother-in-law made plans to return to Georgia. As she dismantled John's shotgun to take with her, she assured me that he truly loved me. John had agreed to go to a psychiatrist at the university, a man much older than he. It would be months before I found out that John stopped going after two visits.

And then, when he cried out his lover's name in a moment of orgasm, my heart hurt even more. As always, he refused to talk about the affair or my feelings. When I did try to talk with him, he would either get angry or lie down on the bed and begin to utter his now familiar nonsensical phrases. I talked with friends, resolved nothing.

Then graduate school was over and John accepted his first job, a temporary position at the University of Washington in Seattle. He phoned me from school to let me know. On the radio I'd just heard of the death of Marilyn Monroe. I lay on the bed and sobbed. I didn't know what I was crying about—the death of Marilyn Monroe, leaving all of my friends and my beloved Philadelphia, or the end of an era that had brought with it a sense of life as I'd never known it before—rich and wonderful things, together with almost more pain than I thought I could bear.

II
1962–1963

In Seattle, we lived in an apartment complex north of the city, filled with young couples with children, many of them around John Elder's age. Our next-door neighbors, the Cranes, had five children. The oldest boy, Dennis, had a hatchet that John Elder envied daily. But even more than he envied the hatchet, he envied all of Dennis's friends. John Elder longed to have friends. Often, as they played, he sat silently on a large rock in the woods as if contemplating the universe.

One day John Elder came running into the apartment, sobbing loudly. I sat down, took him in my arms, and held him tightly. "Why don't I have friends?" he asked, sobbing. "Why won't the boys play with me?"

I was at a loss for words. I could only hug him more tightly.

Sometimes the boys would let him play with them, but more often than not, he played with Dennis's little brother Jeff or held the hand of the youngest child, Mike, as he was learning to walk.

Sometimes Kathy, the oldest at thirteen, came to visit me when her mother was taking a nap and her sister, Diane, was taking her violin lesson. It always distressed Kathy to be in the apartment alone when her mother was asleep.

With five children in a small apartment, Jean Crane needed all the rest she could get. Her efficiency amazed me. The apartment was spotless and the kitchen linoleum shone with layers of wax. And still she had time to sit on the back steps with me most afternoons, smoking cigarettes and talking.

We went together to visit another neighbor, who taught us how to make candles using molds. The neighbor's husband was a mortician. She told us that at the West Coast Morticians Convention that year, the major topic of conversation was the embalming of Marilyn Monroe.

Somehow I was able to put aside the problems of the past and focus on enjoying our new life in Seattle. John taught three days a week, and more often than not we camped the other four. We camped on Whidbey Island in Puget Sound, in the Hoh Rain Forest, and along the Oregon coast all the way to a campground in a redwood forest.

On weekends when we didn't camp, we went on short trips, or spent time at a beach nearby, where John shot at tin cans with his BB pistol, John Elder played in the sand, and I did sketches of them, the sea, and landscapes. Sometimes we went to Mount Rainier, where John Elder sledded in the snow. Once, the three of us climbed to a glacier-fed river on the mountain, and once we went to Hurricane Ridge in Olympic National Park.

It was a year of family activity and exploration.

When the school year was almost over, John was offered a teaching position at the University of Pittsburgh and accepted it. The trip from Philadelphia to Seattle and our many trips on the West Coast with the car top-heavy with camping equipment had worn out our VW. We traded it in for a new Chevrolet station wagon. John Elder cried and cried. He'd loved that little car, and a much larger and more powerful car didn't impress him. The VW had been his friend, and now his friend was gone.

We said goodbye to all our Seattle friends. Jean Crane and I agreed to keep in touch even if it meant only notes at Christmas. For almost a year we had shared our lives daily, talking through the razor-blade slot in our bathrooms, listening to Julie London records on my record player, or sitting on the back steps together smoking cigarettes. And there was the time when we spent the day in her kitchen dipping candles, drinking wine, and laughing ourselves silly over nothing.

John Elder gave his red tractor, Chippy, to Jeff Crane. He had pedaled Chippy up and down the streets of West Philadelphia. And when not riding Chippy, he'd propped him on building blocks, while pretending to fix him with his Playskool toy tools. But John Elder had outgrown Chippy. Now he nursed a dream of owning a bicycle.

As much as I had enjoyed our experiences on the West Coast, I was glad to be going east again. After John backed the car out of our parking space and headed for the highway, I didn't look back.

Chapter Nine

AFTER TWO THOUSAND MILES OF DRIVING, WE WERE FINALLY IN PITTS-burgh, with its hills, rivers, bridges, steel mills, and the tall Cathedral of Learning of the University of Pittsburgh. Pittsburgh had none of the charm of Philadelphia, and we woke mornings to find our windowsills and breakfast table covered with soot from the steel mills. But Pittsburgh was in the East, and for me the East was home.

We rented a house in Edgewood, within walking distance of John Elder's elementary school. He was six years old, and in the first grade. Almost as soon as he entered school, I began to get complaints from his teacher that he wouldn't obey her instructions and was disruptive to the class. She wanted me to "do something with him." I could do nothing except feel bad about doing nothing. I didn't understand my son and felt like a failure as a mother.

The good thing was that almost immediately John Elder made friends with a neighbor named Lenny. They walked to school together, and many afternoons Lenny came over to play. Once they tied a rope to the handle of a battery-operated radio, turned it on, and lowered it down the laundry chute. I stood startled at the kitchen sink as loud music suddenly blared from the wall.

I was always glad that John Elder liked to spend much of his time playing contently by himself, and I never interpreted his inclination to do this as a sign that something was wrong with him. I, too, had enjoyed many hours of playing alone when I was a child. And like my son, I had spent much of that time drawing and reading.

By the time John Elder was in the second grade, he was making incredibly detailed drawings of sailing ships. I was amazed at their precision, and at his skill as a draftsman. He also began to put plastic models together. His first model was a submarine. After finishing it, he left it on the table and went outside. It felt odd that he'd said nothing and hadn't even shown it to me. After a while I became concerned and went to see what he was doing.

I found him sitting on the front steps, crying.

I sat down beside him.

"What's wrong, John Elder?"

He wiped his nose on his sleeve. "I ruined my submarine," he said.

"It looked fine to me," I said hopefully. "Let's go look at it again."

We went inside together. John Elder stood looking at his model while tears welled up in his eyes again.

"See, it's ruined," he said, pointing to a drop of glue that had seeped from the seam on top.

"But you can hardly see that little drop. I don't think that ruins your submarine at all," I protested.

"It's not perfect," he responded with a tone of finality. Then he got a book from the bookcase, sat on the couch, and began to stare at it, though I could see that he was still thinking about his submarine.

Years later I saw that little gray submarine in a place of honor on top of a bookcase in his home after he'd grown up and married, with many interesting jobs already in his past and even more in his future. I was happy that he'd finally seen that his first model hadn't been a failure but a triumph.

II
1965

John Elder was growing up. He was going to be eight years old in August, and I was already twenty-nine. I felt a longing in my heart for another baby. John too wanted another child, and we were happy when I got pregnant almost immediately. My brother Mercer had moved to Pittsburgh to be near us and had an office job in the city. Most days he came over to see us after work. More and more often John encouraged him to drink with him at a local tavern. One night, when John returned home, for no apparent reason he went into a rage, pulled all the drawers out of my bureau, and slung my clothes across the room. By the time I was several months pregnant I finally realized that John was an alcoholic.

He was afraid that the baby might be a girl. He told me again and again that we would have to give the baby up for adoption if it was a girl, as he refused to be father to a girl. I felt terrible about his attitude but could do nothing to change it. Because of it, I too became afraid that the baby might be a girl.

On the late afternoon when I began to have contractions, John came home from the university and insisted that I cook spaghetti for dinner. I didn't feel like standing and cooking and suggested that we go out to dinner (knowing John, I also knew that the dirty dishes would be in the sink waiting for me when I returned from the hospital). Mercer was with us and supported me. We went out to dinner, but John was angry and silent.

After dinner Mercer stayed with John Elder while John took me to Magee-Womens Hospital. After having such a difficult labor and delivery with John Elder, I was determined not to repeat the experience. For months I'd spent time most nights practicing my special breathing exercises and reading about natural childbirth. When the time came, the labor progressed with ease. I felt pressure but no pain.

Magee was a teaching hospital, and many interns sat in the bleacherlike seating and watched. A large mirror hung from the ceiling and enabled me to watch the birth of our baby, thankfully a son. I'll never forget the thrill of seeing his head emerging from my body, his mouth open in a howl even before the rest of him was born.

The doctor handed him to a nurse, who placed him on a table. As the nurses cleaned him, he lay looking at me, our eyes locked together in an unbreakable bond.

In our room, Chris lay in a clear plastic bassinet and slept, while I did drawing after drawing of him. I remember reading someplace that drawing is the next thing to touching, and I believe this is true. With my hand and eyes I traced every contour of his small body. When he cried, I was the one who fed him or changed his diaper. When he opened his eyes, I was the one he saw. I could not have been happier.

John was miserable. Just as when John Elder was born, he was sick with jealousy. He felt burdened by having to take John Elder out for dinner or to cook frozen TV dinners for both of them. John Elder was quite competent when it came to bathing, dressing, and walking to school and back, but I knew John resented what little attention he required. Also, John had to do the laundry, a task he disliked intensely. He arrived every day full of complaints.

I was allowed only three visitors, and Pat King was one of them. I'd met Pat in a drawing class at the Pittsburgh Arts and Crafts Center, and she'd become my best friend in Pittsburgh and—ultimately—one of my best friends in life. She was welcomed not only by me but by my roommate and the nurses. We all needed her light, friendly spirit to balance John's stormy temperament, which threatened to cast a dark spell on everyone.

Mercer was my other visitor. He assured me—truthfully or not—that John Elder was doing all right without me. He was upset by John's attitude, but we didn't focus on that. What mattered was that the new baby was healthy and content.

I brought Chris home on a glorious late-October day, gold leaves everywhere.

Mother hired a nurse to help me for two weeks after we came home, but I wanted to do everything for the baby myself. The nurse was a sensitive woman and quick to see that, so she worked hard cleaning the house, doing the laundry, and cooking dinner, while I gave my attention to Chris. "You're as happy over that baby as I was over my new living room furniture," she commented one day when she saw me standing and looking down at Chris as he slept.

John was upset about having anyone in the house except the family. It was difficult enough that the new baby took so much of my attention, but to have a stranger doing things I usually did was more than he could accept. The second day the nurse was there, he cursed loudly and flung the silver candlesticks across the dining room because he didn't like something she'd cooked for dinner. After that, until the two weeks were over, she cooked an early dinner every day and rushed away before he got home.

I couldn't stop looking at the new baby, and neither could John Elder. He watched me feed him, dress him, change his diapers, and rock him. Sometimes he sat on the couch and held him. I'd had no idea John Elder could be so gentle or affectionate.

John must have paid at least a little attention to Chris, but I can't remember those times. He spent more time at the university than he had before. And Mercer, after being notified that he was going to be drafted into the army, joined the navy and left. I missed him terribly. John continued to go to the local tavern most nights, though alone. More often than not he was drunk by the time he came to bed.

Before Chris was born I'd packed my oil paints and brushes away. I knew it would be too difficult to care for a baby while dealing with the mess of oil paints and turpentine, so I'd made up my mind to focus on drawing and painting with watercolors for the first four years of his life. Sometimes Pat King came over and painted with me. Chris often lay or sat in his playpen and watched us.

It was a time of going to faculty cocktail parties and art exhibits, taking classes at the Arts and Crafts Center, and visiting a neighbor who was also an artist. I was thrilled when a local art gallery took several of my paintings and actually sold two. Despite John and his drinking, it was a happy time for me.

III
1966–1968

John wasn't content at the university. When his friend and colleague Bruce Aune accepted the position as head of the philosophy department at the University of Massachusetts in Amherst, John was glad to move with him. Both Bruce and his wife, Ilene, were friends of ours, and it felt good to be moving together.

We moved in August, before Chris's first birthday in October.

I looked forward to living in Amherst, home of Emily Dickinson, and so was upset when John called me and announced that he'd rented a house on a dairy farm in Hadley.

The Hadley house stood on a hill overlooking a large pasture, acres of farmland, and beyond those, the Connecticut River. A Lyman from Northampton built the house in 1743. He'd lost his family in a fire and wanted to begin again in a place that wouldn't remind him of his tragic past. I don't know how long he lived in the new house before he disappeared. He was found later on the mountain behind the house with his throat slashed. No one seemed to know whether an Indian had killed him or he had committed suicide.

Summer and fall passed, and our first New England winter was bitter. Wind howled through the house, rattling the windows and shaking the attic door on its hinges. The first time I climbed the attic stairs, I was startled to find at the top an old-fashioned high chair with a life-sized baby doll wrapped in plastic sitting in it. The attic, with its old hand-hewn beams, was filled with thousands of dead wasps.

Out the kitchen window were large expanses of snow-covered

pasture, the monotony broken by one bare tree, dark against the white. We were surrounded by snow on every side. Winter was very long.

John spent his days at the university, and John Elder went to the Hadley Elementary School, where his teacher complained about not being able to control him.

I stayed at home with Chris, who, when not napping, required a great deal of attention. Either he was climbing on things that he could fall from and get hurt, or he was putting things in his mouth. Once he tried to eat a handful of Johnson's paste wax while I was waxing the dining room floor, and at Christmas he ate a Styrofoam Santa Claus and had to have his stomach pumped. Sometimes I would take him with me to visit Esther, the wife of John Barstow, the dairy farmer whose house was just yards from ours, but our visits were usually brief, for I had to work to keep Chris from banging on the organ in her living room.

As we sat eating dinner that Christmas, John's parents called. When Carolyn began to speak, John placed the receiver in the sink and turned the disposal on. Then, without saying a word, he sat back down and continued to eat.

After school John Elder often played with the son of John Barstow's brother and partner on the farm, who also lived near us. Once when sledding, the boys had a wreck and John Elder's forehead was slashed open by a blade of his friend's sled. In the summer the two boys climbed the mountain behind the house and got stuck on a rock ledge. The farmer had to climb up and rescue them.

John got drunk most nights and insisted on having sex, though he knew I hated to have sex with him when he was drunk. He also knew that I'd eventually give in out of exhaustion. He had long since ceased discussing philosophy with me, a thing I'd loved. And he was cross with John Elder, criticizing him endlessly. One night, before I could stop him, he slammed John Elder against the dining room wall. I made an appointment for our family with a therapist, but after several meetings I realized he wasn't doing any good at all and we stopped going. I found another therapist, and then another, but no one could help us. John displayed none of his negative behavior in front of the therapists, and John Elder wasn't willing to talk at all.

I spent much of my time lonely and depressed.

Bruce and Ilene came out for dinner occasionally, and we went to their home, but I never talked about my concerns with them.

I was always glad when Mercer, stationed in Newport, Rhode Island, drove up for the weekend, which he did often. Seeing how much John was drinking and how often he slipped into muttering his nonsensical phrases, Mercer understood why I was eager to have company.

Summer arrived and we were given a generous portion of the garden space next to the garage. John loved to garden and spent every moment he could spare from his academic responsibilities working there. We planted corn, beans, potatoes, tomatoes, carrots, onions, lettuce, beets, and bell peppers. What we didn't eat, I froze or canned. And once the apples on the apple tree in the backyard ripened and fell on the grass, I gathered them and made many apple pies for the freezer as well.

John continued to drink heavily, utter his nonsensical phrases, and force his unwelcome sex on me, but we had the garden, and with it came times of gladness between us together and separately.

Jack and Carolyn drove up for a short visit that summer. It was during their time with us that I noticed a red, scaly patch of skin on John's forehead. That was the beginning of the psoriatic rheumatoid arthritis that was to torment him to one degree or another for the rest of his life. Shortly after the skin condition started, his left knee began to collect fluid that had to be drained every week. His pain was acute. He mixed barbiturates with alcohol and often stumbled when he walked and slurred his speech when he talked. I was afraid he would hurt or kill himself. His condition grew progressively worse. His rheumatologist told him he would be in a wheelchair by the time he was forty.

On a cold night in February, Mother called to tell me that Daddy had died. I'd just talked with him an hour before, telling him I wouldn't be coming to visit as I'd planned because we'd just bought a house and I needed to stay and pick out tiles for the bathrooms and linoleum for the kitchen floor. Mother told me that he was happy for me and had paced out the dimensions of our half-acre lot on their two-acre yard before going to Bubba's, and then The Old Home Place, where he died of a heart attack. I'd told Daddy I wasn't going to visit him, and he'd died within the hour. It would take years and writing an entire book of poetry before I was able to deal with my grief and guilt.

Daddy was dead.

Sobbing, I leaned against John, but he was so drunk he could barely hold himself upright. He too was crying. We pulled away from each other, and he made reservations for Chris and me to fly south for the funeral. John Elder always found Mother cold and uncaring and didn't want to go to Cairo with us. I went to the basement and put a load of clothes into the washing machine. Then I leaned against the old stone wall and continued to sob for a while longer before going upstairs to pack.

The next morning the deep snow in the yard was so hard and icy we had difficulty walking from the house to the car without falling. But within hours Chris and I were in Cairo, where everyone was wearing short sleeves, azaleas were in full bloom, and Daddy's body lay in a casket in the funeral home. Everything felt surreal. I couldn't stop crying.

The house was filled with people. After noticing that many of the guests were holding cups of coffee, Chris picked up an imaginary coffeepot and went around the room refilling the cups. Some people thanked him, while others asked for more. He had a wonderful time.

I was grateful that my broad-brimmed corduroy hat covered my face when I bent my head down during the service. I'd never cried so hard in my life. I heard the minister say that Daddy had loved his children. Then someone sang "The Old Rugged Cross," Daddy's favorite hymn, and everyone filed out of the funeral-home chapel to the cars waiting to take us to the cemetery.

Bubba drove the car I was in, with his wife, Anne, in the front seat beside him and Mother and Mercer in the backseat with me. Mother looked a little uncomfortable when Bubba, Mercer, and I each lit a cigarette as soon as we were seated. As the car filled with smoke, she said: "Well, if anyone would understand, your father would."

Beyond the drive, I don't have a single memory until that night, when Mother showed me all the new clothes she'd sewn to wear when she taught school. She was proud of her fine work. There was so much that she wanted to share with me, and I knew she needed me to be with her after the shock of Daddy's death, but I had to fly home the next day to drive John to a Boston hospital for experimental treatment for his arthritis. There was no time for grief.

IV

I drove John to Boston the day after I returned from Daddy's funeral. He was to be one of the first patients to have the drug methotrexate injected directly into a joint. After several days I drove back to Boston and brought him home. The medication was effective. His knee no longer collected fluid, and he suffered less pain, though he was unable to walk without the use of a cane. One day he was even strong enough to walk with me along the property line of our new house.

As always, I'd wanted to buy a house in the town of Amherst, while John insisted on living in the country, as he had with his parents and grandfather. We'd finally settled on a new house being built in the Shutesbury woods, five miles from Amherst. It was the best compromise we could come to. We'd also bought a second car so I was no longer housebound.

We had to wait two months until the house was finished before we could move in. Chris, two and a half years old, kept asking when we were going to move, and I kept answering, "When it's April." After a while he began to refer to it as the April house.

The long living/dining room of the new house had a fifteen-foot cathedral ceiling and a fireplace with an exposed brick chimney. The long wall along the living/dining room and the shorter wall at the end of the dining room were all glass doors opening onto a deck large enough to accommodate two cars under it. The house was built on a lot that sloped so much that being upstairs felt like we were living in a tree house.

Pine, ironwood, ash, hemlock, birch, oak, and maple trees surrounded the house. Chris enjoyed walking through the woods with me. He also often played in his sandbox in the backyard. We had a Ping-Pong table in the game room downstairs. On rare days when John's knee was not causing him too much pain, he sometimes played Ping-Pong with me. John Elder and I played as well. The thing John most enjoyed doing at home was chopping and splitting wood for the fireplace.

But when inside, he sat at the kitchen table and stared at the TV on the counter opposite his chair no matter what program was on. He became upset if he had to sit anyplace except in that chair, and dreaded the necessary faculty parties we gave because he had to leave his familiar chair in the kitchen. But he was a warm and welcoming host, and often entertained our guests with stories of childhood summers spent with his grandparents in Chickamauga. He was a wonderful storyteller; I tried to encourage him to write his stories down, but he never expressed an interest in doing so.

He continued to drink sherry by the gallon daily for a while but soon changed to vodka, which couldn't be detected as easily by students and fellow professors. I had thought he drove the used car he bought while I drove the station wagon because I needed more room to taxi the children, but that wasn't the case. One day, for some reason, I opened the trunk of his car and was shocked to discover it completely filled with empty vodka bottles.

John still initiated sex at least three times a week. Though he no longer had the odor that I'd come to associate with him when he was drunk, I still found it repulsive to have sex with him when he was drunk. Since the time he'd cried out his lover's name during orgasm in Philadelphia, sex had become a silent act for him. And since he'd refused to listen to my feelings about the affair, I had buried them as deeply as I could. But something inside me had died.

V

After living in Shutesbury for many months, I finally made a friend. Paula Thomas lived with her husband, Ben, and her son, Ted, just down the road and up the hill from us. One day, when I was sitting on the deck, Paula saw me as she was taking a walk. I waved and invited her to come up and visit. She was somewhat timid at first, but once we started talking about books, we immediately discovered a common ground. Eventually we talked about our relationships with our husbands, though I could never bring myself to tell her about my sex life with John or the times he was physically violent toward me. We talked about our children, friends, and parents, our childhoods, and ourselves. It was a time of self-discovery and affirmation for both of us.

Chris and Ted also became friends and played together several times a week.

John Elder, too, made new friends. Dwight Allen, head of the university's education department, and his family lived next door to us, and his son Denny and John Elder became friends. Often they roamed the woods and camped together. John Elder also made friends with a younger boy named Greg who lived down the road.

When he wasn't playing with friends, John Elder spent most of his time reading. As he grew older he became interested in learning how things worked, and he took apart radios, a record player, old TVs, and an air purifier. Often he couldn't put the things back together, but he learned a great deal in the process of trying. By that time the carpet in his room was thick with screws, wires, bolts, and nuts, along with many unidentifiable objects.

When he was fourteen he became interested in sound systems and soon was fixing them for friends. He had a business card made, and it wasn't long before he was installing sound systems in restaurants and bars in the area. One of his first commercial installations was in Fitzwilly's, a popular restaurant and bar, in Northampton, a few miles from Amherst. I was impressed that John Elder already had the skill and reputation to install their sound system.

When Chris was four, I enrolled him in nursery school at the Unitarian church in Amherst. There he made friends with Tom Waterman, also from Shutesbury, and I made friends with Tom's mother, Dee. We often took the boys to Lake Wyola, near their home, where they played in the sand and water while Dee and I talked and sunned ourselves. Dee and her husband, Bob, owned the Jeffery Amherst Bookshop across the street from the town common. On the opposite side of the common was the Lord Jeffery Inn, where Dee and I often had lunch.

Chris and Tom made up plays together, and Chris made up plays when he was alone as well. I bought him a chunky blue tape recorder and tapes so he could keep his plays, but he rarely recorded them. My favorite play of his was about Emily Dickinson working at a Burger King in heaven. His wit was brilliant.

He also began to write poetry almost as soon as he could hold a pencil.

He rarely watched TV programs, but he loved commercials. As I was cooking dinner, he often came to the kitchen door and said with the slow Southern accent of the girl in the Shake 'n Bake commercial: "Mama, can I help?" It never failed to make me laugh.

VI

There were many happy days during our early years in Shutesbury. The boys and I had our friends, and John had his friends at the university. I set my easel up in a corner of the dining room and once again began to paint in oils. I knitted mittens, scarves, caps, and sweaters for John and the boys, and sewed slacks and skirts for myself. I also sewed Christmas stockings with tiny bells on them for the boys. I gathered moss-covered stones and plants from the woods and created dish gardens for the kitchen table, changing their contents as the seasons changed. Once a week I hosted a luncheon for a group of my writer friends. And Mercer came up from Newport often until he left the States to be stationed on a battleship off the coast of Vietnam.

Once Mother came for a visit. We took her to Hyde Park, New York, to see Franklin Roosevelt's home. She had greatly admired Roosevelt as president, and seeing his home and many of his personal things was a highlight of her life. It was an event that she grouped with the thrill of touching the Liberty Bell, seeing Marc Chagall's *I and the Village* when she visited us in Philadelphia, and sticking her foot in what she thought of as Mark Twain's Connecticut River when visiting us in Shutesbury.

But family relationships grew progressively more strained. John continued to degrade John Elder and, when I wasn't around to stop him, would hit him or try to hit him with a belt. For the most part, he ignored Chris, though he sometimes took him along when he had errands to run.

John drank more and talked less. I focused on painting and on my friends. But his silence as he sat in front of the TV depressed me. When we did talk at night he often made a game of twisting my words so that I went to bed feeling desperate and confused. Sometimes I got up and sat on the couch writing letters to Pat King, who was with her husband, George, in Turkey. I struggled to find words to adequately express what I was going through. By the time I had written a letter, the floor around my feet would be filled with crumpled papers. The letters must have been terribly burdensome for Pat to read, but she never failed to be a faithful friend, responding with affirmation and support. Though I didn't realize it at the time, those letters played a major role in my development as a writer.

But writing letters to Pat was not adequate in pulling me out of the depression that grew more and more intense. I no longer knew how I could live.

Chapter Ten

My bedroom was dark, curtains drawn. I lay curled up in bed.

"Mom," six-year-old Chris said, coming over to where I lay. "Mom?"

His father had fixed his breakfast, and Chris had dressed and gotten himself ready for school. After all the years of getting up and cooking breakfast, now I lay there, heavyhearted, so depressed I was unable to move.

"Give me a goodbye kiss," I said, struggling to open my eyes.

He bent down and kissed my cheek, as I kissed his.

"Have a good day at school."

"Bye, Mom."

He turned and left my room, walked down the hall and out the front door, to wait at the bottom of the drive for the school bus. (Over thirty years later he will tell me how abandoned he felt, how terribly alone. He will spew out his rage and pain, and I will listen to the man in whom the small boy still hurts.)

That day I turned over in bed and turned on the record player beside it. The voices of Maria Callas and Tito Gobbi filled the room. The opera was *Tosca*. I moved the needle over to Tosca's aria "Vissi d'arte, vissi d'amore." I took a cigarette from the crumpled pack on the bedside table, lit it, and lay back, listening to the music, the tension between Tosca and Scarpia building. Finally he approaches her, expecting to make love in exchange for letting her lover, Mario, go free. As he's signing the papers for Mario's execution, she snatches the knife from his desk and conceals it in her skirt. When he approaches her, she plunges it into his chest. Then she watches as he struggles to rise from the floor. He falls back, begging for help. Tosca asks if his blood is choking him, and taunts him for being killed by a woman. Looking down at the dead Scarpia, she utters the unforgettable line: *"E avanti a lui tremava tutta Roma!"* (And all Rome trembled before him!)

I've memorized this opera with my heart. When I had to paint a poster for a painting class I took, I painted Maria Callas as Tosca standing over the dead body of Scarpia. It was this painting that convinced Ruth, a faculty wife I'd met at a cocktail party where we'd talked passionately about André Schwarz-Bart's book *The Last of the Just,* that my friend Paula had been right when she'd called Ruth and told her that she'd thought I was suicidal. Paula had heard it in my voice on the phone. After years talking to me in person or on the phone almost daily, Paula knew my voice well. Often our conversations went on for hours. She was certain, she told Ruth, that I was suicidal, but that she herself couldn't handle going to my home to help me. Would Ruth please go instead?

Ruth came with her son, Tommy, who was a year younger than Chris. Without knocking, she opened the front door and came into the living room. She stopped and stood for a long time staring at the poster on my easel. Then she came over to where I sat on the couch and sat in a chair next to me. Tommy ran down the hall calling for Chris. I looked at Ruth. It was as if I was seeing her through thick layers of impenetrable glass. Her voice sounded distant.

"Margaret?"

"Yes, Ruth." I heard my voice gone flat and lifeless. It sounded very far away, as if it was detached from my body.

"Margaret, are you all right?"

"I'm all right," I heard myself reply.

From someplace in my memory, John's remorseful voice came back to me: "I've destroyed everything in you that I've ever loved."

And what, I thought, have I destroyed of myself? What of myself have I given up for the approval of John or Mother? What have I sacrificed for the sake of a false peace? How many incompetent therapists have I gone to in search of help for my family? How many wasted hours? How much dashed hope?

Later, Ruth told me that as soon as she'd seen the painting on my easel, she'd known that it wasn't Scarpia that Tosca had murdered; mine was a painting of me killing myself. She'd known that in her heart, she said, with absolute certainty.

Only a year before, I'd spent the morning with Ruth's husband, Matthew, who had spent the night at our house. He had paced the kitchen floor, spewing out rage against Ruth for leaving him and going to New York. Clothes wrinkled, hair uncombed, eyes red, he sat down in the chair opposite me and rocked back and forth. Usually soft-spoken, mannerly, and quiet, Matthew, who was being treated for cancer, stammered out his despair. In my memory his words are eclipsed by the image of the man himself. It was as if everything had been stripped away to reveal the naked, tormented soul that he had become.

The night before, a neighbor had called to say that they couldn't find Ruth, and Matthew had been wandering around the neighborhood acting strange. John had picked him up and brought him home with him. In the morning Chris and John Elder left for school and John for the university. Ruth was on her way to our house to pick Matthew up. I'd called their house to discover she'd not been in New York at all but in their guest room, where she'd gone, desperate for sleep.

Matthew paused in his talk when he looked down and saw that his fly was open. He self-consciously zipped it. "This is the end," he said with an iron-willed tone of finality.

I knew that he was talking literally about the end of his life. Whether he'd been brought to this place by his struggle with cancer, stress in his profession, a combination of these things, or matters that I had no awareness of, I can't say. What I felt certain of was that Matthew intended to kill himself.

I still remember that brilliant, distinguished man sitting slumped in a chair in my living room, eyes downcast, hands limp in his lap. After Ruth arrived, she knelt on the floor, tying Matthew's shoes before taking him home.

"Come home with me," Ruth urged me that afternoon when I sat, suicidal, in my living room.

I finally gave in to her urging. I drove my car, and she followed me to her house in Amherst, the boys riding in the car with her. In her driveway, after Chris and Tommy jumped from the car and ran into the house, I opened my car door and got out. Leaning against the car, I said, in what I hoped was a calm voice, "Listen, I need to be alone for a little while. I think it might help me to do some sketching. Would you mind keeping Chris for me? I'll be back soon." Before I could get back in the car, Ruth grabbed me by my shoulders and pushed me hard against its side, using more force than I thought she had in her small body.

"You're not going anywhere!" she screamed at me. "You want to fight with me? You'll have to fight like hell to get away. You're in no shape to be alone, for God's sake."

Her brute force shook me out of my disconnection with myself. I burst into tears, and the two of us leaned against the car, hugging each other. Soon I began to breathe more calmly.

"Come on in the house," Ruth said. She took my hand firmly in hers and we walked up the front walk and into the house.

For the remainder of the afternoon, we sat in her living room, drinking wine, smoking cigarettes, listening to *La Bohème*, and talking, while Tommy and Chris built a fort of boxes in Tommy's room.

I felt emotionally shaken, but I knew I wasn't going to kill myself that day. Still, I saw no escape short of suicide from the life that I found unbearable.

In my stumbling, self-conscious, and still somewhat emotionally distant way, I tried to tell Ruth about John's violence. I tried to tell her how exhausted I'd become, both physically and emotionally, from John's and my long nightly battles after the boys were asleep. I told her how he twisted what I said until I felt like my brain was nothing but a mass of tangles and knots. I told her that I felt frantic when he denied his nighttime mental torture of me and how, mornings, he would go deadly cold and say calmly: "It's only in your head, Margaret."

John violent?

"No, Margaret," Ruth protested, elongating the word *no* to a purr. "John would never mean to hurt you. He's such a gentleman."

I felt like I would choke with desperation.

"You don't know the John I know. He doesn't act this way around you." I felt my voice go weak. Yes, John was handsome, charming, and mannerly. I was the hysterical wife. I felt frantic to make her understand. "He won't let me sleep nights. I just can't take it anymore."

"Margaret, you're upset. You need a rest. I'm certain that if John realized how tired you are, he'd do everything he could to help you." She took a drag from her cigarette and exhaled. "We'll go get pizza and take it to your house for dinner. I'll talk with John. I'm certain he'll listen to me."

I felt sick. My initial flash of hope went black. No one would believe me. No one except Paula, and she was too frightened to help.

Gentleman John. Ruth didn't believe me any more than she'd believed me a year earlier when I told her that Matthew was going to kill himself.

"Oh, Margaret, you and your imagination." Her tone had been patiently tolerant.

How many times had she said that? How many times had I begun the day by calling her to repeat my fear about Matthew committing suicide? It was a year earlier, on a Wednesday morning, that I made my last call.

"Hello?"

There was a long pause at the other end of the line. Then Ruth spoke in a flat, mechanical voice.

"You were right, Margaret."

Another pause.

"Matthew killed himself last night."

"Oh, God, Ruth, I'll be right over."

By the time Chris and I arrived at Ruth's, she and her friend Dotty were sitting at the kitchen table, drinking coffee and smoking cigarettes. *La Traviata* was blasting from the phonograph in the living room.

Chris and Tommy, who knew nothing of what was going on, were happy to see each other and went to Tommy's room to play. Ruth and I hugged. Then I sat down at the table. Ruth repeated the story that she must have just told Dotty.

She and Matthew had stayed up very late the night before. For hours, Ruth said. Matthew had talked about the many books he'd read that focused at least partially on controlling parents as well as the various characters' struggles with expressing their anger over things gone awry in their lives. Exhausted, Ruth finally went to bed.

Sometime toward morning the Amherst police came to the house. Matthew had slammed the car into a telephone pole.

The music was almost more than I could bear. The volume was deafening. Until that day, I'd disliked opera intensely. It had just sounded like a lot of pompous yelling. Now the music moved through me, and notes of grief swelled in my heart.

Matthew had shattered his skull on the car windshield. On the front seat, the police had found a note scribbled on the back of an envelope: "If you're reading this note, then I've finally succeeded. Tell Ruth and Tommy I loved them."

The note was splattered with blood.

Ruth lit another cigarette. "Dr. Quinlan identified Matthew's body. When the police came to tell me what had happened, I closed the door to the hall so Tommy didn't see or hear anyone."

I imagined Ruth going about the business of pouring orange juice and scrambling eggs as Tommy lay stirring himself awake in his bed, while what was left intact of his father's dead body lay in the funeral home.

After Matthew died, I expected to go back to my dislike of opera. But once my heart had been split wide with sorrow for Matthew, Ruth, and Tommy, once I'd let the music fill me, waking long-dormant feelings, my heart had remained open. Instead of losing interest in opera, I had an unquenchable thirst for it; it became a gift that would enrich, expand, and comfort me for the rest of my life.

Matthew had been dead for over a year, and I was still with Ruth, still listening to opera. This time it was *La Bohème*. Marcello was singing farewell to his overcoat. Mimi was dying. And Ruth was going home with me to eat pizza and talk to John about my exhaustion. Then Ruth and Tommy would go home. But my life with John as it was could not go on. I had reached the limits of my endurance.

II

I lay in bed and spent hours going over my relationship with John. Not the good things—and there had been many good things over the years—but the things that made me want to leave, *have* to leave. And the things that made me *afraid* to leave. All that ruminating in order to postpone facing the inevitable act of remembering what had happened the night we went to our friends Bob and Dee's for dinner.

After dinner, Bob had asked me to dance. John and Dee danced together briefly, then sat down across the room and talked. A fire blazed in the fireplace. Both men drank a good bit all evening, but neither appeared to be drunk. When it was time to leave, John insisted on driving and I didn't argue with him. It wasn't until we were halfway home that he began to yell at me, saying that he knew I wanted to go to bed with Bob, that I couldn't fool him. I wasn't at all attracted to Bob except as a friend and told John that, but he didn't believe me. I didn't expect him to. After years of his jealous accusations, something in me had given up.

That night, after the boys were asleep, I lay in bed listening to the repeated clicking of John's gun. *Click. Click. Click.* He was sitting at his chair at the kitchen table, facing the TV on the counter. I could hear voices from the TV. I stared out the window at the stars above the dark pines, hemlocks, and spruces. I didn't have to go to the kitchen to know what John was doing as he sat drinking vodka. The handle of the empty gun was resting on the floor while John pressed his forehead against the barrel and clicked the trigger over and over.

Click. Click. Click.

John had said to me so many times that he wished he had whatever it took to commit suicide like Matthew had done. "I envy Matthew. I sure as hell envy Matthew," he'd say. Now he was going through his almost nightly ritual. *Click. Click.*

Another click and I was back in the row house in West Philadelphia when John was in graduate school. We'd lived a block from the bus stop, and a couple of blocks from the trolley that ran down Baltimore Avenue.

Click.

The traffic light on the corner from where we lived made that same clicking sound. After midnight, the red and green lights were turned off, and the yellow caution light flashed off and on all night. When I was unable to sleep, I lay in bed watching the yellow light flashing against the bedroom wall. Flash. *Click.* Flash. *Click.*

"Do you love me?" I'd sometimes asked at night when we were in bed. As if his repeating the appropriate words in response to my question would mean anything.

"Yes, I love you."

"Do you really love me?"

"Yes, I love you," he'd repeat, his eyes fastened to the face of some newsman or sports announcer on the small TV screen glowing in the darkened room.

I'd turn over and try to go to sleep. Once the TV was turned off

I could still see the yellow flash of the caution traffic light through the lids of my closed eyes.

After that dinner with Bob and Dee, the clicking of the trigger of John's empty gun went on a long time before he finally stopped, put the gun back in the closet, snapped off the TV, and started down the hall to our bedroom. He was drunk; I could hear his unsteady body hit the sides of the hall a couple of times. Anticipating the probable scene, I felt sick. He'd get into bed, put his hand on my shoulder to turn me over, and wake me to have sex.

"No," I'd say, "I don't want to have sex with you when you're drunk."

"I'm not drunk."

"You are drunk. Leave me alone."

At least three times a week he'd wait until I was asleep, or would have been asleep if I'd not lain anxiously waiting for him to turn off the TV and walk down the hall. Then we would have a futile exchange of words, him getting more and more violent and me getting more and more exhausted. I was desperate for sleep because I had to wake up early to get the boys off to school. Usually I finally gave in so he'd leave me alone and I could sleep. Often that gave him energy to have sex again.

Sometimes it felt like he could go on like that all night, until I said no with enough emotion that he could scream at me: "See! See! You don't love me. I knew it." Then he'd roll over, satisfied that he'd finally gotten what he wanted.

A version of this ritual was what I expected as I heard him walking down the hall that night. My face was turned away from his side of the bed and I tried to give no indication of being awake. *Maybe*, I thought, *this will be one of those nights when he just comes to bed and passes out.* But his feet on the bedroom floor suddenly sounded steady, heavy, and purposeful. He walked to my side of the bed, turned me onto my back, climbed onto the bed, and straddled my body, pinning me down with his full weight. Then he put his hands firmly around my throat and began to squeeze.

I tried to call out to John Elder for help, but no sound came.

John was squeezing the life out of me.

I struggled for a while and then stopped. There was no way I could defend myself against his strength.

I thought: *So it's going to end this way.*

Suddenly I felt no fear. Instead, I was filled with a sense of profoundly calm resignation.

I stopped struggling.

As soon as I stopped, John let go of my throat. He got up, grabbed me by the shoulders, and threw me onto the floor and against the wall. Without a word he left the room. In a few minutes I heard the TV again.

I climbed back into bed.

For the first time in years I prayed. "Dear God," I prayed, "if there is a God anywhere, please help me."

I prayed like I'd prayed every night before going to sleep as a child. Like I prayed before I acknowledged the emptiness I'd found in the organized church. "Dear God," I prayed, all my despair and hope behind my silent words spilling out into the room and beyond it. "Dear God," I prayed, and imagined my words traveling through the night from star to star, from galaxy to galaxy, searching for God. "Dear God—if there is a God—help me. Please." With my mind full of stars and planets, moons and comets, and my heart filled with despair and fragile hope, I fell asleep.

The next day Dandy, John's grandfather, died. I went downstairs to get John's Bible for him. Jack had asked him to speak at the funeral, and John had wanted to read a passage from the Bible. Halfway up the stairs I stopped and opened the Bible. My eyes landed on the words *And the sins of the fathers shall be visited upon the sons and the sons' sons down through the fourth generation.* Yes, that was the answer to my prayer. I had seen four generations in both our families. I knew with all my heart that—no matter the cost—I had to leave John and stop the destructive behavior I'd witnessed and too often been a part of.

After John left for Dandy's funeral, I had time to myself, and I got out my watercolors and did a painting of a violin. Its planes and curves were shattered, fragmented, rearranged, reconstructed. Certainly there was nothing extraordinary about the painting. It was almost a cliché, like those phrases that I sometimes wrote as indications of the meaning that lay underneath and so close to the nerves that I couldn't bear to touch them. But doing the painting gave me strength.

Two days later John came back from Georgia; I drove to Bradley Airport to meet his plane. He had a small carry-on bag, so we didn't have to wait for luggage. We left the terminal and walked together to the car. On the stretch of road from the airport to Route 91, he said with a grim sobriety and a tightly locked jaw: "It's over between us. I could see it in your eyes as soon as I saw you."

"Yes, John," I acknowledged. "It is."

Chapter Eleven

W𝐇ᴇɴ I ᴛʀʏ ᴛᴏ ʀᴇᴍᴇᴍʙᴇʀ ᴇxᴀᴄᴛʟʏ ᴡʜᴀᴛ ʜᴀᴘᴘᴇɴᴇᴅ ᴀʀᴏᴜɴᴅ ᴛʜᴇ ᴛɪᴍᴇ I left John and was eventually committed to Northampton State Hospital, I find many things lost in the blaze of tumultuous feelings. What was clear to me was that, after being with him almost seventeen years, I was leaving him.

After I'd told John, he'd phoned a fellow professor in Amherst, asking him to come out and bring his gun. He was drunk and threatening to shoot himself. I took Chris to Paula's. John Elder was away with friends. From Paula's, I called John's closest friend, Ed Gettier, and told him that I was leaving John and asked him to please come to the house.

When I got home from Paula's, I found John in the bedroom. He announced that he was going to go out and kill himself by crashing the car as Matthew had done. I wrestled the car keys from his hands, and he collapsed onto the bed. Ed arrived a few minutes later. John calmed himself in Ed's presence.

"I hope you can find help for him," I said. "I hope to God you can."

Ed helped John get his clothes and toiletries together. Then he walked with him to the car, steadying him as they walked. He told me he'd get John to a motel and then call for help from there.

Later Ed told me that he'd called Dr. Loescher, our family doctor, who suggested that he call Dr. Roseman, a well-known psychiatrist in the area, but Dr. Roseman was on one of his frequent trips to his guru in India. He had left a Dr. Turcotte on call. Dr. Turcotte called me early the next morning.

"Mrs. Robison?"

"This is Margaret Robison."

"This is Dr. Rodolph Turcotte," he announced. "Do you love your husband?"

"Yes," I replied without thinking.

Then I remembered when, years ago in Philadelphia, John's therapist had told me: "If I were your therapist, I would tell you to run like hell. But I'm his therapist, and I say to you that his life depends on your staying."

My mind snapped back to the present. "But I can no longer live with him," I said.

Dr. Turcotte asked if I'd be willing to meet him at the Howard Johnson's Restaurant by the Town House Motor Lodge out from Northampton on Route 5.

I thought it was odd to meet a doctor in a restaurant.

"I believe this meeting is important to you as well as to your husband." He paused. "This separation has to be handled safely."

At least he was talking about separation, not reconciliation.

"Your husband could well be homicidal," he said.

I was impressed that he actually saw the potential for violence with John that so many others were blind to, and I agreed to meet him.

The cashier at the restaurant pointed Dr. Turcotte out to me. He was seated alone in a booth by the front window, papers scattered on the table in front of him. He hadn't shaved in at least a couple of days, and his clothes were as rumpled as if he'd slept in them, if he'd slept at all. His hair was straight, thick, and almost completely white. When he got up to greet me I was surprised to see that he wasn't the tall man I'd imagined him to be, but short and stocky, with a long torso.

"Mrs. Robison?" He extended his hand.

I took it. Then I sat down opposite him. He began to talk rapidly, without pause. He talked about how his wife didn't understand him and about how she undermined rather than supported him. *Why is he telling me these things?* I thought. Still, I listened. He told me about being unfairly fired from various positions, and how he'd become a scapegoat everyplace he'd lived. He told me about his friendship with Father Gray, a prominent and respected Catholic priest, and about how the priest had investigated the various charges against him and discovered that all were unfounded.

He told me that the Clarke School for the Deaf was being put up for sale and that he intended to buy it. No, he didn't have the money, but he was sure he could find financial backing from other people who believed in miracles, and who believed in him.

He talked with more enthusiastic determination than I'd ever witnessed. He would create his own hospital, where things could be done his way, where people would be cured, not crippled. He talked about how essential the expression of anger was to the healing process, and how important it was for the patient to talk. In his hospital, people would be paid to listen to the patients talk—talk about any and everything, but to talk. He told me a great deal about his beliefs concerning mental health, but what I remember most vividly now is his contagious enthusiasm. Many rooms of the Town House Motor Lodge, he explained, were filled with his patients—all people in extreme crisis—and he and his staff were working almost around the clock.

I told him that I knew that while John did cruel and violent things, I believed the good in John was in exact proportion to the bad, that the behaviors were simply two sides of the same coin.

"You're a very religious woman," Dr. Turcotte responded.

I recoiled, my mind flooded with the many judgmental, hellfire-damnation sermons I'd endured in my life. "No, I'm not religious. This is just something I've found to be true of human nature. I'm sure as hell not going to jump on some church bandwagon," I retorted.

He laughed. "I wouldn't expect you to."

"Now," he said, "I belong to the Catholic Church, but I call myself a positive Catholic." He poured cream into his coffee and stirred it.

That Dr. Turcotte was a "positive Catholic" seemed to be another of the unexpected connections that I was experiencing almost daily now.

I was raised a Southern Baptist, filled with guilt and a sense of not belonging. When I married John, I joined the Presbyterian Church. Both John and I eventually stopped attending church altogether. I didn't miss what the church had to offer and for many years attended no church at all. After we moved to New England, I went to the Amherst Unitarian Church, not because I was a Unitarian—I wasn't—but because of the minister, a black man who taught English at a college in Vermont. His use of literature as well as his large spirit and compassion fed my soul. But it wasn't enough. As my marriage grew closer and closer to the crisis that would result in me leaving John, my spiritual hunger grew more insistent.

It was that hunger that had led me to go to Puebla de Los Angeles—the City of Angels—in Mexico the year before. I'd gone there purely because of the city's name, and the fact that it had so many churches. All of my life I've thought in images. In Puebla de Los Angeles I drew strength from the statue of the Virgin Mary that stood in the sanctuary of every church, row upon row of candles burning at her feet. Hers was the first image I knew that suggested a connection with the female to the divine. I needed to see a woman venerated; I needed the images of Puebla de Los Angeles to connect more fully with myself.

Now I was sitting across the table from this extremely unconventional-looking man with his unconventional beliefs who had also found something grounding and nourishing in the Catholic Church. For all his strangeness, I felt a sense of familiarity. Perhaps the feeling had to do with a mirroring of our common—as yet unacknowledged—manic states. Whatever the reasons, I felt an immediate connection with this psychiatrist I met at a Howard Johnson's restaurant because Dr. Jack Roseman was in India at the feet of his guru.

The waitress came and asked if I wanted to order.

"A cup of black coffee," I said.

When she brought it, I lit a cigarette before taking my first sip. I sat back and listened to Dr. Turcotte as he explained something about the nature of men as he understood it. Especially, he talked about their aggressive and possessive behaviors. He said that it wouldn't be safe for me to simply leave John. Because of Dr. Turcotte's general belief system, or because of what he'd observed of John's behavior, or both, he was convinced that John might kill me and possibly one or both of the boys before he would let me go.

A hard chill moved through me as recognition of that possibility registered in my body. I'd lived with my own private fear of John's potential violence for many years, to say nothing of the actual physical violence. But to have someone else confirm that fear and put it into words made it more real. I felt cold. I also felt relieved. Alone, I'd been to therapists in Pittsburgh and one in Northampton. Of all the therapists John and John Elder and I had been to together, Dr. Turcotte was the first to recognize these things about John.

He said that he believed the wise thing for me to do would be to come to John's room in the motel each day, and he would encourage John, under his supervision, to discharge his anger toward me. Which I did, beginning the next day.

———

Most of the anger John expressed was about my leaving him, breaking up the home he'd built, and destroying his life. I sat across from him and listened as he yelled at me, the doctor encouraging him to express more anger the moment he paused. There was no talk at all, just explosion after explosion of anger. One of the doctor's helpers sat between us to protect me in case John became physically violent.

After most sessions, I went to the upstairs conference room with Dr. Turcotte to review what had happened and to bolster my shaky, unstable self. An hour of John's anger left me feeling like one of those stuffed dolls with the rounded bases that carnivalgoers throw balls at and topple again and again.

It was in the same conference room many weeks later that I met with Dr. Turcotte, John's father, Jack, and his only brother, Bob. Dr. Turcotte had called Jack to tell him that he'd committed John to the state mental hospital, and Jack and Bob had flown up from Atlanta. We sat around the table while the doctor explained what he was doing for treatment besides keeping him confined in the hospital until he recovered from his psychotic episode. John's drinking had gotten completely out of control, and he'd been threatening suicide. He'd smashed every piece of glass he could get his hands on— drinking glasses shattered on the bathroom floor, the water pitcher hurled against the tile wall above the tub. He'd broken Coke bottles into chunky shards in the tub. And intending to hit me, John had slammed his fist into a car's fender. Psychotic, he was also trying to call people in the office of Georgia's governor to help him get out of the country and to someplace in Africa. It was at that point that the doctor had him committed to Northampton State Hospital. Until his brief interlude there, John had spent most of the summer in the motel, while his colleagues in the philosophy department were taking turns teaching his classes.

"We're defusing a bomb," Dr. Turcotte explained to Jack and Bob. Jack lit a cigarette and flipped the match into the ashtray.

"You see, Margaret comes here every day and under my supervision John gets his anger out at her by degrees. It wouldn't be safe for her to just leave him. He'd most likely track her down and kill her."

Jack leaned back in his chair and exhaled a cloud of smoke that hovered above the table around which the four of us sat. "Hell yeah," he agreed. "If Carolyn left me I'd find her and kill her too."

Dr. Turcotte accepted Jack's statement without comment. "Well, we're trying to defuse this bomb. John is homicidal right now, and we want to help him get rid of that anger. The flip side of homicide is suicide."

Jack crushed his cigarette, shook another from the pack. "I don't understand why you don't just take the liquor away from him," he said.

"Alcohol is a tranquilizer to John right now," Dr. Turcotte said. "We have to work with him on his other problems before dealing with his drinking. He's much too upset to deal with the drinking yet. Besides, he'd just go and buy more liquor."

"Yeah," Jack said, "I see." But his tone was doubtful. As if John could or would do what Jack had done with the help of an expensive rehabilitation center and a wife who wasn't about to leave him no matter what.

Jack had been sober for almost a year. Sitting across from me at the round table in the motel's conference room, Jack smiled with a self-satisfied expression. "Hell," he said in a tone of proud disbelief, his Southern drawl thicker than ever, each syllable pronounced slowly, savored. "Daddy died, Margaret left John, and John went crazy all in the same month, and I'm still sober." He took a deep drag on his cigarette and exhaled. "I must be cured."

III

John was in the hospital only a few days before Dr. Turcotte had him released to go back to the motel until he felt it was safe to let him go home to Shutesbury. Over the weeks I'd grown more and more manic under the pressure of John's anger. My mind was racing; thoughts tripped over one another, becoming entangled and confusing me so that my brain raced even faster. I was so emotionally exhausted that I could barely function. Instead of getting away from John, I felt myself moving closer to him in a union of anger and resentment. "Do you love your husband?" Dr. Turcotte had asked. Someplace in the complex of emotions, I was certain that I loved John. But more than love, now what I felt was anger.

Without discussing it with me, Ruth had called Mother, who'd immediately flown up from Georgia. Having Mother with me was a mixed blessing. I was in desperate need of help, especially with taking care of Chris, but Mother's emotional neediness was a constant drain on me. And the relationship that we'd created was one constructed with careful censorship. Clothed in Southern manners and restraint, it was like a large and brittle clay container covered with cracks. Filled to the brim with all our unspoken feelings, it was bound to break apart.

I was worn down. Not only had I been meeting with the doctor and John most days, I was also taking three courses at the university to become certified as a public school art teacher. I'd taken an apartment on Hallock Street in Amherst and rode my bicycle to classes, awkwardly balancing my paint box and canvas in the baskets on the back. John Elder, who must have been around fourteen at this time, had a bicycle, too, and rode it to Amherst, where he had a bedroom in the apartment. But he often preferred to stay with his father in the Shutesbury house, where he had his workroom and equipment in the basement, and his room filled with other projects. I was dividing the care of Chris with Mother, taking him to the public swimming pool or to the playground when I was not in meetings or classes. I was growing more and more manic, my unrelenting thoughts racing faster and faster, exhausting my brain and body.

For months I'd been dealing with John's anger in the Town House Motor Lodge. And living with Mother over the previous several weeks had become increasingly stressful as well. Memories of my last night in my apartment before being committed to Northampton State Hospital are still cuttingly clear.

I came home in the late afternoon to find Mercer—who'd lived with Mother in Cairo since experiencing a psychotic episode while stationed off the Vietnam coast—sitting in my living room. He'd stopped taking his antipsychotic medication and had driven up from Georgia. Being separated from Mother for so long had become unbearable to him. I also came home to Mother's firm announcement that I had to stay in that evening, that I'd been going at too rapid a pace for my own good.

Never in my adult life had she overtly ordered me to do anything. Her control had been subtle, and was internalized when I was very young. Without having realized it, I'd lived much of my life to please her. I didn't know what living my own life would mean. But at that overt command, something inside me snapped.

I picked out a change of clothes and brought them to the bathroom, announcing that I was going to take a bath in case I decided to go out later. Then I locked the door and ran the water into the tub. After my bath I went to the kitchen to fix something to eat. But Mother said that she had cooked supper, and would I please just sit and eat. I sat down and she set a plate in front of me. I looked down at the mountain of scrambled eggs before me and felt like gagging.

Then Mother handed me a tall glass of milk.

It was a handblown glass from Mexico, filled with tiny air bubbles. Because those glasses broke so easily, the one that Mother handed me was one of the few that remained. Whether it was the pressure of Mother's hand around the glass or mine, I don't know. Perhaps it was something else that caused the glass to break. But just as I took it from her, the bottom of it fell out in a perfect circle, shattering on the floor in the pool of spilt milk.

"I'll clean it up," Mother said, rushing to get a handful of paper towels. For a second I saw her frailty and insecurity and felt pity for her. Then I felt anger and helplessness. Then anger again. "No," I said, tearing paper towels from the dispenser. "No, I'll clean it up myself."

I knelt on the kitchen floor and wiped up the milk and the glass fragments.

I was utterly exhausted. I was tired of Mother making my bed each morning after I left for school. I was tired of feeling guilty for not making the bed myself, and resentful because I didn't want to be pressured into making it when a made bed was the least of my priorities. I was tired of her snapping off the lights after me everywhere I went. I was tired of her doing things for me constantly when I wanted to just be left alone. I was tired of feeling her enormous need, tired of feeling sorry for her.

I was tired of always feeling inadequate.

The longer she stayed, the more the apartment felt like it was Mother's rather than mine. I was tired of having to leave early in the morning so I could sit in a coffee shop at the university and have half an hour alone before beginning classes.

I cleaned up the milk and glass. Mother and I ate silently. I kept thinking of how frantic she'd looked when the glass broke, and I felt guilty as I was filling myself with the eggs I didn't want. Forkful after forkful of eggs, just as I'd eaten to please Mother when I was a child.

After supper I got up. "I'm going to take a nap now," I said, walking to my bedroom.

Mother pushed herself hurriedly back from the table and got up. "I want to take the phone from your room. I don't want you to be woken by a phone call."

"I need the phone," I responded stubbornly. "I'm expecting a call." Then I closed my door and locked it.

Mother beat on the door for a while, demanding to be let in. Then she stopped. I lay on my bed, smoking a cigarette, too upset to sleep.

In a little while Paula called, as I'd expected her to. Talking, I felt a rush of grief. Over the summer she'd grown closer to Mother as she'd grown more distant from me. And she'd recently said to me: "I don't know how to relate to you anymore. You've become like a therapist to me and I don't know what to do."

I crushed my empty cigarette pack and put it in the ashtray by my bed, got up, and unlocked the door. I handed Mother the phone, saying that it was Paula and that I was going out for cigarettes. Then I rushed out before she could stop me.

I walked the couple of blocks to the Pizza Tower restaurant across Pleasant Street. I had exactly enough money for a pack of cigarettes and a Diet Coke, which I sat in the restaurant drinking while I smoked.

Before I'd finished my Diet Coke, Mercer came to my table and sat down.

"Please come home, Sister," he said in his thick Southern drawl. "Mama wants you to come home."

"I can't. Don't you remember the things you wrote me when you were having your breakdown, Mercer? Don't you remember how she hurt you?"

He crushed his cigarette in the ashtray and lit another. "I was crazy then, Sister. Mama didn't mean any harm. She didn't know any better. Please come home." He took a long drag from his cigarette, then exhaled. A cloud of smoke swirled between us.

"I can't, Mercer."

He got up then, turned, and walked away, his shoulders rounded in a permanent slump of defeat, smoke trailing around and behind him.

What could I do?

"I Don't Know How to Love Him" from *Jesus Christ Superstar* wailed from the jukebox.

Where could I go?

In a few minutes Mother came into the restaurant, walked back to my table, and stood looking down at me. She spoke in a firm, authoritative voice: "Come home, Margaret."

"I can't."

Her body trembled with rage, and her neck, engorged with blood, looked as if it had swollen to twice its normal size. But her voice was still controlled, measured, and deathly calm. In the dimly lit restaurant, I looked up at her.

"Come home and take care of your son."

I'd never heard her voice sound so cold.

Now "Lucy in the Sky with Diamonds" blasted from the jukebox.

There was no way I could care for my son. I thought of Dee and Tom, and how many times the boys had played together while Dee and I visited with each other.

"Mother," I said, "please just call Dee to take Chris. She'll do that for me."

My voice was as controlled as Mother's. Anger was battling with guilt. But I couldn't go home.

Without saying another word, Mother turned away from me and left the restaurant.

I'd spent my last dollar on cigarettes. I was too upset to go to friends who lived in town. And I couldn't go home. Would Mother send someone to look for me? Yes, she probably would. I had to get away from her. I needed to be alone. I needed to slow my racing thoughts. I desperately needed to rest.

Where could I go?

I left the restaurant and walked down Pleasant Street toward the university. *Where can I go? Where can I go?* The question repeated itself in my mind faster and faster, and I walked faster and faster as if to keep up with my thoughts. Suddenly I tripped on a sandal and nearly fell. It was then that I realized that I'd rubbed blisters on the soles of both feet. Stopping, I leaned against the side of a tree and unbuckled and removed the new, handcrafted sandals that Mother had bought for me, much too expensive for her poor budget, and much too large for me.

Too large. Of course they were too large. Then they weren't sandals at all; they were a metaphor for my whole life and what Mother expected of me. Of course the sandals were too goddamn large! I flung one out into the darkness. "Damn you!" I flung the other in the opposite direction. "Damn you!" Two beautifully crafted sandals forever separated. "Damn you!" I cried out into the darkness.

Then I turned and walked back toward town.

After a while, I reached the gate to West Cemetery. I knew I would be safe from Mother in the cemetery at night. The night was starless and dark. I heard the low, long growl of a dog. Then the dog itself appeared, walking cautiously among the tombstones toward me. It was a large German shepherd. He paused and stood observing me. *Walk calmly on up the hill,* I told myself. *Don't give it any indication of fear.* Then I thought of Saint Francis and his ability to communicate with animals, his kindness and compassion. His image had come to me so vividly when I was pregnant with Chris that I did an oil painting of him to celebrate the life of my unborn child. Now I imagined Saint Francis walking quietly beside me as I continued on up the hill.

Soon the dog turned and walked away.

I knew exactly where Emily Dickinson's family plot lay enclosed by an old black iron fence. I couldn't say now what thoughts were racing through my mind as I walked through West Cemetery that July night. As an adult I'd read little poetry. But as a girl, I'd read poetry almost daily and had especially loved the work of Emily Dickinson. After moving to our house in the Shutesbury woods, I bought a record of her poetry being read aloud. As I cleaned hand and paw prints off the sliding glass doors that enclosed the living/dining room on three sides, or—with an extension brush—raked cobwebs off the wood beam that ran along the apex of the cathedral ceiling, I listened to her words.

> *I never saw a moor,*
> *I never saw the sea*

> *This is my letter to the World*
> *That never wrote to Me.*

> *The Brain is wider than the Sky*

> *You cannot fold a Flood—*
> *And put it in a Drawer.*

The more despair I felt in my daily life and marriage, the more I turned to Dickinson's poetry as comfort and companion.

> *Pain has an Element of Blank;*
> *It cannot recollect*
> *When it began, or if there were*
> *A day when it was not.*

> *I felt a Funeral in my Brain,*
> *And Mourners to and fro . . .*
> *And then a Plank in Reason, broke,*
> *And I dropped down, and down—*

The Dickinson plot lay straight ahead. I opened the gate and went inside. To my right two tall cedars twisted their way toward the stars like the cedars in Van Gogh's paintings. To my left stood the Dickinson family tombstones. I walked past the stones of Emily Dickinson's grandparents and parents. I walked past the stone of her sister, Lavinia.

At Emily's grave, I sat down. I could not hear one sound, only Emily's words in my heart—

> *There is a pain—so utter—*
> *It swallows substance up—*

I stroked the grass growing over her grave—

> *Then covers the Abyss with Trance—*
> *So Memory can step*
> *Around—across—upon it—*

A slight breeze rattled nearby branches.

> *As one within a Swoon—*
> *Goes safely—where an open eye—*
> *Would drop Him—Bone by Bone.*

In the deep silence there, I lay down and sobbed into the grass and dry earth.

After a while, I got up and left the Dickinson plot, closing the gate behind me. I walked down the little dirt road to the other grave-yard entrance, this one with a chain hung between the gateposts to keep cars out. The road went past the older, hilly section of the cemetery, with sandstone and slate tombstones planted centuries be-fore: Mrs. Sarah, the wife of Dr. Ebenezer Dickinson, 1743; M. Ephraim Kellogg, 1777; Nehemiah Strong, 1772; Mr. Solomon Boltwood, 1762. Stones leaning in the earth.

I climbed over the chain between the gateposts. To be certain that I didn't run into Mother out looking for me, I walked behind the stores on Pleasant Street and across the parking lot of the Mobil sta-tion, built where the house in which Emily Dickinson and her fam-ily lived from 1840 to 1855 once stood.

Before I had time to decide where to go, I saw Dr. Turcotte's wife, Claire, parked in front of the gas station. It was as if she'd known ex-actly where I'd been and was waiting there for me all along.

Jim Clark, who worked for Dr. Turcotte, sat in the front seat be-side her. Jim had been Dr. Turcotte's patient in the Brattleboro Re-treat, a Vermont psychiatric hospital at which Dr. Turcotte had worked briefly before being fired. Now Jim lived in Dr. Turcotte's house, and as a job, he listened to patients talk out their anxiety, stayed with patients who were not disturbed enough to be commit-ted to a hospital but were still in crisis, and ran errands. Seeing me walking barefoot across the Mobil station parking lot, he opened the door, got out of the car, and headed toward me.

"Hi, Margaret," he said. His dark eyes were sensitive and search-ing.

"Hello, Jim."

"Come for a ride with us," he said, gesturing toward the open door.

"I'm not going home, Jim," I said. "I can't."

"No one's going to make you do that. We'll only go for a ride. It's just not safe for you to be out alone this late at night. We won't take you anyplace you don't want to go. I promise."

I believed him. For the previous two months I'd spent hours talking to him in a small room off Dr. Turcotte's main office. We'd both talked about our lives. He told me about beatings from his father, and how his mother had held his head under the running water in the kitchen sink while whipping his head and face with an old enema hose. I told him about John's drinking, violence, and threats. I told him about my depression. Jim was a good listener, attentive and compassionate. I'd grown to trust him.

I got into the car beside Claire. She turned it around in the Pizza Tower parking lot and drove through Amherst. Then she turned right on Route 9 and headed for Northampton. I had no idea what to say to her. She was a warm, well-meaning woman who talked incessantly, words that I blocked out as I sat smoking, staring out the window, wondering what I was going to do now.

Where had the night gone? I must have walked around Amherst much longer than I'd thought. All the restaurants and coffee shops were closed, and Northampton looked deserted.

"I surely would like a cup of coffee," I commented, lighting another cigarette.

Claire responded agreeably, not even appearing to take note of the late hour.

It must have been around that time that I began to grow more confused, for as well as I knew Northampton, I had no idea of the location of the diner that Claire finally found open. We pulled into the parking lot, and the three of us got out of the car and walked into the diner. Small stones ground themselves into the broken blisters on my bare feet. I could hardly walk. After sitting down in a booth, I saw that I'd left bloody smears across the floor.

How long did we stay there, talking? When trying to remember this episode, the closer I get to the period of my incarceration in the state hospital, the more blank spaces I experience in my memory. At some point Claire left the diner and a man named Al, who was on the doctor's staff, took her place. Al was a middle-aged bachelor with dark hair and clear blue eyes. A man who'd been sitting on a stool at the counter came over and began a conversation with him.

My next memory is of walking down the street with Jim and two young men who'd also been at the diner. I still remember the intensity of the conversation, but not a word of content. Then we were in someone's basement furnished with a shabby couch and a bare mattress on the floor. Jim and one of the young men were sitting on the couch talking. I slipped out of the basement with the other man. I'll call him Bob, though I've no idea what his real name was. I do know that with his red hair and beard, I thought he looked like a young Vincent Van Gogh.

We walked for miles through unfamiliar neighborhoods. Like a faithful dog, Bob followed me up and down the streets. Everything felt like a maze, reflecting the confusion in my mind, confusion so great that it negated awareness of the pain in the soles of my feet. A gray dawn began to define details of neighborhoods—gingerbread trimming on an old Victorian house, a cluster of clay pots of geraniums on a front porch, an old-fashioned porch swing on another.

As the sky turned a delicate peach color, we found ourselves in a field, the sunrise casting a warm glow on the dew-covered grasses. We sat down on the damp ground and smoked. I was convinced that Vincent Van Gogh was communicating—or trying to communicate—with me through Bob's voice. I kept insisting that he listen to the voice straining to come through him and tell me what he heard. God knows what he thought of me, a woman with her passionate crazy talk, long dress, and blistered and bleeding feet.

I remember my acute surprise when I stood and saw that the field in which we'd been sitting was directly across the highway from the Town House Motor Lodge. I felt enormous relief and wonder at the fact that, with all the seemingly meaningless meandering through one strange neighborhood after another, I'd ended up exactly where I needed to be.

Walking across the highway, I was also relieved to see Al leaving a patient's room and heading for the Howard Johnson's. He saw me almost as soon as I saw him, and came to meet me. I told him I had no money or shoes and was in desperate need of cigarettes. He cursed loudly at Bob, as if he'd been responsible for my disappearance, and demanded that Bob leave. Then he took me to a room at the motel, where I waited until he came back with cigarettes and coffee.

The day passed in a blur of faces as one person after another came to be with me. For two months I'd visited John at that motel. Now—at least momentarily—*I* was staying there as a patient. I felt as much at home there as any place I'd been since I'd left John and our house in the Shutesbury woods.

I spent a restless night, the last night before my incarceration in Northampton State Hospital.

The next morning Al arrived early, bringing a suitcase full of my clothes that Mother must have packed. "Dr. Turcotte wants to see you. He sent me over to drive you to his office."

I put my cigarettes and matches into my purse and eased my feet into the loafers my mother had packed.

Ethel, the doctor's part-time assistant, sat at the desk in his waiting room, bent over what looked like accounting books. Jim was sitting on one of the couches with a patient who was playing "Puff, the Magic Dragon" on his guitar. They acknowledged me. Then the patient began playing and singing "Blowin' in the Wind."

I sat down on the other couch, but before I could say anything, Dr. Turcotte opened the door to his office and walked out with a patient who left the room quickly. The doctor looked at me. "Margaret," he said, ushering me into his office. He sat down in his chair. I sat down in the chair opposite him.

"Do you know what day this is?" he began his questioning. He asked me about the month and year, and who was president of the country.

I dimly remember answering his questions with metaphors that had nothing to do with what he'd asked. What I remember clearly about the meeting is that Dr. Turcotte's gray pants were worn around the cuffs, and that he was wearing black shoes that came to points at the toes. I was staring at his shoes when he got up, went to his desk, and called Northampton State Hospital, telling the person on the other end of the line that he was sending a patient for admission.

I agreed to sign myself in. Dr. Turcotte had no privileges at the hospital. He had been kicked off the staff some years before because, he said, of clashes with the chief doctor on staff who, he claimed, was schizophrenic. But he explained that he would be able to come to the hospital to help me because Ethel still held a position in administration there.

PART THREE

Roses and the Pineapple Doctor

Chapter Twelve

ETHEL DROVE ME TO THE HOSPITAL IN HER PALE BLUE OLDSMOBILE.

From what I'd heard over the years, Northampton State Hospital for the Insane was more a place of torment and abuse than one of healing. In my mind, I associated it with the movie *The Snake Pit*, starring Olivia de Havilland. I saw the movie at a drive-in theater with my parents and brothers when I was a girl, and it frightened me terribly. I can still see de Havilland as the fragile and confused Virginia looking up at the inmates behind walls of bars, thinking they must be animals in a zoo. At some point in the movie someone explains that long ago they used to throw insane people into pits full of snakes, thinking that what would drive a sane person crazy might drive a crazy person sane.

Riding with Ethel, I was remembering the images of the insane people in the movie, the camera moving farther and farther away until I was looking down into the earth at the mass of tormented humanity and writhing snakes.

I felt like vomiting.

Ethel turned into the driveway of the administration building, pulled the car up in front, and snapped off the ignition. "Let's go," she said, dragging her heavy purse across the seat and slamming the door. I opened my door and got out. Ethel was already at the entrance.

She was a practical, down-to-earth woman, with a large, strong body and a commanding presence. I followed her into the admissions office, where I was told to sit in a straight chair across the desk from a small, dark-haired nurse. Ethel sat in a chair by the door.

The nurse asked for my wallet, watch, and ring.

"May I keep my cigarettes?" I asked, twisting my wedding band off my finger and placing it on the desk next to my wallet.

"Yes, but not the matches."

I unfastened my watchband and laid my watch beside my ring and wallet.

She asked me a lot of questions, recording the answers on the admissions form: name, age, marital status, number of children, home address.

Then she took me into a small room with an examination table and a pair of scales. She weighed me: 130 pounds. Then she measured my height: five feet, seven and a half inches. She had me sit on the examination table while she took my blood pressure. She recorded all of this information on the paper on her clipboard.

"So you're suicidal," she said.

"Suicidal?" I responded, shocked.

"That's what it says on the papers Mrs. Swift brought from your doctor."

"Suicidal?" I repeated, incredulous. I stretched my arms out before me, wrists up, exposing the veins. "But look," I said. "I have no scars."

She ignored my statement and without giving me a chance for a backward look at Ethel escorted me across a large, high-ceilinged room crowded with inmates milling about, lost and dazed expressions in their eyes, resignation in their posture. Most of them looked like people who'd been abandoned here for so long that they'd forgotten who they were, if they'd ever known. There were skinny, bent old men shuffling along, muttering; women with ravaged faces, full lower lips hanging loose over chins sprouting long hairs, bellies grown large and soft from years of eating instant mashed potatoes and white bread; a tall, thin young woman with pale frightened and frightening eyes. The room felt like Penn Station as Goya might have painted it in his last years when he was old, sick, and deaf, and his inner darkness and fear had become almost palpable in the coarse strokes of the thick, dark paint.

As I followed the nurse, Goya's most horrible images filled my mind. Then I again focused on the image of Penn Station. Then on the trains there. For a few seconds, I could imagine the steam and hiss of engines as if all the tormented human beings in their churning confusion were actually about to embark on a journey. But where were they going? *Auschwitz,* I thought. *Buchenwald. Treblinka.*

Where were *we* going?

I followed the nurse through the maze of humanity crazed by life, dulled by genetics, or both. Coming to a closed door, I waited while she unlocked it with one of the many keys on the ring that hung from her belt by a chain. My mind was spinning. Another image from *The Snake Pit* rose to my consciousness—an enormous lock and key. All the years of my growing up and marriage, that image had been stored in my mind. Waiting.

But this must be some sort of special opportunity, I thought. *Soon Dr. Turcotte will appear, and together we will save all these tormented souls. Yes,* I assured myself, *soon Dr. Turcotte will arrive and everything will be all right.*

The nurse told me to sit on one of the straight chairs lined up against the wall in the corridor. Then she gave my papers to the nurse at the nurses' station, unlocked the door, and disappeared.

What we were waiting for?

Two policemen brought in a middle-aged woman and placed her on the chair next to mine. The woman was tall and bony, with frizzy hair dyed a garish red, a slash of matching lipstick on her thin lips. She wore open-toed, black sling-backed pumps that revealed red nail gloss on her toenails like that on her long fingernails. She tugged at the sleeve of one of the policemen, pleading, "What will happen to my cats? I tell you, there's no one else to feed them. Dear God, there's no one to feed them but me." The tears streaming down her face were black from mascara.

"Calm down, lady, those cats will be just fine. Just fine," he said. He disentangled himself from her grip. "Here are her papers," he said, handing them to the nurse. Then he hurriedly left through the door that the nurse unlocked for him.

Another nurse pulled a chair up to the woman, took one of her hands, and, with a pair of nail clippers, began to clip the nails off— *snap, snap, snap.* One after another, small, red, crescent-moon shapes fell to the floor while the woman continued to weep her black tears. "Oh, no," she wept. "Oh, no." But it was clear that she expected nothing now. Her words were only incredulous utterances of grief.

I stared down at the scattering of fingernails on the floor. How meticulously she must have shaped and polished those nails, taking care to avoid breaking them. And her cats, what of her cats?

It was as if my skin had been stripped away and I was nothing except raw nerves exposed to any and all of the horrors that came my way. There were no boundaries between the woman and me. Her pain was my pain, her isolation mine. Her despair drove itself deep into my own heart. My vision began to change, colors intensifying like nothing I'd ever imagined. For a few minutes I was diverted from my emotional pain by my fascination with the change in my vision. *This must be like some sort of drug trip,* I thought, excited by the colors' intensity. *The colors—how beautiful they are!*

Then a young woman was seated to my left.

"Hello," I said.

"Hello," she responded, looking down at her lap.

"Are you from Northampton?" I asked, reaching for a human connection in that alien environment.

Even as I asked the question, my eyes were drawn to the thick scars that followed one another from her left wrist to her shoulder. I'd never seen anything like it. How could she have slashed herself with such determined violence? And so deeply so many times?

"I have no home," she responded flatly. She paused. "My name is Margaret. What's yours?"

"Margaret," I replied. Then I saw myself as that young woman facing me. Which was I? Or was I both? My mind swam with confusion.

"I have no home either," I told her, though in reality I had a very nice apartment. An apartment, but not a home. At least not my own home. It had become more Mother's than mine. Mother, who had done her very best to help me.

The other Margaret ran the fingers of her right hand up and down over her scars. I sat, fascinated by the tenderness expressed by the same hand that had done such violence to her arm.

I felt my eyes brim with tears. I longed for such tenderness to console me.

A nurse came and took the other Margaret away, and I was alone, two empty chairs beside me.

Then I was admitted to a ward for people in extreme crisis.

II

It has been many years since I was in that hospital, and I still struggle to claim those experiences as mine. Yes, I tell myself, I was the young woman who sat on the floor, embracing an old woman who wailed and wrung her hands while frantically muttering what sounded like some strange foreign language. I was the young woman who thought that the newscaster on the TV in the lounge was speaking directly to me. I was that young woman with the desperate belief that I could do something to save the whole world—someone had to! I was that young woman with wires of connection in my brain blasted apart by pain, the blaze and spark of energy gone haywire.

I was that young woman singing aloud, singing to block out the feeling of terror that rose in the silence of my throat while a macho nurse stood, arms crossed over her heavy breasts, watching me shower. There was no shower curtain to protect me from the assault of her eyes. Some song about love on Jupiter and Mars. Singing with all my heart.

My friend Ilene came to visit me on her way to Boston, where she was going to have open-heart surgery. I was still in the first ward with its enormous room full of beds. Ilene came with a dozen red roses. "Thank you," I said awkwardly, taking the vase from her hand. Then we sat side by side on my bed.

Seeing Ilene in that context made me feel terribly self-conscious. Jim, Al, Ethel, Dr. Turcotte, and his other patients and family members were all a part of the world in which I now functioned. Ilene was a part of the academic community, with its faculty cocktail parties and dinners for visiting dignitaries, a world in which I'd always felt uncomfortable and inadequate. Ilene was the perfect model of a good faculty wife, devoted mother, and contributing member of the community at large. She was also terribly sick.

I began talking rapidly. I told her I wanted to mend her damaged heart with the new powers of my mind that I had recently acquired. But almost as soon as the words poured out of my mouth, I realized that what I was saying was crazy and they trailed off in a self-conscious mumble.

"What did you say?" she asked, puzzled.

I felt relieved that she'd not understood my words. Shamefaced, I looked down at the roses.

"They are very beautiful, Ilene," I said softly. I no longer remember how that awkward conversation ended, but I shall never forget Ilene's visit and how I longed to help her the way she helped so many others.

As soon as Ilene left, a nurse came and jerked the vase away, saying: "Patients aren't allowed glass."

"Are patients allowed roses?" I asked.

She glared at me. Then she handed me the roses, their long stems dripping in my hand.

I gave them to the women on the ward—one to the woman who

begged for cigarettes, one to the woman who wanted to save the world. I gave one to the woman who paced the corridor, her rapid turning like a snapping whip. I gave one to the woman who sat on the floor doing nothing, and another to the woman who wept continuously. I gave roses to the women who asked for them.

Twelve roses to twelve women.

Then one woman began to walk down the corridor, and the others followed. They walked silently in a strange parade, each with a rose like a torch in her raised hand.

III

The picture was printed on cardboard with simulated brushstrokes like those in the framed paintings that you could buy at the five-and-dime when I was a child: bowls of fruit, bouquets of flowers, seascapes with waves crashing against the rocks. This one was a bowl of fruit—apples, bananas, grapes on a dark walnut table. What I remember about it most clearly is darkness. And a sense of lifelessness. I couldn't imagine those fruits ever having known sunlight or rain. I couldn't imagine them ever nourishing a human soul any more than the cardboard on which they were printed.

Two nurses sat talking in the nurses' station in the hall. The picture hung to the right of the lounge door, just out of their field of vision. I paced back and forth across the room, smoking one cigarette after another, stealing glances at the picture. The longer I looked at it, the more monstrous it grew in my mind.

At the upper right-hand corner, a speck of cardboard was exposed where a part of the image had been nicked or torn off. For a few thoughtful seconds I stared at the exposed cardboard, an area smaller than the nail on my little finger. Then, seeing that the nurses were still engaged in conversation and paying no attention at all to me, I went over to the painting, dug my fingernail into an edge of the torn area, and peeled away a small section. Then another. And another. The more paper I pulled off the print, the easier it became. But pulling the print off the cardboard wasn't enough. In spite of all my effort, nothing of substance was revealed. Behind the bowl of lifeless fruit and dark wood lay no promised land. I felt a mounting rage.

I tore and scratched at the picture—ripped apples, shredded bananas, fragments of grapes. Still I clawed at the cardboard. Then, in place of the damaged fruit, I saw the torn and bleeding faces of Mother and John. Furiously I tore at bloody flesh that gave way to bone.

Only then I heard my own shrill scream.

One of the nurses came running into the room.

"What in the world?" she exclaimed. Then, seeing the mutilated picture, she clamped her hand over her mouth. Tears spilled from her eyes. "Why?" she pleaded. "Why did you do such a thing? And such a beautiful picture. I bought it with my very own money to try to pretty up the place. I should have known better than to even try with the likes of you in here." Then she went and got a broom and dustpan and swept up the scraps that lay on the floor.

With the arrival of the nurse, the faces had disappeared. Once again the picture was only a simple print of a bowl of fruit, now damaged beyond recognition.

"I'm sorry," I said limply.

The nurse took the ruined picture from the wall and wordlessly walked away with it under her arm. Then a scream like none I'd ever heard before came from someplace on the ward. I rushed from the room to see what had happened.

Down the hall two male orderlies were wrestling a screaming woman into a straitjacket. I caught my breath. I'd never seen anyone handled so violently. The woman wasn't especially large, nor did she look physically strong, but the men were jerking her around roughly with a force I could only call an assault. Her eyes were open wide and filled with terror. "Please!" she screamed. "Oh, please!"

I turned to the nurse at the desk and blurted out: "For God's sake, what she needs is comfort, not attack."

"Mind your own business, lady. You don't know what you're talking about. It's time for you to brush your teeth and get ready for bed."

With the mention of my toothbrush, I forgot about the woman. My entire mind filled with the image of that toothbrush in its cellophane packaging.

Where *was* my toothbrush? It was the third toothbrush I'd lost. My throat constricted with panic. I felt like I was losing my whole life.

"I can't find my toothbrush."

Disgustedly, the nurse pulled open a drawer, got another one, and handed it to me.

"Now you keep up with this one, you hear?"

I took the toothbrush. Then I looked down the corridor to find the men dragging the straitjacketed woman to a padded cell.

"No!" I screamed to no one. "No!"

Was this when everything began to have a purple haze around it? Was this when the orderlies came toward me? Was this when I rushed to stand behind a chair as if it was both fortress and weapon? Was the glare in my eyes so defiant, so threatening to those large, muscular men?

Here my memory is shattered to fragments—a man's large hands, his hairy wrists, flashes of white uniforms, nurses yelling. Screams.

Then I was a child again, lying on my stomach on the living room rug, listening to the record player and to someone reading Lewis Carroll's *Alice in Wonderland.* Then I myself was Alice falling down and down for miles, wondering how I would get out of such an unexpected dilemma.

Was this when I was tied hand and foot to my ward bed, no longer Alice, but not certain who I was? My heart pumped as rapidly as when I was a little girl, always in a hurry, while Mother looked at me as she mimicked the White Rabbit's words in a syncopated beat: "I'm late. I'm late. For a very important date."

Was this what I'd been hurrying toward?

Mother must have been back home in Georgia by then. She'd gone without so much as a phone call to me, much less a visit. John told me later that just before she left Amherst, he and Mother had stood by my brother's idling car, arguing over which one of them had driven me crazy.

IV

"These straps are *not* too tight," the night nurse grumbled, jamming her index finger between the leather strap and the skin of my wrists and ankles. "Not too tight at all." I struggled, still spread-eagle on the bed to which she and an attendant had strapped me after I'd torn pieces off the picture in the patient lounge.

The restraints felt unbearable. I opened my mouth in the loudest scream of my life. I screamed for Dr. Turcotte, who would have never—I told myself—put me in this awful place, if only he knew its terrors. I screamed because I knew he knew very well its terrors and still he had put me here. I screamed because there was nothing else I could do. A nurse came with a hypodermic needle and, with the help of an aide, twisted me just enough to inject a tranquilizer into my hip.

Soon everything felt far away. After a while I stopped struggling to free myself. *Perhaps it doesn't matter,* I thought. *Perhaps none of it matters.* The ceiling light blazed in my eyes like a captured, shrunken sun. *Maybe I'll leave this body soon and go into another. Come morning, who knows where I'll find myself?* I looked across the aisle at the woman in the next bed. Except for me, she was the only patient awake in the whole room. Her eyes were dull with layers of rage like layers of compressed sediment in ancient stones. Her hair was stringy and greasy, and on her high, round forehead an enormous pimple rose in the middle of a mass of swollen red flesh. Looking at her, I thought: *I could wake in the morning and be this woman. I might this very minute be looking into my own tormented and hardened eyes.* I felt a knot in my heart. *I could be this woman,* I repeated to myself, and the knot loosened a little. What I felt was a seed of compassion. *Tomorrow I could be this woman.* How inadequate a thing mere skin is to contain us. I looked down at the woman's hairy legs, at her toes with their thick, yellow nails. I looked at her fingernails with their cracked and chipped scarlet polish. *Tomorrow,* I said to myself, *I could be her,* and I felt the compassion deepening. Compassion for her, compassion for me, compassion for the nurse scowling at the door.

The woman screamed to the nurse: "Get that fucking bitch to stop staring at me, she's driving me bonkers!" Then to me she shouted: "Stinking cunt, you give me the creeps." And she gathered all the spit in her mouth and spat the whole wad into my face, where it clung to my skin before beginning its slow journey from the corner of my eye and down my clenched jaw.

I looked at my feet. They had turned a bilious green. Perhaps I was dead already. How could I tell?

V

Morning brought an aide who set a breakfast tray beside my bed: cold eggs and limp toast. She offered me a forkful of eggs.

"Please let me feed myself," I said.

"Don't start giving me trouble again. Just eat your breakfast." She tried to jam a forkful of eggs against my tightly closed lips. Then she slammed the fork down on the plate.

"Please just unfasten my right hand and let me feed myself," I said, hating the pleading tone in my voice.

"You're not going to feed yourself. You're going to let me feed you, or you're going hungry. No skin off my back, sister. You're nothing but a troublemaker from the word *go.*"

I looked hard at her face. Why hadn't I noticed before? Shock raised gooseflesh all over my body. "I did an oil painting of you," I said. "For nearly a year I worked on it."

"Nut!" she screamed as she picked up my tray and left the room.

I felt relieved when the nurse left. I lay thinking about what it meant to be a human being, wondering what part of the human being is mortal flesh and blood and what is a part of eternity, or if flesh and blood, spirit and soul, cell and celestial configurations, aren't all part of the boundless being of God.

The room was full of women lying quietly on their beds. So far as I knew, no one had kicked up a disturbance like I had. They all looked so peaceful. Maybe not peaceful, but resigned, and obedient, like well-trained dogs. Drugged. Why couldn't I get so drugged I didn't care about anything either?

I was pulled quickly away from my thoughts by the sudden appearance of the Pineapple Doctor standing over my bed and looking intently into my eyes.

"Hello!" he said and smiled.

"Hello, Pineapple Doctor!" I called him that because he wore a shirt woven from fibers of pineapple leaves. He'd told me about his shirt when I'd admired it the day before. I returned his smile.

"How are you feeling this morning? You look better."

The doctor was Filipino, short and stocky with dark eyes and hair. His round face was one of those faces that would look forever young, even after he had grandchildren and great-grandchildren. He wore a chunky tiger's-eye ring on his right hand, which caught my eye. "Nice ring," I said.

"I'm glad you like it." His smile felt like a blessing.

I stared at the complex weave of his pineapple-fiber shirt.

"I don't know why we can't have the restraints removed," the Pineapple Doctor said, calling to an aide to unfasten me. The purple haze that all night had surrounded everyone—patients and staff alike—had disappeared, and the morning light was as ordinary as on any other morning in my life.

VI

Paula didn't visit me in the hospital, but she wrote me a note that she gave to our mutual friend Kay to deliver. She wrote that she didn't know how to visit me without losing her identity. She also told Kay to ask me to tell her what my experience was like. "Tell her it's like living in Eugene O'Neill's *Long Day's Journey into Night*," I said. "Only worse. Much worse." I thought of the Tyrone family—father and sons drowning their pain in alcohol, the frail and ghostly mother with her pills and futile stays in sanitariums. Then I thought of how the young, sensitive, and mortally ill Edmund Tyrone wanted to be lost in the fog. I had memorized his words about feeling like he'd drowned long before, and how peaceful he felt "to be nothing more than a ghost within a ghost."

I certainly didn't feel peaceful. I felt a torment I'd not known existed. Edmund's words echoed in my mind. I longed to be *nothing more than a ghost within a ghost*.

Kay visited me only once more, but Dee Waterman was a faithful and supportive friend. She was neither judgmental nor overtly afraid, though she later told me that her husband, Bob, had waited in the hospital parking lot for her during each visit. Afterward they went out to lunch while she recovered from the shock of seeing me psychotic, as well as seeing the other patients—the thin young woman who sat alone all day rocking and rocking, chin resting on her folded legs held together by her frail arms; the old woman who paced and babbled incoherently while bouncing a red rubber ball; and the woman who pleaded into her mirror for the long-dead John Kennedy to save us. "See! See!" she'd exclaim. "He's right here in my mirror. If only he'd come out and help us. Oh, Mr. President, please!"

Despite the upset, Dee came. She came bringing me bags of nuts

and fruit. She came bringing me books. She came with her exuber-
ance and her deep summer tan, silver earrings catching the sunlight,
soft rose nail polish gleaming on her toes.

Judy, a friend I'd met through Dr. Turcotte, came and brought me
a blank journal, but after that, she left for her family vacation and I
didn't see her until I was home from the hospital.

During the time when John and I had been meeting with Dr. Turcotte, Judy and her husband, Tom, had begun to go to him too. I met
them at a dinner that the doctor arranged for a large group of his patients at the Northampton Hilton. Judy and I were seated next to
each other at a long table. I was surprised when she leaned over and
asked in a whisper, "Will you go with me to the bathroom?"

"Of course," I replied, pushing my chair from the table. As soon
as we left the table, she began to cry, the story of her troubled marriage spilling out in sentences punctuated by sobs. By the time we got
back to the table, I knew more about her and her family than I knew
about some friends I'd had for years.

Judy had spent weeks staying at the motel along with other patients. I'd often visited her when I went there to meet with John.
Some weeks after she was able to go home, Judy had invited me to
her beach house for the Fourth of July weekend.

"You can't leave me here alone," Mother had protested. "I'm
afraid of John."

Hurt and anger rose inside me. Mother and John. Mother, who
forbade Daddy to drink, had jokingly commented to John, "Your
new house would be perfect for you if only all the faucets ran with
liquor." John, who waited for Mother to go to sleep before he began
tormenting me with his drunken forced sex and false accusations.

"If you're afraid of John," I said to my mother through clenched
teeth, "go to a motel for the weekend."

I brought Chris with me to the beach house, and Judy brought her
son too. Judy's sister, Martha, was there also, along with their
mother, Mabel, who, according to Martha, roamed the house at all
hours of the night, carrying on animated conversations with herself

or her long-dead husband. Mabel was a warmhearted woman, and I enjoyed sitting on the porch with her talking, as we four women drank whiskey sours while the children watched the fireworks in the distance.

"See that blue light blinking across the bay?" Judy said to me, pointing in the opposite direction of the fireworks. "It marks the place where the house stood that Eugene O'Neill lived in when he wrote *Long Day's Journey into Night*. The house was destroyed in the hurricane of 'thirty-eight."

Mabel sighed. Light from the fireworks sparkled for a moment on her earrings, tiny carousels that made gentle tinkling sounds like miniature wind chimes. She turned to face me. "You know," she announced with sad appreciation, "I've always loved Eugene O'Neill and musical comedy."

Fireworks burst again in the night sky above the water. The children yelled exuberantly while we chain-smoked and drank. My broad-brimmed hat was lying on a table, and Martha asked if she could try it on. "Of course," I replied, then felt my heart plummet when I saw how charming she looked with my hat tipped back on her head, revealing her smiling face. It had never crossed my mind to wear my broad-brimmed hats—and I had many—tipped back. I always wore them low over my forehead, shading my eyes.

"Keep the hat, Martha. It looks much better on you than it does on me," I said.

"Are you certain?" Martha asked, surprised.

"Of course I'm certain. The hat looks wonderful on you."

I felt miserable. I wore my hat as if to hide from the world, as if to conceal my fear and sorrow in the shadow of the brim. Suddenly I felt totally undeserving of it. Why wasn't I refreshingly pleasant like Martha? I accepted another drink when Judy offered it.

The evening became a whiskey-soaked blur.

Mabel, Martha, and the children went to bed. Somehow—I've no idea how—Judy and I ended up lying on the living room rug with me unbuttoning the five or so buttons at the top of her blouse. She fumbled at the buttons, pushing each clumsily back into its button-hole as I slowly became aware of another presence in the room. I looked up to see Tom, Judy's husband, towering over us. He had never looked so tall.

While Judy screamed furiously at Tom for having come to the beach house uninvited, I sat up, overcome with embarrassment. How could I possibly have dared to do such a thing as to unbutton those buttons?

Judy demanded that Tom sleep on the couch in the living room. She and I slept in her bed. By the time we'd gotten undressed and crawled in, a storm had risen. All night, a hard rain beat at the windows while a wild, howling wind ripped at the roof shingles.

By daybreak the storm had subsided, while the storm in my mind raged more furiously than ever. My thoughts were racing wildly. I remember only one thought, and that was vaporous and fleeting like the tail end of a dream caught just after waking. I was thinking about reality and how most of us are unconscious that we are living in a dream from which we are waking, if at all, so slowly we can hardly notice the changes taking place in ourselves and the world around us.

Tom made a phone call to Dr. Turcotte, but I heard nothing of the conversation. I only know that, after their talk, we all got ready to drive back to Northampton. I packed Chris's and my clothes.

Then I waited, sitting on a large stone in the water thinking about how Shakespeare said life was a dream within a dream, and wondering when I might wake from the dream altogether. My feet dangled in the surf, while an empty beer can made a knocking sound as the water sloshed it against the stone.

Tom called out to me that everyone was ready to leave. I wanted him to come to where I was sitting so that I could tell him that I truly understood Shakespeare's meaning and that I was waking to a whole new level of consciousness and feeling elated at my new insight. Then I thought better of telling him. He wouldn't understand what I was trying to say. I would end up looking like a crazy fool.

Tom, Judy, and I rode in one car while Martha and the children rode in another. I sat in the front seat with Tom, and Judy sat in back. All the way home, I talked at a manic pace, wildly spilling out metaphors and similes in an attempt to explain what was happening in my mind.

Two days later I was in the insane asylum.

VII

Now Judy was gone. Paula was at home, unable to visit me. Ruth was in Italy, drenching her soul in opera. Dee would come on Thursday. But now I was alone, and being alone, I sat at a little table in the ward lounge, splashing violent reds and purples on a sheet of watercolor paper and—with a fine-pointed sable brush—defining the features of the patient across from me, who sat caressing a large wooden cross in her hand.

I again remembered the weekend at the beach house, and my humiliation at unbuttoning Judy's blouse. I'd revealed a part of myself that I had denied, rationalized, or buried all my life. I remembered how the young and ailing Edmund Tyrone had loved the way the fog hid him from himself and the world, but the fog in my own life was growing thinner and thinner.

"Bisexual." I tried the word out in a whisper. "Bisexual?" The old rationalizations and denials began playing themselves out in my mind. Once again I was the young teenager listening to Mother telling Daddy that she didn't know how she could live if I was a lesbian. I slung a thick blob of scarlet on the painting. Again, I felt the shame that told me that Mother and John were better than I was, that I deserved the pain that life had given me. But even as I felt these negative things about myself, I also felt an acceptance I'd never known before. Even as I was forced by the nurses and attendants to obey the hospital rules, I felt a new freedom growing inside me.

Chapter Thirteen

I

1971

IN AN OLD MAGAZINE IN THE OCCUPATIONAL THERAPY ROOM I FOUND A color print of Vincent Van Gogh's *Wheat Field with Crows,* one of his last paintings before he put a pistol to his chest and pulled the trigger. It is a painting filled with turbulence of brushstroke and thick pigment. In it a road curves through a field, then stops as if at some invisible barrier. A chaos of black wings rises from the wheat. The painting inspired the attempt at black humor that caused me to title my hospital journal *How Not to Paint Blackbirds.*

I spent a large part of my life in the struggle to become a painter. My effort had raised questions and conflicts, confusing and frustrating me. When I wasn't painting but filling my days with cooking, sewing, knitting, gardening, reading, and being mother to my two sons, I wondered why I ever put myself through the inevitable emotional pain of trying to be a painter. When I was painting, the process itself felt like life to me, no matter how poor or ineffectual the final product.

There was no confusion or frustration about writing or being a writer. I *was* a writer. Whatever I didn't know about myself, I knew this as surely as I knew that day follows night. A dream gave me this realization, though I have no recollection whatsoever of the content of the dream. I dreamed it one late afternoon while taking a nap on the living room couch in Shutesbury. I woke with the certainty that I, Margaret, was a writer. I felt my identity as a writer with the same assurance that I felt my identity as a human being. Though I had no idea how I could know that with such certainty, I had no doubt that the revelation that waked me from my nap was true.

After the nap, I felt disorientated and a little crazy. Since my marriage, my only writing had been academic papers and letters to friends, especially to Pat King. Those things didn't make me think of myself as a writer, only as a person who sometimes wrote. *If I'm a writer*, I said to myself, *then I want to see what I can write.* I went to the desk, got a pen and a legal pad, and sat back down on the couch. Without thinking, I scrawled on the first line of the legal pad: "A lost skate key." *How odd*, I thought. "A lost skate key." Then I remembered the many afternoons of skating back and forth on Grandmother's paved sidewalk with my cousins and neighbors. All the bruised knees and bending down to tighten the skates with a skate key came rushing back to consciousness. "A pittosporum bush," I wrote, remembering biting through the dark green leaves on the bush growing at the edge of Grandmother's yard. I wrote: "June bugs. Roscoe the pig. Grandmother churning butter on the shady side porch." One after another I wrote images from my childhood: " . . . the mimosa tree, mint leaves wet with faucet water, my sister's shoes, handfuls of dirt . . ." But what did they mean? Was this being a writer? I felt awkward and puzzled. Still I wrote: "Old wallpaper and spider webs. A bicycle. Bamboo and starlings."

Then I heard John's car turn into the drive. Quickly I jammed the legal pad under the couch. I would have been embarrassed to have him see what I'd written. In the morning, after he left for work, with shame I destroyed the writing, an action I grew to regret years later when I discovered that what I'd written had been a list of the key images of my first book of poems, *The Naked Bear.*

Now I was in the state hospital with doctors who—with the exception of the young Filipino doctor—paid no attention to me, and nurses and attendants who were insensitive and sometimes abusive. I sat at a table in the lounge of the new ward, my journal open in front of me. Until now I'd not kept a journal since I was a startled teenager facing my distraught mother lying on my bed, arm thrown over her eyes, body shaking with sobs. "What have I done to deserve such a daughter?" Mother had wailed, clutching my diary in her hand. She'd read that I'd had a beer on the beach with the girls. She was also hysterical about what I might have meant by "being indiscreet" with the boy I'd been dating and whom I adored. I lied to her, saying that I had been "indiscreet" about something I said about his former girlfriend. I had in fact let him touch my breast through my sweater, and—though I felt terribly guilty for having committed such a mortal sin—it mattered so much to me that I felt compelled to acknowledge it in my diary, even if I had to conceal the real event and its excitement in formal and vague language. But watching Mother in her misery, I felt sick with guilt. Guilt for letting the boy touch my breast, guilt for drinking the beer, and—most of all—guilt for upsetting Mother.

But whatever anger I might have felt at Mother's coming into my room and reading my diary evaporated when the back door slammed. Someone had forgotten: because of the sharp and sudden sound, my sister, Harriet, would be having a convulsion. Mother jumped up and ran down the hall to her. Had Mother said these words to me, or had they just repeated themselves in my head again as they so often did? "You with your mind, you with your talents and gifts and your sister lying up there in that bed unable to raise her head or utter a word. You with your mind . . ."

Except for a few abstract poems that would have made no sense to Mother, I destroyed all my writing that day. After that I only wrote an occasional poem, making certain that my words were vague enough to keep her from understanding what I was talking about. In time, I pushed writing from my mind altogether until madness broke through the thick walls of repression and gave me back that forgotten and essential part of myself.

I remember little of what I wrote in my hospital journal. I do remember that the writing gave me strength and—by degrees—clarity. My journal gave me reason to wake in the mornings. But later, when I went through periods of feeling shame over my episodes of madness, I took my scissors to the journal and, over time, mutilated it. What remains is a faded green construction-paper cover. On the upper left side is a dirty piece of adhesive tape with my name misspelled on it and some faded identifying numbers. Upside down under this is the partial question "look at this painting?" Under it in smaller letters is: "Think about it for a moment," followed by "how much do you see," and the single word "how." All of the letters have been cut from magazines. In the lower right corner a portrait of Van Gogh stares out in all his red-bearded intensity. The back of the cover is a piece of less faded red construction paper. These words, also cut from a magazine and glued to paper, instruct the reader: "Now look at the painting again." On the lower right side is a brilliant sun painted by Van Gogh. To me, the message on the cover meant that I'd gone through a near-suicidal struggle and—through writing the journal—had come out on the other side. I had learned how not to paint blackbirds. What follows is the little that remains of that hospital journal after shame and scissors censored it:

August 2, 1971: God. I am so tired of this hospital, this worse than prison place, this institution for dehumanizing human beings fighting to be human. Each day I've thought that today could be the day I'd get my walking papers out of this nut house. Each day I've held hope in front of me like a carrot held before a horse or donkey or whatever kind of animal it is. But, damn, I'm not a horse or donkey. I'm me, Margaret, and I don't want any more carrots. My eyes are quite good enough to see all

I care of pain. If I could run fast enough would it help my eyes to not see the pain that is already there?

One has to have one hell of a big sense of humor to live in this place. Another patient is looking over my shoulder, telling me I have confused thoughts. Where can I go to be alone and write? Someone is calling me now. I hope she doesn't find me. She's the patient who thinks I'm her mother. And I can't be mother to my own children now. Dear God.

I have just chosen to sit in OT and write. Of course, I couldn't make that choice until Mr. Buttons decided to unlock the room. Thank you, Mr. Buttons, for unplugging the fan because I needed music and there weren't electrical outlets for both fan and phonograph to run at the same time. Thank you, Mr. Buttons. Thank you, West Side Story. I need "Maria." I need to feel pretty. I need to know that somewhere there's a place for me, too.

But surely not this abominable place, I thought, and looked around me. Sitting at the table next to me, staring blankly at the blank TV across the room, was the young woman who had tried to electrocute herself by poking a fork into a toaster after her parents insisted that she break up with her boyfriend because he was a Jew. At an old upright piano a woman stumbled over notes to a hymn familiar from my Southern Baptist childhood. "Stay away from her," a nurse had hissed in my ear earlier. "We're almost certain she's a lesbian."

Beneath the barred window next to me stood an old rattan table, someone's sad, worn castaway. On it sat one of those tall, sharp-speared plants that teachers so often had on their desks when I was a child, those mottled green-leafed plants that seemed to thrive on neglect and dust. One of the patients was kneeling her thin, bent body before the table, scrub rag in hand and a bucket of suds beside her. All morning she knelt before the table and rubbed the rag up and down first one, then another of the table legs, working hard to wash away the dirt and grime accumulated over the years. Around and around the table she moved. Each time she approached a leg as if for the first time, settling in patiently, giving each the same meticulous care she'd given it just minutes before. Even with her thin, stringy hair and state-supplied cotton housedress she had a monumental quality about her. I thought of Lady Macbeth washing and washing her hands.

At the far end of the hall a nurse and two orderlies were dragging a resistant woman across the floor. "Come, cooperate with us, Mary," the nurse whined, but the woman only stiffened her body, her shoes scraping the floor. "Mary!"

"*Mistress Mary, quite contrary,*" I thought, surprised at the eruption of that old nursery rhyme in my mind. I was surprised also at my pleasure over the woman's defiance, and how I enjoyed her stubbornness until the nurse and aides succeeded in getting her into the dreaded room and slamming the door. At that point the woman let out such a desperate scream that I could hardly stand it. But it was over my heart, not my ears, that I wanted to clamp my hands.

I wanted to enjoy the idea of being contrary. I had never been "Mistress Mary Quite Contrary" as a child. Fueled by fear, I'd always been a good girl. In an elementary school play I'd been Little Miss Muffet sitting quietly on her tuffet and eating from a large blue bowl until a cardboard spider came onto the stage with chubby little-boy legs walking beneath the thin spider legs. In mock fear I dropped my spoon and bowl to the floor and ran off stage left.

Now that cardboard spider and the mock fear collided with my memory of being locked in a padded cell just days ago—cold clotted oatmeal shrinking from the sides of its pale blue plastic bowl, congealed blob of rancid butter on top—while a solitary spider made its way up the cracked plaster wall.

"Please, someone come and take me to the bathroom," I pleaded from the cell. "Please." But no one came. I sat in a pool of menstrual blood while passersby gawked at me through the small square window in the door. In the new ward, I bent over my journal recording my fear and humiliation.

"What a good girl you are." Mother's words came back to me.

Being a good girl meant living a lie.

Sitting at a table, my journal open before me, I picked my pen up with an unfamiliar firmness and, feeling anger rising as if from within the bowels of the earth herself and up through me, grinding my teeth, I wrote, "Mother, you must be glad." Then—deeply shaken and overwhelmed by intense and confusing emotion—I stopped writing and closed the book.

II

"This place is driving me crazy!"

The words burst from my mouth in an explosion of frustration when the Pineapple Doctor stopped me in the corridor and asked how I felt.

"To tell you the truth, there are days when I feel like it will drive me crazy, too," he responded, smiling, and then continued on his way.

What I'd said was true. Something had shifted inside me. I'd awoken that morning with the conviction that any more time in the hospital would hurt me beyond hope of recovery, that it would push me into a pit of madness too dark and deep for me to ever find my way to the light again. I felt frantic to get out.

I went to my room and got pen and paper from the bureau. Then I went to one of the tables in the corridor, sat down, and wrote a letter:

Dear Dr. Turcotte,

I have endured 21 days in this hellhole. I have been strapped spread-eagle to a bed, locked in solitary confinement where I was refused use of the bathroom. I've been condescended to, spat at, and forced to clean toilets. I have reached the limits of my endurance. I fear for my sanity if

I have to stay here. I can feel myself about to break under the strain of this place. I need to get out NOW. I am truly desperate.

Margaret

I folded the letter, put it into an envelope, sealed it, and wrote Ethel Swift's name on it. Under her name I wrote, "Please get this to Dr. Turcotte today. Thank you, Margaret." Then I persuaded a nurse to take it to Ethel.

It was only a couple of hours before Ethel came up to the ward to tell me that I'd be released from the hospital that day. She brought several cardboard boxes with her, and we worked together packing my things into them. First, we packed my clothes from the bureau. Then we packed the other things that I'd accumulated during my three-week incarceration—books, notebooks, postcards and letters, pens and pencils, paint and paintbrushes, and many sheets of heavy handmade French watercolor paper. There was also a small portable typewriter borrowed from Al.

After we finished packing, Ethel asked an orderly to help her carry the boxes and load them into her car. It took them two trips.

When she returned from the last trip, Dr. Turcotte was with her, as well as John, there to sign me out against doctors' orders. I was only beginning to comprehend that I was really going to leave the hospital. When I saw John, I collapsed against his chest and sobbed aloud while he held me.

Then we pulled apart.

The four of us walked down to the end of the corridor, where we waited while a nurse unlocked the door, then stepped aside to let us leave. Without looking back, I walked down the hall to the elevator. Ethel pushed the button, and we waited in silence. Then we filed through the open door.

When we got out at the main floor Dr. Turcotte shook my hand and said that he and John would be leaving. Ethel would drive me to the motel, where he wanted me to stay for a few days before returning to my apartment. Ethel and I stopped by the admission desk, where I got my wallet, watch, and ring. Then we too left the hospital.

The trees were green and the sky blue. Sunlight spilled its blessing on my face. Once more my life was my own.

III

I was out of the hospital now and staying in Town House Motor Lodge in Northampton. There were several other patients there. An old, alcoholic priest slipped out at night to dispose of his vodka bottles in a public trash container. There was the wife of a professor from one of the colleges who was tired of playing faculty wife. A young woman who studied astrology had visions of a Renoir-like child visiting her at night with her arms full of flowers.

But before going to the motel, Ethel had taken me to Dr. Turcotte's office, where he had questioned me.

"Why do you want to go home?" he asked.

"To take care of the boys."

"And?"

"To pay the bills."

"And?"

"To water the plants."

I thought of the huge pots of banana trees and aspidistra leaves and how kind Dee had been to keep them watered all this time.

"And?"

"To do the laundry."

"And?"

"To paint and write."

He looked at me with clear blue eyes that so often seemed to see through me and beyond to someplace altogether invisible to me. Chris and John Elder had been staying with my in-laws in Georgia for six weeks and were still there. Carolyn and Jack wanted to keep them and adopt them legally, and told Dr. Turcotte of their intention. I was terrified that I would lose my sons forever. The arrangement made before my hospitalization had been for Chris to live with me while John Elder, at fourteen, would be free to move between the family house where his father lived and my apartment.

Two weeks later I was sitting in a straight chair, smoking a cigarette. My right leg was crossed over my left, and I was shaking my foot in an agitated frenzy while Dr. Turcotte leaned against his desk, dialing the phone. My father-in-law answered. He wanted to know if I was sane enough to take care of the boys.

Dr. Turcotte cleared his throat. "I've examined Margaret, and I see no reason that the boys can't return."

The two men talked for a few minutes longer, while I sat stunned with relief. My sons were coming home. I began to cry. I'd spent twenty-one agonized days in a nightmarish state institution, strapped to the bed, locked in solitary confinement, and then confined to a locked ward. I'd been condescended to, manipulated, ignored, humiliated. Now, after gradually reclaiming myself in the motel, I was going to be able to go home. And I would not lose my sons.

I reached for a tissue from the box on Dr. Turcotte's table and blew my nose. Then I covered my face with my hands to muffle my sobs, my whole body shaking.

Dr. Turcotte asked Jim Clark to drive me back to my room at the motel. On the drive over, Jim talked and talked about Carl Jung, about whom I, at the time, knew little. Dr. Turcotte appeared to harbor animosity toward Jung. At one point I shared with him what was to me an important dream. I no longer remember anything about the dream except that the circle was a prominent image in it. I was interpreting the dream in the context of what I'd been reading in Jung's book *Man and His Symbols*. Dr. Turcotte waved my interpretation away without consideration. "You had circular images in your dream because you have a round face. It's as simple as that."

I accepted his dismissal without protest. By that time I had given him authority over much of my mind and life. I—after all—was the mental patient, the one who'd thought the moored boats in a painting in the lounge were really rocking in the water, had seen them knocking gently against the dock. And such intense colors! Nothing a sane mind could see. Of course I accepted Dr. Turcotte's dismissal without protest. I was the one who had been locked up and medicated, wasn't I? Wasn't I the flawed child grown into the flawed woman?

How do you live when you can't believe what your own mind tells you?

You find someone else's mind to believe in.

It wasn't altogether different from my childhood when, between three and four years of age, I began to block my own perceptions because they weren't like those of my parents, and I wanted my parents and other adults in my life to accept me. I'd lived in constant fear of abandonment.

Turning into the motel parking lot, Jim was still talking about Carl Jung, and I was listening with fascination. Jim was introducing me to a world that would enrich my life. But that would come later. Now I had been freed from the locked ward and would soon be going home. That was more than enough for now.

IV

By the time Ruth returned from Italy and I got out of the hospital, everything had changed. She had strongly disagreed with the way Dr. Turcotte had encouraged me to put a firm emotional distance between John and myself when John was begging me to come back to him, and threatening again to kill himself if I didn't.

"Poor John," Ruth had said to Dr. Turcotte. "He needs her so. This is cruel."

We were sitting together in Dr. Turcotte's office. He'd asked her to come talk with him. Dr. Turcotte said that her support of John's pressuring me to come back to him was undermining his work to effect a safe separation.

He looked at Ruth and retorted: "If you're nursing a baby and he begins to bite your nipple off with his teeth, you better get your breast out of his mouth in a hurry."

That was the last time Ruth accompanied me to his office.

Shortly after my release from the hospital, Ruth and I leaned against my car parked in her driveway and smoked cigarettes, while Chris and Tommy chased each other around the yard. She told me that I was much too involved with Dr. Turcotte, and that she thought I was either the sanest or the most insane person she'd ever known and she couldn't tell which. Then she told me about how once as a volunteer in the state hospital she was engaged in a conversation with someone she assumed to be a staff member. The conversation was interesting, and she had been enjoying it until an orderly came to take the patient to the dining hall for lunch. Ruth was so horrified that she'd not been able to tell a patient from a staff member that she never went back to the hospital.

I assumed she was telling me that she was afraid of me. I called Chris and we went home.

I remember one last phone conversation with her. I told her I had begun to write poetry and read her my latest poem. She said it made her think of Carl Sandburg. She was polite and reserved. She said it was a shame I wasn't painting. She never called me again, nor did I call her. My son and I had each lost one of our best friends.

V

Now I was back living in the Shutesbury house with John, from whom I'd tried to get away for years. When I was in the hospital, Dr. Turcotte had brought John with him so I could discharge my anger toward John just as he had done with me when he was in the motel. Even though it was made of anger, the emotional bond between John and me was growing stronger. My pain was so great that I was willing to do almost anything to rid myself of it. If expressing anger at John was what the doctor ordered, expressing anger was what I did.

I stayed in my apartment for a few weeks after I left the hospital before moving back into the house with John. He and I continued to go together to Dr. Turcotte's office. Usually the doctor saw John for quite a long time before inviting me to join them. Then he would encourage me to express anger toward John. Often I didn't feel anger, I just felt depressed. But, with the doctor's encouragement, I would try to find something to express anger toward John about.

Then he would instruct John to say: "Margaret, your anger is beautiful."

That angered me most of all. I wanted John to speak for himself. He looked like a puppet mouthing the doctor's words while maintaining an absolutely blank face or sometimes a face twisted with a mixture of pain and rage. But I too was following Dr. Turcotte's instructions; I too was a puppet.

"What are you feeling now, John?" the doctor always asked. John always replied that he wasn't feeling "much of anything."

More and more I felt that Dr. Turcotte was focused on getting John and me back together. A whole family was involved. Of course it would be better for our sons if John and I could get along, if we could remain a family.

But—

The word hung heavy in the air.

My depression made me almost totally dysfunctional. I didn't know how I would be able to cope with Chris and getting him to and from school. Going to the Laundromat felt like an impossible task. And I was grieving over the loss of Paula, who no longer called me at all. More and more intensely I felt John's pressure to "come home." Since he'd been working with Dr. Turcotte, his behavior *had* improved. More important, he had actually taken all the anger I'd hurled at him. Maybe we could find a way to live together after all. Maybe if we built an addition onto the house, a place I could call my own . . . Dr. Turcotte had given me hope that even my marriage to John might work, that we together with the children might truly become a healed and whole family.

With the great loss of confidence in my sanity, feeling the stigma of mental illness, and brokenhearted by both the loss of my friends and Chris's, I went home to John. I went home to months of depression so severe that I was hardly able to get out of bed.

One afternoon Chris came home from school to tell me that Paula's son Bob had told him he was no longer permitted to play with him because his mother was "mental." Chris was devastated. He and Bob had played at our house or at Bob's several days out of every week ever since we'd lived in Shutesbury. I couldn't bear to see his pain when I was helpless to do anything to comfort him.

All the years of friendship between the boys had dissolved overnight. I struggled between feeling terribly hurt by Paula and feeling guilt for having had the psychotic break. Paula's first husband, Tom, a racing-car driver, had been killed in a car crash. She'd told me there were times she was barely able to function. I remembered the phone calls when she would talk about looking in the bathroom mirror while watching her image slowly dissolving into smoke. Once she called frantic, saying that the trees outside her window had begun to walk across her backyard. I listened, thinking of *Macbeth* and "Birnam Wood do come to Dunsinane," a soldier hidden behind each moving bough. I wondered what threats hid behind the walking trees in Paula's yard. I asked her to tell me more about the walking trees, and listened until she had talked herself back into a calmer place.

"You really should go back to school and become a therapist, Margaret. You're so good," she'd often said to me.

"No," I'd always replied. "I want to be a writer and a teacher of creative writing. I don't want to be a therapist."

But now I was "mental." Chris and I were untouchables. The years of friendship were over. Paula ignored Chris's feelings, and her fear about her own instability had hardened her heart against both of us. But understanding this did little to ease the pain.

Chapter Fourteen

LONELY FOR MY FRIENDS AND STRUGGLING WITH DEPRESSION, I FOCUSED on writing and in the writing found a renewed sense of life. Despite all my self-doubt and confusion, this much I felt certain of: I was a writer. It was the clearest sense of my identity that I had ever had.

Much of what I had to write was painful. Knowing that I would be tempted to find excuses to avoid the pain, I made an agreement with myself. Monday through Friday, just as soon as the boys and John left for school, while breakfast dishes went unwashed, beds unmade, furniture undusted, I devoted three hours to writing. If words wouldn't come, then I sat and stared at the paper until an image finally rose from its blank white like something long submerged in the sludge on an old pond's bottom.

Sometimes what emerged was a phrase, as in, *This is the season of the rain,* when I remembered a slide taken of Chris and me on a sacrificial altar near the Pyramid of the Sun at Teotihuacán in Mexico during the rainy season. Sometimes a compelling rhythm came into my mind so strongly that I followed it as if I were writing lyrics to someone else's song. Sometimes an image would emerge like that of Mother buttoning my Roman sandals with a buttonhook, or the image of the old battered teakettle hissing and steaming on the woodstove in Granddaddy's house. Most of the images were from my childhood.

One day, while lying on my bed, suspended between wakefulness and sleep, I became aware that to unlock my creativity as a writer, I had to connect with the scared little girl inside me, the little girl fighting to hold her feelings inside in order to behave the way her mother wanted her to, the little girl who, even after all those years, tugged at my heart with her immeasurable loneliness.

Perhaps the dream that had told me I was a writer had also given me this information about the connection between creativity and childhood. But how was I to connect with the child when I could hardly remember my childhood at all? This question was on my mind when I lay down that afternoon and began to try to remember. How does one remember what one has forgotten for so long, what has been shoved behind the years and years of living away from the South, away from my family of origin? How could I get through and behind the psychotic visions and newfound rage to find the child?

The creative drive let loose must be like that of a homing pigeon set free on a foreign shore. It must know deep inside its being where home is and how to get there. That impulse in me that wanted to write, that *was* a writer, had been set free and was looking for its source. Somehow I knew that the source lay in childhood.

The afternoon was quiet. Sunlight fell through the glass doors onto my half-asleep body as I began to seem to float backward toward childhood, shadowed images glimpsed in the periphery of my vision. I felt my mind opening like the wings of a magnificent butterfly, all pattern and color, grace and fragility. It was as if time was expansive and moving, yet as flat and still as a broad field in which I could walk or—like a butterfly—move from blossom to blossom, from blade to leaf. Childhood images came and went. Something was growing in my mind, and, while I didn't know what it was, I lay warm in the sunlight, letting it take form.

When I got up, I went to my desk and wrote "The Child Wakes," a poem that was included in my first book. Other poems and prose poems were written in the same way—by lying down and allowing myself to go into what seemed to be a semi-hypnotic state, freeing my mind to release whatever images or memories the quiet gave me.

In the quietness and stillness I was finding myself.

II

While my psychotic episode in 1971 was the longest and most terrible of all, it was during that episode that I *came to myself* as a writer. Pain like a blade slashed through my brain, releasing not only memories of childhood, but memories of my adolescent attempts at writing as well. I remembered that I had written a poem about my sister that began: *While other children run in fields of daisies and in sand / I've often watched her longing eyes and her clenched hands.* I had hoped Mother would like the poem. I'd imagined her sending it off to the cerebral palsy newsletter that she subscribed to. Maybe they would even publish it. But Mother responded to it with her "That's nice" comment used to dismiss anything that I shared with her that didn't really matter to her.

Books were one of the most important things in Mother's world. She loved good writing. But what I wrote either upset her or seemed to fail to touch her. I wrote a long poem that ended with the lines

> *Footprints in sand, footprints in time—*
> *I know the two are one. Footprints on moonlit beaches do not fade,*
> *and I must turn away and run.*

This last poem was an attempt to find a way to express myself with words and images that would be inaccessible to Mother. It was also written to be mysterious, like the poetry of T. S. Eliot. I'd been reading his poetry and, without understanding it, loved it just as I did my favorite classical music. In the state hospital, too, I'd remembered Mother's invasion of my private diary and her extreme upset with me, and how—except for the few poems—I stopped writing then. I was fifteen years old.

But my reason for ceasing to write went deeper than Mother's reaction to my diary. It went back to the shame I'd thought so much about but had never understood. It was the shame that had made me feel that I had absolutely nothing worth writing about, nothing that anyone would ever want to read. Nothing that really mattered.

After the psychotic experience, the reason for that old shame didn't matter so much. And unlike my uncertainties and questions about painting, my reasons for writing were quite clear: I wrote because I was a writer. I wrote to find out what my feelings and thoughts were, and to put those thoughts and feelings into forms that would allow me not only to hold them consciously and sanely but to express them to others. I wrote to be myself.

Sometimes I was afraid of what the writing might reveal about me. What if I discovered something unbearably bad about myself? What if I discovered I was bisexual or a lesbian after all? Fear haunted me. Despite it, I wrote. And through writing I discovered a new and deeper understanding of and compassion for my humanity, and for all humanity.

III
1975

Suzanne and I were graduate students at the University of Massachusetts, both working toward our MFA degrees in creative writing. We were both around forty, both married with children. Suzanne had two girls. I had two boys. John was a professor in the philosophy department at the university. Her husband, Bob, in human services, was director of an Amherst community-living complex. There were seemingly unsolvable administrative problems in the organization, and Bob spent half his time struggling with those, and the other half trying to come up with a totally new profession in middle age. John was struggling with the recurring and potentially crippling arthritis that had flared up again after several years of respite. Though he'd finally stopped drinking, he still often behaved as if he was drunk. One night he slung the candlesticks across the dining room because I hadn't baked corn bread.

Suzanne and I were both in crisis.

Suzanne had written off and on all her life. I'd hardly written at all until the dream followed by the psychotic episode in 1971 reminded me that I was a writer. Since that time I'd written constantly, with confident determination. Now we were both looking forward to receiving our MFAs. Suzanne was an organizer, involved in the many lives of the people in the housing complex. I was a more private person, battling chronic depression and episodes of psychosis. I spent most of my energy trying to survive. Often I fought panic as I felt that I'd explode, burst through my skin. Other times I felt like all the protective tissue had been stripped off every nerve in my body. Daily I confronted the stigma of mental illness. I also daily experienced more deeply new feelings of self-discovery.

I had written poems about my incarceration in Northampton State Hospital and read them in writing workshops, sometimes to the shock of the other participants, who sat around the table in speechless fascination. Then Anne Sexton died, and I took a long, thoughtful look at her poetry and career again. It seemed to me that she had become a "crazy lady" with a voyeuristic public feeding on her sensationalism and her painfully visible vulnerabilities, while she'd written more and more for their voracious appetites. I felt sad and embarrassed for her, even as I admired her gift. I also felt immense gratitude to her for writing about her craziness and her personal struggles. Except for Robert Lowell, I'd not read another poet who dared make verses from his or her insanity. Sylvia Plath had expressed her own emotional agony with compellingly brilliant language but had stuck her head in her oven and killed herself before I'd become aware of her. Anne Sexton was still alive and writing when I began my own writing, and her poems gave me the support I needed to write about my psychotic experiences.

But after I read in the newspaper on October 4, 1974, that she'd eaten a tuna fish sandwich with Maxine Kumin and gone home and killed herself with carbon monoxide from her car, I decided that I wouldn't run the risk of becoming another professional "crazy lady" poet who committed suicide. I decided that I wouldn't write more about my psychotic experiences until I could look back on them from a stable place.

Now, instead, I wrote about my childhood. I began to be invited to give poetry readings and was always surprised when listeners were so supportive and emotionally moved. I hadn't realized that by writing honestly and openly about my own childhood feelings and experiences, I would touch something in their lives as well.

I also wrote about my marriage, my relationships with friends. I wrote a poem about standing "in a tense embrace" with Suzanne in front of the fireplace in her study. Remembering both poem and embrace after all these years, I can see the obvious passion between us. One poetry workshop leader said to me: "Margaret, write more poems about your relationships with women. There's a hell of a lot of feeling in those words."

One afternoon, when I arrived early for my prose workshop, Suzanne was sitting at the table alone, sobbing. I sat down beside her while she told me of a criticism another workshop leader had made of her work, and what he suggested she do. I disagreed with him, and made a totally different suggestion. She said she would try to do as I suggested. A week later she came to my home in Shutesbury to share what she'd written.

Suzanne and I sat on the couch in my study while she read aloud the chapter I'd encouraged her to write. After she finished, she hurled her notebook across the room, slamming it hard against the closed door. "This is the worst writing I've ever done. It's just awful! I'm ashamed I read it to you."

The notebook lay open on the floor, loose pages scattered around it. Suzanne burst into tears.

I walked over, gathered the loose papers, picked up the notebook, and brought them back to the couch. I sat down again. "This is your very best writing that I've read, Suzanne."

Her eyes were red from crying, and she was blowing her nose on a tissue pulled from her purse. She fumbled at the loose papers. "Do you really believe that?" She folded the tissue and blew her nose again.

"I know so," I said, lighting a cigarette, taking a slow drag, then exhaling just as slowly. Smoke swirled in the room's still air. The writing was bone solid and real. It had that strength that only comes from authenticity.

What she'd written about was terrible. It was about living in horrible circumstances when she was a child, about living in shame. Hearing of Suzanne's childhood pain evoked feelings of my own childhood. Our circumstances were different, but we shared the feelings of shame. In order to write about her childhood, she'd moved so close to it that the adult Suzanne, still carrying that shame, couldn't see through it to the fine quality of the writing. She couldn't distinguish between her terrible experiences and terrible writing.

"This is wonderful writing," I said again. "This is damn important writing. It really is."

IV

Suzanne and I were seated in the balcony of the theater in the Fine Arts Building at the University of Massachusetts, watching a production of *West Side Story*. Sometime during the musical, I realized we were holding hands.

Afterward, we walked to her house, hand in hand. Then we got into my car to drive someplace where we could be alone. A hard downpour began. We parked beside the Amherst Common and talked, all the while caressing each other's hands.

"This isn't sex," Suzanne stumbled, shocked and confused by the intimacy that we shared. "And is," she contradicted herself.

We talked for hours, our hands making love to each other, while the rain streamed unceasingly down the windshield. There was no one else on the common that night. Only the drenched trees and the darkened storefronts across South Pleasant and Main streets bore witness to our presence, while a couple of blocks away stood the house where Emily Dickinson wrote her poetry—*Oh, Future! thou secreted / Or subterranean woe*—and the only visible moon was the glowing clock face on the town-hall tower.

Chapter Fifteen

"To dream the impossible dream," Dr. Turcotte boomed as he rummaged through the stacks of papers on his table like a blundering, boisterous Don Quixote. His shirt pockets bulged with his underlining markers of many colors. The front of his shirt was covered with so many slogan buttons that he looked like a caricature of a brigadier general displaying a chest full of war medals. However, Dr. Turcotte's buttons had nothing to do with war; they were peace signs, rainbows, and smiley faces. One supported Mairead Corrigan and Betty Williams and their work for peace in Northern Ireland. He greatly respected the two women and their work.

Betty Williams was the housewife who had rushed from her home when she heard the shot that mortally wounded an IRA gunman, causing him to lose control of his car. The driverless car killed three children and critically injured their mother, the four of them out for a leisurely walk in Belfast on that August day in 1976. The sight of the broken and bloody bodies of the dead children changed her forever, and she was moved to take a dramatic stand against violence. She and Mairead Corrigan, aunt of the dead children, worked together, and in 1976 they were jointly awarded the Nobel Peace Prize.

In honor of the women, Dr. Turcotte began to walk many miles a day. He carried an umbrella as a reminder of the umbrellas the women had used as shields against stones thrown at them as they walked for peace. Often he carried a bouquet of helium-filled pink-and-blue balloons for the children.

"Each step I take," he said, "is a prayer for world peace."

On Sundays I sometimes joined him, his daughter June, Ethel, Jim, and other group members on his walk. June, in her late twenties, usually carried a sign that said something about world peace. She also sometimes carried things her father found along the way—a bent hubcap, a matchbook, a twig, or a tattered piece of fabric worn by weather and faded. Mona, a young woman with long greasy hair and large unbrushed teeth thick with a film the color of nicotine, occasionally joined the group. The small, straggling parade could have been lifted whole from a Fellini film.

Dr. Turcotte always led the way. In his eyes, everything that he found, from a discarded gum wrapper to a half-eaten sandwich, seemed to be a sign from God. He would stop and expound on the sacred and personal meaning of each discovery. He crammed his pockets full of his precious findings. A used tea bag could seem as significant to him as the tablets Moses brought down from Mount Sinai.

Occasionally the doctor stopped walking to look up at a formation of clouds, reading a message from God in it as one might read the leaves at the bottom of a cup of tea, or in the toss of coins for the I Ching.

I remember with special vividness the Sunday he saw Winnie-the-Pooh among the other puffy white cloud shapes. As hard as I tried, I couldn't see any shape that reminded me even remotely of Winnie-the-Pooh. Furthermore, I would never have given the image the meaning—long forgotten—that he gave it. Looking skyward, I felt spiritually inadequate, as if I should have seen what he saw in the sky that day. I felt like an ignorant patient in great need of Dr. Turcotte's spiritual and emotional guidance.

I only have to look at the one instance of Winnie-the-Pooh in the clouds to see with painful clarity how insecure I was with my own mind. If I'd been insecure before the psychotic break, my new label of mental patient had further eroded my self-confidence, even as the psychotic experience itself continued to expand and intensify my understanding of myself and life.

Now Dr. Turcotte finally found the article he'd been looking for in the chaos on his table. It was a copy of the sermon he'd written for Father Gray to deliver to his congregation that Sunday. He wanted to give it to Ethel when she joined the group in its walk from Northampton to Florence; though he'd dictated it to her, he wanted her to have a typed copy. He folded it and put it in the inside pocket of his jacket. Then we walked through the waiting room, where a poster of Albert Einstein hung. Under the portrait were Einstein's words: "Great spirits have always encountered violent opposition from mediocre minds."

The doctor locked the office door behind us, and we walked down the stairs, out of the building, and to my car. I drove past Smith College and parked across the street from John M. Greene Hall, where we were to meet the other participants for the peace walk. Ethel was slamming the door to her car and turning to meet us. Mona was standing on the curb looking down absentmindedly as she blew an enormous bubble with the wad of bubble gum crammed in her mouth. Jim was talking with Al and a couple of new patients with puzzled looks on their faces, as if they'd somehow been transported to a foreign land where they knew neither customs nor language.

"Ho!" the doctor yelled in greeting as he got out of the car. He opened the back door and took out his umbrella, which he snapped open before getting the large bunch of balloons that had hovered on the car's ceiling.

June, almost always late to everything, came running down the sidewalk, breathless, her peace sign flapping against her legs.

The doctor gave Ethel the copy of the sermon and took his place along with her at the head of the group. Then we began to walk. Dry brown leaves made a scratching noise as a gentle October breeze tumbled them at our feet.

Gustav Barth was the first to follow the doctor. A brilliant and scholarly old man, he'd grown so compulsive and fearful over the years that, until recently, he had rarely left his room over a store in Northampton. He spent his days studying William Blake and D. H. Lawrence and writing copious notes on his interpretation of the whole of Blake's theology as he understood it. He also spent hours each day scrubbing and scrubbing his tiny efficiency kitchen. After Dr. Turcotte's faithful daily visits to his room for three years, Gustav had dared to go out in the light of day. Many people said it was nothing short of a miracle that the doctor had been able to get Gustav out of his room and able to buy his groceries in a grocery store rather than sneaking out at night to a convenience store for potato chips and sandwiches from a vending machine. Sometimes he even sat on a park bench and discussed poetry with some of the other writers who lived on Social Security and sat outside writing in little pocket notebooks.

Now, though this was the first and only time he joined the peace walk, he was participating in the most social event he'd been involved in since his wife had died thirty years before. In preparation, he'd Scotch-taped his glasses to his face and put on white surgical gloves so his hands wouldn't become contaminated by touching an unclean surface.

He walked as closely behind the doctor as he could without actually running into him. His tall, thin frame was bent permanently like a birch tree shaped by many New England winters of ice on its bowed trunk. In an almost inaudible whisper he repeated Blake's lines as he walked:

> *Each Man is in his Spectre's power*
> *Until the arrival of that hour,*
> *When his Humanity awake,*
> *And cast his Spectre into the Lake.*

Perhaps Gustav's humanity was waking to throw his ghosts into the lake forever. I'll never know. In December, only a block from where we were walking, a car slid on a sheet of ice and hit Gustav, dragging his injured body yards before he was crushed against a tree.

But that day in October, Gustav walked with more freedom and determination than I'd ever seen in him. Whatever else Dr. Turcotte did in his life, both positive and negative, he'd wakened in Gustav the strength and fearlessness to take a walk for peace with us on that Sunday afternoon, and for that I always loved him.

I loved his stubborn determination; his blatant disregard for criticism hurled his way, his defiance of any social amenities that stood in the way of his intentions. I loved his support of the underdog, the scapegoat, the misfit, those who, like him, lived on society's fringes, some of whom, like Gustav, would never—without his help—have known sunlight on their faces and fall leaves at their feet.

Chapter Sixteen

I

1977

WHEN PAULA BEGAN TO FACE THE POSSIBILITY OF HER MARRIAGE END-
ing, she once again turned to me for friendship and support. For
years we'd lived down the road from each other, with trees, ponds, the
hill, and a deep—for me—painful silence between us. Now we were
talking as if nothing had ever happened. I was grateful to have her
back in my life.

I say she was beginning to face the end of her marriage, but that's
not quite accurate; I have no idea what she was conscious of facing.
What I did know was that, as her marriage to Tom grew more and
more difficult, her rouge grew redder. The intensity of her rouge
was always the most accurate barometer I had of both her feelings
and her degree of denial, or simply her lack of awareness of her
feelings.

I remember her coming to my door one morning and excitedly
announcing that she and Tom were headed to New York City for the
weekend. They were going to a play and out to dinner. Everything
between them felt better than it had in ages. In fact, they were going
to two plays. Wasn't it wonderful! She stood defiantly at my front
door, a beautiful woman who carried herself with a rigidity that

could pass as dignity. Her rouge was more intense than ever. It hurt to see her looking so unconsciously vulnerable.

"I hope you have a good weekend," I said, while Tom waited for her, the car engine running.

She would hold on to the illusion of her marriage for months to come, but my own marriage was rapidly coming to an end.

The closer I got to completing work for my MFA, the more John reverted to his old jealousies and feelings of being threatened by my painting and writing. And now there was the new possibility that I might get a job and leave him. Much of the progress he'd made while working with Dr. Turcotte for so many years seemed to have been erased overnight.

When John saw that I was doing a watercolor of the family of Dee's husband, Bob, he angrily picked up my watercolor box and brushes and threw them, as well as the photographs from which I was working, across the room.

After years of struggling, I felt hope suddenly grow thin as a thread. I was painfully tired. Paula and I went away together; we spent two days and a night talking in a motel before returning to husbands and children, and me to the end of my marriage.

Over the years, Paula and I had raised our sons together, critiqued each other's writing, exchanged and discussed favorite books. We'd talked about our lives to each other so often that images from her childhood were almost as familiar as images from my own. But we'd never touched. Or rather, we'd only touched once, when, in a moment of lonely despair, I'd reached across her breakfast table to take her hand. For a minute we sat, our clasped hands resting on the table's gray Formica surface, while she whispered nervously: "I would never hold any woman's hand except yours."

I understood clearly then—as I'd intuited earlier—that even touching another woman upset and threatened her. After that, no matter the intensity of emotion between us, I never embraced or touched her, not even after long absences. At those times we stood, facing each other awkwardly, our words rushing to fill the space between us like ocean water rushes to fill a hole dug in the sand.

Which is why her touch that night in the motel surprised me so.

We were in our separate beds talking when, beginning to cry, I turned away from her. She came and sat on the edge of my bed. My nightgown had narrow straps, and I remember even after all these years the shock of feeling her hand on my naked shoulder, her hair brushing against me as she lay her head on my back. Then she jerked away, stood, and looked down at me. "If anything sexual were to happen between us, I couldn't live with myself," she said, and quickly climbed into her bed, where she lay on her side staring at me, wide-eyed, the sheet pulled tight under her chin.

I looked at her and laughed inside at us, laughed at life's absurdities. My friend, who'd had sex with several men after her first husband's death and before her marriage to Tom, lay frozen with fear at the thought of sex with a woman. Paula mirrored my lifelong fears and questions about my own sexuality. Even as I looked into the mirror of her love and fear, my questions dissolved while my expanding heart embraced us both.

Who one loved was what was important, not the sex of that person. It was that simple. I remembered the pain I'd experienced all of my life because I was so afraid to let myself know who I loved if that person was another girl or woman. If Paula looked ridiculous with her rouge circles of denial, I *was* ridiculous with my denial of my feelings for fear of Mother's disapproval. Mother's disapproval, and the disapproval of most of the people I knew.

All my life I worked to deny that under the intense emotion I felt for other women, I'd often felt a sexual attraction as well. Somehow, with constant effort, I'd managed to keep one of the most important secrets of my life from myself.

How critical I'd been of Paula! I felt ashamed of myself. With Paula frankly stating her fear that she couldn't live if anything sexual were to happen between us, a veil had lifted in my own mind. Of course, I loved women. I'd loved girls and women all of my life. I began listing them, beginning with childhood and adolescent play-mates, and ending with Paula with her dark and frightened eyes.

II

I hardly slept the night after I returned from our weekend. Knowing clearly that I could make love with a woman had changed my entire understanding of who I was. Finally, I had realized that sex was about expressing love and had nothing to do with gender. It was such a large realization about myself that I knew I had to tell John. It felt dishonest not to.

But I was afraid. For a long time in the middle of the night, I stood at the bathroom window, feeling my fear and looking at the pines and hemlocks, a sliver of moon visible through a clearing in the woods. The worst thing I'd imagined about myself turned out to be true. But instead of the shame I'd expected, what I felt, along with fear of facing John, was relief.

I told John after the boys left the house. He said nothing but was grim and silent on the drive to Northampton to see Dr. Turcotte. He was in the office a long time before I was invited in. Dr. Turcotte had calmed and reassured John by telling him that I had not had sex with a woman, that I'd only told him about feelings, and that people have all sorts of feelings. In essence, what I'd told John was without im-portance. I was relieved to see John calm, though for Dr. Turcotte to dismiss my self-discovery so easily upset me. But I was too pressured to confront him. I had to keep my focus on my oral examination. Passing it was the last requirement before receiving my MFA.

III

Toward the end of my preparation for my orals, John's behavior dis-tressed me so much that I couldn't focus on my work. Again and again he came into my study and demanded that I stop studying and have sex with him. When I did as he demanded, he would have sex repeatedly until I refused him. Then he would insist that I didn't love him and begin the nonsensical talk that I thought he had stopped. I finally went to a motel to study, while Chris swam in the pool or watched television.

When the day of the examination arrived, Paula and I discussed what I should wear to face the male professors. Together we decided on my professorial tweed jacket, a brown turtleneck sweater, and brown wool pants. I also wore a pale shade of lipstick, mascara, eyeliner, a handcrafted silver bracelet, and silver earrings. I felt tired but confident as I sat down at the table with the men with whom I'd studied for three years. It felt more like a necessary ritual than an examination. By now they had an idea of what I knew. A few minutes into the process, I relaxed and enjoyed the dialogue.

My orals over, degree assured, and a first book of poetry completed and published, I met Paula at the Lord Jeffery Inn for a drink. I'd done what I'd set out to do. After the waiter brought our drinks, we clinked our glasses together in a toast and drank, late-afternoon sunlight flashing on their rims.

The moment stands out in my mind like a jewel.

IV

In bed one night, I told John that I needed him to acknowledge his aggressive behavior when I was preparing for my orals. I needed him to claim all his violent and mentally and emotionally hurtful behavior to me. It wasn't a matter of blame, I said. It was a matter of my needing him to validate my experiences so I wouldn't go through any more of my life feeling so alone. Especially, I needed him to acknowledge the years in Philadelphia that had been so painful.

His body stiffened as he stared at the ceiling.

"Driving home this afternoon," he said in his strange, faraway voice, "I saw a large golden hexagon floating over the O'Rourke house."

"Please don't do this to me again, John. I'm desperate for honesty." I felt frantic. "Please, John. I'm not blaming you. I just need you to own up to your behavior. Then we can go on with our lives. You have no idea how lonely it is for me when you deny what you've done."

"I would never have done those awful things to you, Margaret." His voice was flat, and he continued staring at the ceiling.

"But you *did* do them, John, and I really need you to just validate my experience. I'll never even mention them again. I swear it!"

"I told you, Margaret, I never did those things. *He* did them, and he lives in my body." His voice was sinister and frightening.

I gave up and turned over in the bed. All night I lay awake, images rushing through my mind like images on TV that advertise the news—one rapid clip after another of murder victims, multiple births, trials, tornadoes, famines, plane crashes, missile attacks, bombed buildings. I had no control over the images—the memory of John throwing me across the living room, ripping my blouse as he yelled at me, then storming out of the apartment. His phone call begging me to forgive him, please forgive him. John throwing my easel down the basement stairs, the painting on it smeared beyond repair. John slapping me hard across the face and accusing me of having a lover. His affair, his denial of it, and finally his admission of it. John saying that now that he had told me about the affair, he would never talk about it again, nor would he allow me to talk about it with him. Carolyn trying to reassure me that John truly loved me as she dismantled his shotgun to take it home to Georgia with her. The razor blades and the Statue of Liberty. Then the train back to Philadelphia, the sound of the wheels, their rhythm and click and how they seemed to echo the words "A safe way out, a safe way out, a safe way out. Stay with him. Stay with him until you find a safe way out."

A safe way out.

I bowed my head and prayed.

My nerves were raw and ragged, and my heart was racing by the time morning came. I had finally reached my breaking point. I had no energy to go on. I was going to leave John.

V

The next morning I called Paula, who told me that she had Valium on hand.

I could see the fear and rage in John's eyes as he realized that I might finally be leaving him forever. He said he would drive me to Paula's new house in Pelham. "You're too upset to drive," he said, heading out of the house to the car.

I called Chris to come with us. He came running, excited that he would get to play with Ted.

By the time I picked up my purse, opened the door, and walked down the steps, I saw that Chris was in the front seat next to his father. Before I could get in, John backed out of the blind driveway at a suicidal speed. Chris began to scream. It was the most piercing scream I'd ever heard in my life. Hearing his scream in the deepest place in my heart, I began to scream that same piercing scream, the two of us connected by that terror-filled sound as the car sped down the road.

Then Chris's screaming stopped abruptly. There was only the sound of the speeding car fading in the distance. I raced down the driveway and toward Chris's scream. There he was—Chris running toward me as I was running toward him. Then he was in my arms, sobbing and shaking. "My father said he was going to kill what you loved most," he sputtered. "He said he was going to kill me. I had to jump from the car."

There was not even time to comfort him. What if John were to turn the car around and come after both of us? I took Chris's hand and together we ran down a path in the woods. We came to a large fallen tree, moss-covered, decaying in a field of ferns. We lay down on the moist earth behind it, out of sight of the road, both our hearts racing.

We lay there for a long time before I decided that John wasn't coming back. We ran to the house and got into the station wagon. Driving in the opposite direction from John, I took the road to the center of Shutesbury. I tried to think clearly. Where to go? I drove to Greenfield. I felt desperate and my eyes stung. I couldn't believe John would actually kill Chris, but I'd seen the way he drove out of the driveway, and before that, the rage and fear on his face. Chris looked so vulnerable. Something in his spirit seemed crushed.

Our world was falling to pieces.

I parked the car.

"Let's calm down," I said, speaking to myself as well as to Chris as we got out. "Let's go window-shopping."

No. That didn't feel adequate.

"Let's look for a new ring for you. A special, protective ring."

Chris's eyes brightened. Ever since he was five or so and in Mexico with all its silver rings, he'd loved rings. "Yeah! A ring. I'd love a special ring."

We looked in store after store before Chris found the right one. It cost more than I could easily afford, but I had to buy something beautiful for him. It was a large tiger's-eye set in silver.

"This is a very special ring," I said, making a great show of the purchase. "A very special ring for a very special boy."

VI

There are occasions when trauma has torn my memory apart, leaving fragments of images, minefields scattered throughout my consciousness. What happened after Chris's terror-stricken screaming was one of those times. After buying the ring, I took him with me to Paula's.

I remember sitting at Paula's kitchen table, talking about Emily Dickinson's poetry. During my most painful times, I always turned to Emily Dickinson.

> *Much Madness is divinest Sense—*
> *To a discerning eye—.*

> *I measure every Grief I meet*
> *with narrow, probing Eyes*
> *I wonder if It weighs like Mine—*
> *Or has an Easier size.*

The next thing I remember is sitting on the edge of the motel bed with Ethel threatening to plop her heavy body on top of me and force some antipsychotic medication down my throat if I wouldn't cooperate and take it. The doctor sat in the chair opposite me, watching.

"You're going to take this medication," Ethel said in a hard, stubborn voice.

I took the pills followed by a glass of water.

Later Father Gray came in and reported that John was holding his own in intensive care, but they still didn't know what he'd taken to bring about the bleeding in his stomach. *John in the ICU? Did I know that? Who'd told me? When?* Well, I'd done my best. I really had, no matter how inadequate my best might have been. After all the years of therapy, the fighting and talking, after all the negotiating, maybe John could live without me. But whether or not he could, I couldn't live with him again.

I tried to block Chris's screaming from my mind.

Dr. Turcotte and Father Gray went outside. Ethel got up and sat in the doctor's chair. Overcome with a desperate need for sleep, I took my shoes off and crawled under the covers. I lost consciousness almost immediately.

I must have slept for hours.

When I awoke, several people were in the room talking. Without opening my eyes, I recognized Jim's voice. Then Ellie, a young student at the university, June, Jim, and a new patient whose name I couldn't recall. Eyes closed, I listened with fascination. Supposedly they were talking about me—sometimes agreeing, sometimes arguing—about my condition and how they could help me through my crisis. But in the context of focusing on me, it was clear to me that they were in fact working on their relationships with themselves and one another.

In my mind I saw a great wheel of clay, hands reaching out to partially formed faces and bodies all around the wheel, each individual shaping the one in front of her or him, molding fingers and thumbs, noses and mouths, and eyes that could take in the whole night sky with its galaxies filling the domes of their magnificent emerging heads. *The Great Wheel of Creation at work in this ordinary motel,* I thought, and felt humility at the earnestness of that group of young people focusing on me while becoming themselves.

Then I lost consciousness again.

It was dark when I woke up. I opened my eyes. Suzanne was sitting on top of the dresser at the foot of my bed.

I shut my eyes again. I felt exposed and defenseless. "How did you find me here?" I asked, puzzled.

"I was worried when I didn't hear from you and got no answer when I tried to phone you. I called the house, and John Elder answered and he said you were here. He said it would be okay for me to come to see you."

Then I realized Dee was sitting in a chair across the room.

"Hi, Dee."

"Hi, Margaret. How do you feel?"

"Drugged. Drugged and hungry."

I got up and went to the bathroom. I washed my face, brushed my teeth, and ran my fingers through my hair. Then I came out of the bathroom, got a cigarette from the pack on the bedside table, lit it, and sat staring at patterns in the smoke. I called my attention back to Dee and Suzanne.

"Let's go to Howard Johnson's and get something to eat," I said.

Suzanne jumped up from the dresser. "Dr. Turcotte told me that you weren't to go anywhere."

"I'm certain he didn't mean I wasn't to go out to eat," I said impatiently, walking toward the door.

Suzanne stood in front of the door, her feet spread apart, her hands on her hips. The two of us faced each other, our eyes locked in a defiant glare. It took every ounce of self-discipline I could muster to refrain from forcibly pushing her aside. She stood, stubborn, and solid as stone. She wasn't about to relent without a physical confrontation.

I took several deep breaths. Then I sat down on the bed. "Suzanne," I said through clenched teeth but in what I hoped was a calm voice, "would you please phone Dr. Turcotte and ask him if I can go to the restaurant to get dinner."

She made the call. Then she put the receiver back in its cradle.

"He said it would be okay for you to go get some dinner."

"I expected him to say that," I responded sharply. I took my purse from the bedside table, put my cigarettes in it, and snapped it shut. "Let's go."

I don't remember now if it was because of our confrontation at the door, or if it was something I said in the restaurant, but Suzanne rushed off to the bathroom in tears shortly after we got to the restaurant. I followed her, apologizing for whatever I'd done. We hugged each other and went back to the table. I felt more comfortable being with Dee. We'd known each other for years, and she'd supported me through the 1971 psychotic episode. Suzanne was new in my life and—in spite of our intense feelings for each other—I didn't feel altogether comfortable with her.

After dinner we walked back toward my room. Dee stopped at her car and said she had to go home to her family. We hugged goodbye. Then Suzanne and I went into my room, which was still filled with stale cigarette smoke.

"I told Dr. Turcotte I'd spend the night if it's okay with you," she said. "He doesn't want you left alone."

"Thanks," I responded, and we got undressed and ready for bed. I got into my rumpled, unmade bed.

"Would you like me to rub your back?" Suzanne asked.

"That would be wonderful."

I turned over on my stomach. She lay down beside me and began to massage my right shoulder. After a while, she got up and knelt over me, her strong hands massaging my back.

"Fools rush in where angels fear to tread."

To this day I can't remember which of us said that.

The next morning Dr. Turcotte said he was going to have me committed to the Brattleboro Retreat.

Jim, sitting in a chair beside the doctor, leaned toward him. "No," he protested. "I'll stay with her every minute. I'll take speed to stay awake. I'll do anything. Anything. I won't let you put Margaret in a hospital again."

Suzanne interrupted, saying that she wanted to take me home with her. Dr. Turcotte said he thought that would be a good idea. He would come to Suzanne's to work with me.

"Here," Suzanne said to me. "I'll help you gather your things together."

In the meantime, John had passed his crisis. *Three times in the ICU for taking overdoses of one thing or another, and he's still here,* I thought. *Well, he will live after all, but never again with me.*

VII

I'd just gotten out of the car after sitting and talking with John. Suzanne stood at her door, watching me walk toward her. John got out of the car and began to yell. "The cars are mine!" he yelled. "The house is mine! The land is mine! The furniture is mine!"

When I reached the door and turned around, I saw that his face was red and his hands were trembling.

"What's Margaret's, John?" Suzanne shouted angrily.

I was stunned by her question. I hadn't thought of cars, house, or furniture. I hadn't thought of the land with its thick woods and stream.

"What's Margaret's, John?"

The words thundered through me. Then my hands were trembling.

A question emerged from the core of my being. It was one of the most important questions I'd ever asked myself, and it reverberated through me until I was filled with a great and sober calm. *Is the story of my life mine?*

Ever since I was a girl I'd felt a strong need to tell the story of my life. When I was a freshman in college I wrote a short autobiography for my English class, for which I received an A. But when I went home to Cairo I destroyed it because I didn't want Mother to read what I'd written.

After I was married and living in Philadelphia in the late 1950s, I told bits and pieces of my stories to friends. In the early 1970s— after my first psychotic episode—I found relief by telling stories about my Georgia family. But under the telling, under all the separate stories, was the question *What is the story of my life?* Finding the answer had seemed crucial. Certainly the story of my life wasn't just the collection of the stories I'd written and told over the years.

The stories were just that—stories. They were attempts to make sense of my life as I examined it—one thing happened as a result of another thing that happened before it, and so on. What I had really been looking for was the answer to the question *Who am I?*

I hadn't been able to find that answer. But that day in front of Suzanne's house, I had another important question to consider: *Is the story of my life mine?*

Was the story of my life mine if to tell that story meant to tell things about other people's lives that they preferred to keep private? Was what I wrote truly the story of my life if I changed names and circumstances to protect the privacy of friends, if I did the best I could to grasp and hold the essence of what I saw as my story?

And John?

The memory of his trembling hands and his useless claiming of material things broke my heart. Whether he was conscious of it or not, he wasn't talking about things at all. He was fighting to hold on to things because he was losing his family and was desperate. Looking back, I feel more compassion for John than I can bear.

John has been dead for years now, and we've been divorced for more than thirty years. He married again shortly after our divorce and lived with his second wife until his death. In all these years I've not yet stopped dreaming at night that we are still together. Sometimes in my dreams he divides his time between his wife and me. Other times he and I are together alone. Often I'm upset to see that he's built a much more beautiful house for her than he ever built for me. Or, if he and I are living in the same house together, he's built an incredibly beautiful and extravagant study for himself. His is always the most beautiful room in the house.

Even so, I'm almost always glad to be with him.

John is no longer here to tell his story even if he wanted to. I can only tell my story, and the story of us from my perspective, and I am well aware that this story is a mix of my personal observations and feelings, thoughts, memories, and whatever part imagination plays in calling back the past and translating it into words.

And my dreams? In my dreams John and I are together, no matter how difficult or rewarding the circumstances. Mornings I wake after being closer to John than we ever were when we slept together, his arm around me tightly, no matter what our day or night together had held.

Is the story of my life mine? What is the story of my life?
Page by page I am finding out the answers.

VIII

When I try to remember my life just after leaving John and going home with Suzanne, I see fragments of memories like pieces of a jigsaw puzzle scattered on a table, with no picture on the puzzle box to guide me. I have no memory of going to Suzanne's. I have no idea when Chris and I moved into one of the student houses that her husband managed. When I try to remember images from that time, my mind is almost as blank as the snow-covered ground outside my window as I write.

My high school history teacher said: "Dates are hooks on which to hang history."

I've never been good at remembering dates. I seem to remember my own history through the particular images that I associate with significant events: waking in the motel room to see Suzanne sitting on the dresser, looking at me. Me sitting on a stool in Suzanne's kitchen, watching her stir the stew bubbling on her stove. Today's snow falling and falling.

I have no idea how long Chris and I stayed in student housing. I have only a few memories of being there. In one, Chris and I are sitting at the table in the kitchen. We are drinking milk and eating thick slices of Suzanne's homemade bread, spread with butter and strawberry jam. It's very late and the house is quiet. Chris and I whisper to each other so we won't wake anyone. We are alone together, but it feels like a secure aloneness, with all the sleeping people behind their closed doors.

In another memory, I'm lying on my bed looking at my life-sized poster of Charlie Chaplin hanging on the dark door of the old walnut wardrobe. I've lain here for so long looking at him that I feel almost as if I have become Chaplin. I reach for a cigarette, light it, and look at the poster again, grateful for the image, and for the memory of his signature exit line: "Buck up—never say die. We'll get along." And the title of the poster: "Waiting for Inspiration."

I have many memories of Suzanne rubbing my back. Her hands were strong from years of kneading bread, pulling weeds, digging in her garden. As long as Suzanne's hands were on my back, I could relax and breathe deeply.

IX

John wrote me a letter in which he explained why he should have the car, the house, the furniture, the dishes, the books, and so on. His words were as cold and logical as one of his papers for a logic class when he was a philosophy student. There wasn't a hint of emotion, not a word of caring for Chris or me.

I decided to answer the same way he had written to me. Suzanne and I worked on the letter for hours one night, careful to use his format with all its As, Bs, and Cs, and references back to one letter of the alphabet or another. It was difficult to write such a cold, calm argument when I was feeling so much emotion. How could John not see that Chris needed his own home and school, especially at a time when so much of his life was changing? I controlled my emotions and worked on the letter.

The next day I mailed it. The following day John's reply arrived. He wrote that my argument was logical and he had no choice except to agree to it—the house and station wagon were mine.

X
1978

John moved into an apartment in Amherst, and Chris and I moved back into the house. It felt good to be in Shutesbury again, along with John Elder, who, at twenty-one, had moved back into the house with his girlfriend and future wife, Mary, after by now having lived on his own for some time. Being with his brother was a comfort for thirteen-year-old Chris, but there were many desperate occasions with him when I felt helpless to ease his pain and could find no way to comfort or reassure him.

One night he answered the phone to John's pleading to let him come home.

"Dad," Chris begged, "please hang up the phone. Please stop pleading." His father, who had begun to drink again once I left him, continued to plead.

Chris hung the phone up.

It rang again. Before I could reach the phone, Chris answered. Again it was John. I took the phone from Chris and asked John not to call back. As soon as I hung up, it began to ring again. I picked the receiver up and put the phone back in its cradle. Again John called. Chris answered and begged his father to hang up, but John continued his drunken pleading. Chris left the phone dangling from its cord on the wall.

Even from the living room couch I heard John's voice. I looked up to see Chris standing in the hall, between the kitchen door and the side of the fireplace. His feet were apart in a defiant, determined stance. He looked me resolutely in the eyes, but what he communicated was vulnerability and fragility.

I felt the color drain from my face. I sat deathly still.

Chris was holding one of our largest, sharpest kitchen knives against the side of his throat.

"I'm going to slit my throat," he said in an even, calm voice. "I'm going to kill myself."

"Chris," I said as softly as I could. "Chris, please put the knife down."

"No. I'm going to kill myself," he repeated.

"None of this is your fault," I said, rising from the couch slowly, carefully watching his response.

Dr. Turcotte had told me, "He could kill himself without giving himself time to think. Upset adolescents often act impulsively." Now his words filled my mind, repeating themselves as a nightmarish chant. I felt like I was walking a tightrope with Chris's life in my hands.

"You've done nothing wrong, Chris."

The knife's blade pressed against his jugular vein.

"Please, Chris."

I was almost close enough to touch him.

"Chris," I repeated softly. "Chris."

He lowered his hand and the knife fell to the floor.

Then he was in my arms, his thin body leaning against mine as he sobbed into my shoulder.

The house didn't feel large enough to hold the intensity of the two of us.

I was afraid to let him be by himself, and John Elder and Mary were out. I spread blankets on the thick shag living room rug and encouraged him to lie there with me, in front of the woodstove. When I touched him, he was trembling. I was trembling, too. I rubbed his back for a long time before we both fell asleep there on the floor.

Chapter Seventeen

I

1979

I HELD THE HANDRAIL TO STEADY MYSELF AS I WALKED DOWN THE COURT-house steps. I'd had no idea what a brutal confrontation the hearing would be. John had gone through all my papers, making copies of the pen-and-ink note cards I'd made for sale, and had presented a carefully thought-through case for my ability to make a living with-out the need for alimony. All those years he'd never let me get a job, pay the bills, or handle the money. He didn't even tell me how much money we had. Now he was trying to convince the judge that I was competent to walk out of our twenty-three-year marriage and live as if I'd always been an independent woman, that *he* could walk away from the marriage with no sense of responsibility at all.

What a fool I've been, I thought. *What a naïve, thoughtless fool.*

My lawyer said he'd never been involved in such a long divorce hearing. The divorce was finally granted for reasons of cruel and abusive treatment. I was to receive $125 a week for alimony, $50 a week for child support, health insurance for Chris and me, and half of whatever the house brought when it was sold, which had to be done within the year.

My lawyer and I shook hands. Then I got into my car and headed to Northampton for an appointment with Dr. Turcotte. But first I stopped at Carburs on Route 9 for a sandwich. I was late for the lunch crowd, and except for a few people at the bar and a couple in a far corner of the dining room, the restaurant was empty.

I sat down at a table near the door. The waiter came and took my order for a tuna fish sandwich. I lit a cigarette. Through the smoke I noticed a ceiling fan revolving slowly and thought of an old black-and-white movie and the feeling of heat and humidity. What was that movie with Humphrey Bogart and Ingrid Bergman? I couldn't even remember his famous line as he watched her board a plane to fly away from him forever.

Forever.

I took another drag from my cigarette.

Casablanca. That was the movie's title.

The waiter set the plate on the table in front of me. He must have been around John Elder's age. "Anything else, miss?"

I wondered if *his* parents were divorced. "No, thank you. This will be fine."

I unfolded my napkin and spread it on my lap, took a bite from my sandwich, and chewed thoughtfully as the ceiling fan revolved its broad blades slowly. What was that Bogart line? What did it matter? Two hours ago I'd been an unhappily married woman. Now I was a divorced woman. I practiced saying the words in my head—*a divorced woman.*

"Can I get you anything else?" the waiter asked politely, hesitantly, as if afraid he was intruding on my thoughts. His cheeks were slightly red, and he averted his eyes from mine.

"No," I assured him. Then I realized that my sandwich lay uneaten on my plate.

I lit another cigarette and sat, looking at the fan blades in their slow rotation.

I was a divorced woman without any idea of how to play the part. It was as if I'd spent my entire life reading someone else's lines. I'd learned quite well how to play the unhappy wife. Mother had taught me that from the beginning. But the divorced woman? The independent woman?

Then I remembered Bogart's line: "Here's looking at you, kid."

And Bergman's "I wish I didn't love you so much."

I remembered twenty-three years of cutting John's hair and how well I knew the way it grew, how my fingers felt as they ran through it, the snap of the scissors, hair falling at my feet. The angry divorce scene dissolved in my mind, and—just as some people say happens to you before you die—image after image of my life with him came flooding through my mind. Not the nightmarish confrontations, the mental torment, or the violence, but the good things about John and me and the children. The first snow we saw in Philadelphia when he woke me in the middle of the night and together we went out to the backyard in our pajamas and robes and lifted our faces to the sting and tickle of the first snowflakes we'd ever seen. John Elder flying his kite at Valley Forge while John and I sat on the grass, talking. The three of us in a boat on the Schuylkill River. Camping in the Poconos, roasting unhusked corn in the coals, and camping along the Oregon coast, with postcard sunsets and the surf pounding. Year-old Chris sitting on John's lap, eating an ear of corn from our garden in Hadley, Massachusetts.

I remembered the day John came home carrying a brand-new Olympia electric typewriter for me and how nervous I was, wondering if I could possibly ever write anything to deserve such an expensive machine.

I remembered our trips to Hyde Park, Tanglewood, the Bay of Fundy, Old Sturbridge Village, and up the dramatic coastline of Maine. There were the plays we saw in Williamstown. And, when John and I were very young, the trip to New York, where we saw Anne Bancroft and Patty Duke in *The Miracle Worker.* Tears streamed down John's cheeks as he watched. Image after image flowed through me until I thought I might get caught up in the flow and go on forever seeing images of John and me and the children until my heart broke open and I sat paralyzed with grief.

I fumbled in my purse for money to leave in the tray with my bill. Then I crushed my cigarette in the ashtray, fought the panic rising in my chest, and went to my car to continue on my way to Dr. Turcotte's, not as part of a couple but as a woman alone.

II

Driving, I thought of Suzanne. Since the night in the motel with Paula, I had accepted the idea of sex between two women with none of my old guilt, or the feeling that something was wrong with me. The more I was with Suzanne, the more clearly I understood that sex simply had to do with love. And beyond my immeasurable love for my sons, I was consciously learning more about love than I'd ever known.

Suzanne was an orthodox Christian who went to the Congregational church on Sundays and tried to live according to the principles of her church, and the Bible as she understood it. She was also married. Her own father had left her mother when Suzanne was a young girl. As an adult, Suzanne believed that a happy, fulfilled life lay in having a husband and children.

I was raised in the Southern Baptist Church, had gone through periods of agnosticism, followed by searching in the Presbyterian, Unitarian, and Catholic churches for spiritual sustenance. After my psychotic experience in 1971, I came to believe everything came from and was a part of God. I felt the ground under my feet as holy, just as the housefly buzzing annoyingly at my ear was holy. My spiritual growth continued to widen and deepen, with troughs of doubt and confusion followed by periods of reaffirmation of a faith that didn't fit into any formal belief system or church.

Unlike Suzanne, I had finally gotten a divorce. As an adolescent, I'd felt torn by the way my parents tormented each other. I'd wished with all my heart that they would divorce and go in search of their own separate happiness. Wisely or unwisely, having reached the end of my endurance, after twenty-three years of marriage, I had taken the step I'd wished my parents had taken when I was young.

I was also getting more and more involved with a married woman who was weighted down by guilt and filled with longing and confusion. Suzanne's inconsistency and the varying limits she put on our expressions of our love only served to intensify my longing. Looking back, I can see that, more than anything else, it was the longing that gave life to the relationship for me, the longing that gave me reason to live another day, despite my grief and depression.

III

During all the years of going to Dr. Turcotte I'd sat in the waiting room for ages while he talked with John. Now it was I alone who went in to talk with the doctor. John told me that Turcotte blamed him for the breakup of our marriage and wanted nothing more to do with him. It was I who kept my relationship with Dr. Turcotte.

He told me that he was my brother, my God-brother; that his would be the shoulder I could lean on when my burdens grew too heavy for me to bear alone—that I would never be alone. I looked across the cluttered table at him, his clear blue eyes always looking just a bit past me.

I looked down at the stacks of old magazines, half-burnt candles, books, boxes of Kleenex, and dirty ashtrays.

Dr. Turcotte was my brother? Why didn't I feel any brotherly love in his voice? It was as if he'd thought things through and decided that he should say those words. Maybe, feeling confusion about his relationship with me now that John was no longer there, he'd opened his Bible for an answer. Maybe his index finger had landed on the word *brother*. Whatever brought him to tell me that he was my brother, I felt sad at the absence of feeling behind the words. I wanted a brother. I needed a brother. Mercer didn't have the emotional strength to relate to me, and Bubba and I had rarely spoken in years. But was Rodolph Turcotte my brother? I wanted to believe he really was. As I left his office that day he embraced me, but the gesture felt empty, and distrust began to work its way up into my consciousness.

IV

My relationship with Dr. Turcotte gradually changed. Some of the changes were good. I had the opportunity to begin to know him better, and to discuss his beliefs more thoroughly. Often I just enjoyed his company, which was everything from compassionate and wise to outrageous, funny, and blundering. There were disturbing changes, too, although I fought, often successfully, to deny them. As my denial grew stronger, so did my depression.

Driving home from a meeting of the Massachusetts chapter of the Society of Religion and Mental Health one afternoon, I began to talk to him excitedly about a new insight I'd had about the creative process. He gripped the steering wheel with ferocity. "I wouldn't know about the creative process. I'm too damned busy treating mentally ill people."

I was shocked by his anger, and by a bitterness I'd not heard in his voice before. I was surprised that he didn't realize that his teachings in relation to mental health contained many of the basic principles of the creative process as I'd grown to know them. By encouraging me to accept my depression rather than fight it, he had allowed me to bring some of my best writing out of that darkness. I told him that I'd never come out of a depression without bringing a gift back with me. His encouraging me as well as his other patients to keep talking no matter the content was an important thing I applied to writing. I discovered that if the stream of writing ran on long enough, sooner or later I'd discover gold in the flow.

I'd become friends with more of Dr. Turcotte's patients, as well as with Jim Clark and two of the doctor's five daughters, June and Amy. All were involved in writing to one degree or another. Both sisters painted, and Jim was a serious photographer. After the Shutesbury

house was sold on October 1, 1980, Chris and I moved to an apartment on Dickinson Street in Amherst. June, Amy, Jim, and several
patients met in our apartment on Sunday evenings for a potluck supper and conversation. Several members of the group also participated in my Thursday-evening writing workshop. One group
member was Helen Jackson, a young woman whom I had worked
with on her writing and who'd come to stay with me while on vacation. Shortly after she arrived, I realized she was deeply troubled.
She'd heard Dr. Turcotte give a talk in Amherst and wanted to see
him as a patient, which she did. Because she didn't feel up to going
back to college, she became a permanent member of my household
and of the group. Our home was always filled with creative people
coming and going—sitting at the dining table writing, making collages on the kitchen table, Jim developing film in the basement, people spending the night sleeping on the couch or on the shag rug.

One Sunday evening during dinner, Dr. Turcotte called from
Philadelphia, where he'd gone with Father Gray. "You're trying to
take my practice away from me!" he yelled.

"What?" I exclaimed, unable to believe what I'd just heard.

"You're trying to take my practice away from me with those meetings of yours," he repeated.

"I'm not trying to take your practice away from you. I teach people about the creative process. I'm not a psychiatrist."

It was true that everyone in the group was becoming more open
and emotionally expressive as they were growing more creative, but I
saw no one pulling away from him. However, *my* relationship with
Dr. Turcotte continued to change.

V

Chris was visibly nervous when he and Jim came into the kitchen
where I was sitting at the table writing. I closed my notebook and lit
a cigarette. Still standing, Chris explained that Jim had something to

tell me. "I have to go to town. I'll be back soon," Chris said, hurrying from the room.

Jim sat down on a kitchen chair.

I can't remember a word he said to me, but I remember his message with searing clarity—he and Chris were having a sexual relationship. Dr. Turcotte had already told me this, but to hear it in Jim's words made the fact painfully real. This man whom I had known and talked with for years in Dr. Turcotte's office, discussing my troubled marriage, his troubled childhood with abusive parents, and, hour after hour, the life and ideas of Sigmund Freud, Carl Jung, and Georg Groddeck; this man who had supported me when I was in Northampton State Hospital and—years later—had said he would stay with me night and day to keep the doctor from committing me to the Brattleboro Retreat; this man who had attended my Sunday-night potluck dinners and Thursday-night writing workshops, and who developed his film in a darkroom he'd created in my basement, was having a sexual relationship with my fifteen-year-old son.

When Dr. Turcotte told me about the relationship, he had warned me that I would risk losing Chris altogether if I opposed it. And he told me that Chris had been sexually active long before his relationship with John.

I remembered how—two years before that night—Chris had threatened to become a male prostitute in Springfield if I wouldn't do something he wanted me to do. I had no idea that he even knew what the word *prostitute* meant. We settled whatever conflict we were engaged in, but that he had known enough to make that threat concerned me.

Now he was having a sexual relationship with Jim.

As I sat once again attempting to accept the fact, Chris burst into the kitchen with enthusiasm.

"I've bought you a gift, Jim," he said, and handed Jim a gift-wrapped box.

Did Jim open his gift? Did Chris say anything to me? Did I say anything to him?

I do remember that his feeling of relief was palpable. I remember him touching Jim's shoulder.

The rest of my time with them that evening is a blur, though I have a vague memory of them leaving the apartment together.

Life continued as always in the Dickinson Street apartment—the potluck dinners and writing workshops, the Turcotte girls and Helen and her friends coming and going, Jim developing film in the basement, and Chris sitting upstairs writing poetry or writing in his journal, while I too wrote. But somehow, nothing was the same after that night.

VI

After Dr. Turcotte returned from Philadelphia, nothing more was said about the accusing call he'd made. He invited me to go out to dinner with him one night, and I accepted. He often invited patients to join him for lunch or dinner. Usually the patients were either interested in or involved with one or another of the doctor's projects, or they were in distress or in need of extra attention. Often he invited patients to accompany him because he needed someone to listen to and support him.

Over dinner that night he began to tell me a story about him being a lonely high school boy who was grateful for the attention of one of his teachers. The details of the story are gone now. What I remember is the image of him sitting across the table from me in a rattan wing chair. Whatever Dr. Turcotte's teacher had said or done seemed to me to be such a small thing that it magnified his great emotional need. As he talked, his eyes filled with tears that spilled over and streamed down his face in a torrent of grief and gratitude.

"I don't know," he said, pulling his handkerchief from his pants pocket and wiping his eyes. "I've never talked about these things. For some reason, you're so easy to talk to." He blew his nose and continued to cry.

In addition to compassion for him, I felt puzzlement and surprise as well. This doctor to whom I'd been going for so many years had not lived according to his own theories. He had never talked with anyone about these painful things in his childhood and youth. All those years his old unacknowledged pain had gnawed into his perceptions until they were like slices of Swiss cheese, each hole creating a blind spot in his vision. Surely we all have many blind spots, but that someone with such power over confused, distraught people was so unconscious of the lack in his own perceptions about himself frightened me. Now I saw Dr. Turcotte, whom I'd thought the most perceptive and creative therapist I'd ever known, as also the hurt child holding a heart full of unacknowledged grief and unfulfilled emotional need.

Had he been one of my students, I would have suggested that he write the story he'd just told me. I would have told him this, believing that finding a form for his pain would make it a story rather than a series of disconnected sentences spilled out through his tears; writing the story would be a second step toward his healing, just as his awkward and emotional telling me over dinner had been the first.

He finally stopped crying. He wiped his eyes, blew his nose again, put his handkerchief back into his pocket, picked up a piece of meat loaf with his fork, and lifted it to his mouth. I sat stunned at the realization that my therapist had explored his own childhood and youth less than many of the young people in my writing workshops had explored theirs. The realization made me feel less secure with him, but he was still my therapist, and I wasn't ready to let that relationship go. I wasn't confident enough to claim myself as person rather than patient.

VII

I began to take more short trips with Dr. Turcotte to different Catholic churches, and visits with priests, meetings of the Society for

Religion and Mental Health, and short excursions to unknown destinations. Sometimes he'd follow his heart from one town to another. I thought of Saint Francis, who, I'd read, often tossed a coin to tell him which direction to follow when he reached crossroads in his travels.

Once the doctor pulled the car over to a large pond and sat for a long time, looking. On the pond floated more ducks than I'd ever seen gathered in one place. "What an example of the abundance of God's creations," he said with wonder. Then he started the car and pulled out onto the highway again.

Trip by trip, bit by bit, I began to piece together the story of his life, at least some of the highlights and major shaping events, or at least those things he felt moved or willing to tell me about. Dr. Turcotte told me that he'd never been able to please his father and how much that had hurt him. He said little about his mother except that she had actively engaged in life until her death.

He told me about the first patient assigned to him when he was still in medical school. She sat in a chair on the ward, smoking cigarette after cigarette, staring off into space, saying nothing. Her hair was unwashed, and her dresses were someone's ill-fitting castoffs. Her eyes were vacant, her body skin and bones. "I sat in a chair facing her," he said. "I tried every way I could think of to get a response out of her, but nothing worked. So I just sat there and she sat there. I returned the next day, and the day after that. Day after day we sat there together that way. One day I looked at her, that woman stripped of personality, and it was like she was naked. That woman had nothing, absolutely nothing left but cigarettes. Then I saw her. I really saw her. And I thought: *I'm looking into the face of God made visible.* It was a holy moment." There was tenderness in his voice. "I was humbled by the experience," he said. "It changed my way of looking at patients from that day on."

He went on with his studies until he graduated and became a board-certified psychiatrist. He told me that he was certain that the first patient he had after graduating from medical school was determined to kill him once she got out of the hospital, and how afraid he'd been, both of the patient and the patient's brother.

There was the story of a patient who was a priest, who, Dr. Turcotte claimed, was determined to set fire to the rectory. The doctor could convince no one of this possibility but shared his thoughts about the priest with everyone in the diocese, trying to convince them of what he saw as imminent danger. The priest finally packed his things and left the diocese altogether.

The stories came in bits and pieces, but after hearing various fragments, I began to see that two themes emerged: that of patients out to kill Dr. Turcotte and other patients who were going to set fires, possibly killing themselves and others. While I wished no one harm, I did wish that something visible would happen to prove the doctor's beliefs—a fire started, but extinguished before damage was done, a written death threat to the doctor that could be traced to the patient he claimed was threatening him. I wanted to visibly see that he was right about his patients, that he knew what he was talking about and wasn't a paranoid manic-depressive who survived by projecting onto certain patients, while putting other patients in the position of supporting him and his delusions. He'd saved my life, and I still wanted to believe in him.

VIII

Dr. Turcotte fell in love with a patient, a young divorced woman with several children. He talked about her to anyone who would listen. He claimed that falling in love with her made him feel more in love with his wife, Claire, and with Ethel, whom he considered his "second wife."

Claire must have been well aware of his long relationship with Ethel. He made no secret of his belief that men often needed more than one wife. Ethel worked part-time for him, and had become increasingly devoted to him and his teachings, both psychiatrically and theologically. Their emotional bond grew stronger. He told me of their struggling with what to do about their feelings for each other, their praying and reading the Bible. He said that a scripture convinced them to consider themselves husband and wife. According to him, they repeated vows to each other and made love. Ethel became his second wife. I suppose he wanted the patient as yet another of his wives.

I never knew Claire's or Ethel's response to this. Claire probably went on with her life as she'd learned to do years before. She was a loyal Catholic who would never divorce her husband no matter his behavior. If she was grief-stricken, brokenhearted, jealous, or angry, she was as silent about her emotional state as her husband was loud and public about his.

Patients' problems paled in comparison with the doctor's needs. Many therapy sessions turned into opportunities for him to talk incessantly about his new love. "My heart," he announced repeatedly, "is bursting with love." After his proclamation of love to her, the young woman—I'll call her Sally—stopped going to him. Dr. Turcotte went to her brother, begging him to persuade her to return to therapy. She refused. He called her, wrote notes to her, phoned her. He told her how much she needed him. He drove back and forth in front of her house.

Then he called me one evening and told me he needed to get out of town for a few days. Would I drive him? I threw some clothes into a suitcase and picked him up at his office. He was visibly shaken. Sally was going to have him killed. He was certain of it. She and her family had hired a Mafia hit man to execute him. She was also going to set fire to her house and kill the children along with herself.

His two great fears had been brought together in one person. He frightened me. So many of the things he'd said about people had seemed insightful and true, but this was too much.

Yet I went with him.

Chapter Eighteen

I
1980

WE ATTENDED A SPECIAL MASS AND HEALING SERVICE IN A CATHOLIC church in the eastern part of the state. He gave one of the priests a letter about Sally and her plans to burn her house down, trying to persuade the priest to intervene and avert a potential tragedy. The priest scanned the letter with no apparent interest, shook the doctor's hand, and wished us well.

After the mass, Dr. Turcotte told me that he wanted to take me to Cairo to talk with my Aunt Curtis, Mother's sister, who'd suddenly and without explanation cut off the financial support she'd been giving me since my divorce. I was shocked that she'd taken a major source of financial support away from me, but that she'd taken her emotional support as well left me devastated. I'd plunged into a more intense depression than I'd experienced before. I agonized at the thought of Dr. Turcotte going to Cairo to talk with her but agreed to go even though I felt certain that she would think him an outrageous, blundering, totally unacceptable man. My depression was dark and intensifying.

The doctor's paranoia was also intensifying. Many times we'd rushed out of one restaurant or another because he was certain there was someone there who would pull a gun at any minute and kill him. That day, the day he decided to go to Cairo, I sat slumped in the car, smoking cigarettes, while sinking deeper and deeper into a depression that grew to psychotic proportions. By sundown we'd reached Newport, Rhode Island. Dr. Turcotte pulled the car into a parking space in front of a motel that faced the sea. "We'll spend the night here," he announced, and snapped off the ignition.

II

As usual, Dr. Turcotte was broke. He slapped Ethel's American Express card on the motel counter and signed us in as Mr. and Mrs. Harold Miller. Then we went to the room, which had two double beds. I went to the bathroom, while he opened the Gideon Bible in the bedside table drawer to do what he called a "Bible dip." I'd never heard the phrase "Bible dip" before he used it, but even as a teenager I often looked for guidance by opening the Bible at random and reading whatever verse to which my eye was drawn. I assumed Turcotte was looking for guidance about how to save his life from Sally's deadly revenge. The story felt like a cheap crime novel. I didn't ask what the Bible had told him. Then the two of us went to the motel restaurant for dinner. The table he chose was next to the bar.

A woman about my age was sitting on a stool, talking to the bartender. She had long, chestnut-colored hair, a few freckles across her nose, and a Southern accent much like mine. "Excuse me," I said to her during a lull in their conversation. "You sound like you're from the South. So am I."

She responded in an open, friendly manner. "Yeah, you sound like you're from Georgia, too. I grew up in Dalton."

"I grew up in Cairo," I said.

"I've never met anyone from Georgia up here!" she exclaimed.

"Neither have I! Would you like to join us?" I asked.

"Yes," she said enthusiastically, and came over and sat down next to me. We introduced ourselves. Then she began to talk in a rapid, animated way. She was divorced, had no children, and wrote songs that she sang, accompanying herself on her guitar. We talked about Georgia clay, live oak trees, and Spanish moss. I told her I was a poet. Maybe we'd write a song together. I was having a wonderful time when I felt a heavy darkness descend on Dr. Turcotte.

He turned to Jeanie, my new friend, and announced: "Margaret's sexually attracted to you." This was clearly intended to shock and intimidate her, but she dismissed him and his remark as casually as she might have flicked away a fly that had landed on the sandwich she'd brought with her from the bar. Without missing a beat in the cadence of our conversation, she continued: "Margaret, wouldn't it be fun to write some music together and take it south?"

The doctor was clearly left out of the conversation. He sat glumly eating, while Jeanie and I talked about Georgia and music. At the end of the evening, she gave me her phone number and address, and we agreed to get together the next day.

From here on, the story of my stay in Newport with Dr. Turcotte is filled with memory lapses caused by shock and increasing psychosis.

We went to the room. Dr. Turcotte took his clothes off and stood at the window in his undershirt and underpants. I got ready for bed, got into my bed, and pulled the cover over me. Dr. Turcotte walked across the room, pulled the cover of my bed back down, and climbed in. I sucked my breath in and held it. This wasn't supposed to happen. He said he was my brother; I'd always felt physically if not emotionally safe with him. Now he was pressing his body against mine. My heart beat rapidly and my breathing was shallow.

"How voluptuous you feel," he said, kneading my flesh. His fingers dug into me with such force that I imagined him bruising my bones. There was such hatred in his touch. Hatred. I felt frightened and confused. Nothing in our relationship had prepared me for this. Suddenly he was all over me, his frenzied hands everywhere, digging and digging. What was he trying to do? I tried to push his hands away, but he was determined and strong, pinning my body down with his while I fought to twist myself from under him. Almost thirty years have passed, and still I can sometimes feel the hatred in his hands. I remember him stopping to take a shower while I fell asleep, exhausted. Then I was once again startled awake as he climbed onto me and resumed the struggle.

I lost all sense of time. Many days and nights could have passed. Or only one or two. Once he went away and returned with some antipsychotic drug and I took it without protest. Then another drug. Once he returned with a little tin of candies. I opened the tin and became violently sick from the smell.

He undressed and got into the other bed.

"Come here, Margaret," he commanded, stretching his arm toward me and sweeping it back toward himself. "Come here."

He acted like I was an animal that he was determined to train to mute obedience.

In a chair across the room sat a large crocheted clown. I remember trading my heavy, beautifully wrought Celtic cross for it in the gift shop. *What an ugly thing that clown is,* I thought. Yet my eyes fastened onto it steadfastly, as if my life depended on it.

I looked at the crocheted clown and thought of Daddy. How hard he had worked to make us children laugh. I must have wanted the clown because something about it made me think of Daddy's sense of humor. Thinking about Daddy made me feel secure. I learned what love feels like through Daddy's touch.

"Come here," Dr. Turcotte commanded, again stretching his arm toward me and sweeping it back toward himself. This time, I thought of Nazis marching by the thousands, then their salute: "Heil Hitler." Dr. Turcotte's gesture became the Nazi salute. I felt nauseated.

And lost.

Then darkness, a deep, thick darkness. And silence that felt like strangulation.

Then I was in another room in the motel. Helen was lying on the bed beside me. Chris was pacing back and forth. Talking quickly in intense metaphors, I was telling him about how he himself was the Future. Jim was there too. I got up and began to sprinkle some sort of bath powder over the room, explaining that I was performing a spiritual ritual, though I have no idea what I might have meant.

Dr. Turcotte came into the room. Seeing him, I threatened to hurl my heavy Frye boots through the picture window. "No," he said firmly. "Don't throw those boots."

I turned to Jim, and he and I went down the hall and into the room that Dr. Turcotte and I had shared earlier. We sat at a table by the window and talked. The draperies were open, and sunlight flooded the room. I said nothing about my struggle with the doctor. I felt ashamed. Had I done something to provoke him? I didn't ask Jim why Dr. Turcotte had called them all to come down. I thought the doctor was afraid of how upset he'd made me.

After my talk with Jim, I went back to my room and lay down. I lay there in silence a long time.

Days and nights become one long, thick fog. *Maybe everything is my fault.* The thought churned in my mind, which became a confused tangle of self-condemnation and fear. I thought of Suzanne. I thought: *If I focus on her hard enough, will she feel my thoughts and come to get me?* For hours I lay on the bed, eyes closed, my mind focused on Suzanne.

Of course Suzanne didn't come.

For days I got up from the bed only to go to the bathroom. I neither ate nor bathed. I closed my eyes and thought of Suzanne. *Please come get me,* I pleaded silently. *Please.*

"You have to get up and take a bath."

Whose voice is that? I asked myself. *Dr. Turcotte's voice with the same com-*

manding tone he'd used when he said, "Come here, Margaret." I don't want to think of that. Keep your eyes closed, I told myself. *Keep your eyes closed.*

"Do you want to take a bath?"

It was not Dr. Turcotte's voice this time.

I felt a hand on my thigh. The touch was firm but gentle.

Trustworthy.

Jeanie's touch.

I opened my eyes.

"Hi, Jeanie."

"Hi, Margaret. Someone found my phone number in your purse and called, asking me to come over. They say you've not been out of bed in days."

"Yes," I said. "I'd like to take a bath. Would you stay with me in the bathroom?"

"Of course I would, honey." Her thick Southern drawl felt like a warm hug.

I got my clothes together while she ran the bathwater.

She sat on the toilet, smoked a cigarette, and talked with me while I bathed.

I got out of the bathtub, dried myself, and dressed. It felt good to be clean.

I brushed my teeth.

Again there are blank spaces.

Now we are all in the restaurant. Brightness. I was aware of brightness everywhere. Out the window the sky was cloudless with a scattering of gulls. The ocean stretched its blue to the horizon. Lunch was over. The young people left Newport for Northampton.

The doctor and I remained seated. I was writing something in my notebook about the sky being the blue of one of Grandmother's china teacups. I was still drugged, but my mind, like the day, was clearer. Dr. Turcotte took Ethel's credit card from his wallet and handed it to the waitress. Once more he'd become the familiar man I knew. His eyes no longer frightened me like they did when he'd looked from his bed to mine, commanding that I obey him. *Don't think about that,* I told myself. *Don't think about that.* He was calm now, and self-assured. How could he have possibly . . .

Denial took root in my mind. Even before we left Newport, it sprouted and began to grow wild and rampant like the kudzu vines I saw in Georgia when I was a child. How rapidly it covered everything in its path.

III

On our way out of Newport, Dr. Turcotte drove me to Jeanie's apartment. He rested on the living room couch while she and I sat in her kitchen and talked. She kept telling me that she didn't trust Dr. Turcotte. She told me that she was very psychic and had led the police to a murdered woman's body just by holding the woman's scarf.

"Believe me," she said, exhaling a cloud of smoke and inhaling again. "That man isn't someone to put your trust in." I couldn't make myself tell her what had happened with Dr. Turcotte. My voice was rapidly growing weaker, and to talk at all was a great effort. It was easier to listen to Jeanie.

For dinner, she scrambled eggs, fried bacon, and made toast. I looked around her kitchen at all her knickknacks, but the only thing I remember is a large, pale blue crescent moon. It hung on the wall over—I remember now—a small maple table with its captain's chairs.

That meal was one of the few that I remember when Dr. Turcotte didn't monopolize the conversation. Perhaps he sensed Jeanie's distrust of him. He buttered his toast quietly and ate in silence. We spent the night there. Dr. Turcotte slept on the couch. I slept with Jeanie, who gave me an enormous terry-cloth teddy bear to hold as I went to sleep.

The next morning Dr. Turcotte and I left for home. By that time, I could only speak in a hoarse, labored whisper. He was driving my car. As he spoke, his tone made me think of a puffed-up rooster in the chicken yard.

"You know, when we got to Newport, I opened the Bible and my finger landed on a verse that said, 'Do not touch this woman,'" he said, pausing as if consciously giving me time to take in what he'd said. I felt the energy drain out of my body and spirit.

He glanced at me. Then he turned to face the road ahead. "But I was curious," he said flatly.

Curious? Fragments of memories of his hands on my body, probing, digging in my flesh, flashed across my mind. Curiosity. Cruelty. His touch had been more cruel than John's touch had ever been. In some way, John had cared. To Dr. Turcotte, I'd been a puzzlement. And somehow a threat.

I lay down on the car seat beside him and closed my eyes. Drugs still sedated me. I felt such relief that the doctor had returned to his normal self. It was like John coming back to his normal self after a night of drunken cruelty. It was like, when I was a very young child, Mother's voice returning to normal after she'd said in a strange, shrill voice: "Your mother has left this body, and I—the wicked witch— am your mother now."

The doctor drove. I slept. When I woke, I pretended to be asleep until I could no longer bear the cramped position I lay in. I sat up, relieved to see the Springfield skyline.

I'd soon be home.

Chapter Nineteen

I
1980

I CAME DOWN WITH AN EXTREME CASE OF THE FLU. FOR DAYS I LAY IN bed with a fever, cough, and stuffy nose. My whole body ached. I only got up to go to the bathroom. One afternoon someone left the TV on. I couldn't make myself get up and walk across the room to turn it off. I lay there, miserable, listening to some soap opera I didn't want to hear. Finally I reached for pen and paper on the bedside table and wrote a satirical poem about the soap opera. I ended by saying that I wished that I, like the woman on the show, could fall into the arms of the handsome police officer who would make everything all right. After I actually did get involved with the police I realized that in the poem I had known more than I'd recognized consciously.

But that came much later.

I lost track of time. Was it a year or more that I was depressed? Two years? I continued seeing Dr. Turcotte, never talking with him about Newport. I knew he'd deny what had happened just as he'd denied other things. Father Gray was a prominent and respected priest. Who would believe me with Father Gray on the doctor's side? I did talk to Helen, but she didn't believe me. She'd begun to work part-time for Dr. Turcotte, and I could see that her commitment to him was growing stronger as she was moving away from me. Chris, too, wouldn't listen when I tried to talk to him about Newport. I guess he thought it was just more of my craziness. Or maybe he was afraid that what I claimed was true and he couldn't face it.

II

1980

Dr. Turcotte had driven me to the Brattleboro Retreat, my friend Helen and Dr. Turcotte's daughter June on either side of me. Chris sat in the front seat by the doctor. I no longer remember when or why I was moved from a room in the main ward, but the room I was moved to felt nightmarish to me. It was small, windowless, and cold, and the bare mattress on the cot was hard. There was nothing else in the room. I was barefooted and had only my raincoat to cover my naked body. "There was no such room," my friend Helen later insisted. "Not in that hospital." But in my memory, I lay on a cot in a small locked room.

I called out, asking for a blanket.

There was no answer.

I got up and walked to the door, hugging the raincoat to me. I turned the doorknob. The door was locked. My teeth were chattering.

"Help me," I pleaded. "Please help me!"

No answer.

I called louder, beating on the door with my fist. "Help!" I screamed. "Help!"

No one came.

"Someone, please bring me a blanket! I'm freezing!"

Footsteps approached, paused, and then went on past the room and down the hall.

I called out again.

Waited.

Called out again.

Finally, I gave up and went back to bed, pressing my back against the wall for what warmth it might have held. There was only the hard smoothness of the cold plaster against my backbone. How long could I endure such cold? Even in the state hospital the temperature had been comfortable in the solitary-confinement cell. And I'd had all my clothes on then. *Why was I stripped of clothes here except for this raincoat?* I thought. *Who would permit staff to strip and freeze a patient like this?* Once more I called out.

No one came. No one came just as no one had come when I was a baby and screamed for hours, stopping only after my whole body was sweat-drenched, my nose running with mucus, my hands sticky with it, my breath coming in shallow gasps, and I had no energy left for screaming.

"Your screams still haunt me. I should never have left you alone crying so much. I only did what the books said for me to do," my mother told me in her old age, her voice heavy with years of remorse.

But I was no longer in that crib in my grandfather's house with its slanted floors and dark rooms. Now I was in a mental hospital in a small cold room that my friend will tell me did not exist. I don't know how long I waited, or why. Hour after hour I lay on the cot, staring at the door. I didn't know if it was night or day. The only sound was that of occasional footsteps in the hall. I was numb with the cold.

I don't know what made me turn my eyes away from the blank wall across the room to stare at the door, but when I did, I saw a flicker of motion beginning in the wood's grain, then another. As I watched, flames seemed to move through the locked door as if it had no substance. The flames hovered several feet above the floor, and inside them I saw Joan of Arc, her young face radiant with her own burning.

"I, Joan the Maid, the Lily Maid of France, am bound in chains,"

I had recited in a high school monologue. Memorizing the words, I had repeated them over and over until they had moved through my mind and body, and out through my mouth as if they were mine. "Try it once more, Margaret," my drama coach would say, suggesting a pause, correcting the prolongation of a vowel. But high school was over, and college, and graduate school. Marriage was over, too, and I was in a locked room that my friend told me never existed. I was looking into the face of Joan of Arc, and nothing felt real and everything felt more real than I could bear. My own face felt the flames' heat, while her face was consumed by fire. And then there was no face at all, just the door, and in front of it, the flames in which my sister's clenched fists emerged, then her face with her blue eyes, blond hair blazing. And I thought that she had been waiting all these years for me to take her in my arms again and walk with her the way I did when she was a baby with pressure on the brain, and screaming. A part of me escaped my skin and moved out of my body toward her. Molecules of me were leaving their home of flesh and blood, tendon and bone, moving through the skin and out into the air toward her. But my sister's flesh was becoming flame even as I approached, no face now, no body, no clenched fists rising. I saw only her burned bones. I thought: *How many years have they been burning? Burning. And begging for skin.*

This is a memory: It was 1951 and my sister was four years old and had pneumonia. Mother stayed at the hospital with her most of the time. She sat in a straight chair beside my sister's crib. Sometimes she lay down and rested on the adult hospital bed that stood by the crib. After school I went to the hospital to keep Mother company.

I dreaded the walk down the hall to my sister's room. It meant I had to walk past the room of the burned boy. I didn't know his name or how old he was. Always he was screaming. And the stench coming from his room was human and terrible. Passing his room, I tried not to imagine what it must feel like to have the skin burned off your body. I was glad I didn't know his name. I thought it was easier for me not to know his name. I didn't know that his scream and smell would be with me all of my life.

I wish I knew his name.

"They locked me in solitary confinement, and no one came," I told Helen later. "I'm certain they did." Still later, I drove north again to the hospital, that time alone. I spent a long time parked in the hospital parking lot looking up at the windows, trying to remember the floor plan of the ward, trying to imagine where the locked room might have been, wanting to know what of the experience of that room was dream, what, if anything, was waking reality.

III

Psychotic visions and dreams were intruded on by aides bringing meals on trays, or nurses with their carts full of medications. Or by frequent and welcome visits from my friends June, Amy, and Helen. Or by Chris, who had already learned to mask his own pain with a blazing intelligence and a searing wit.

That day June brought me a bag full of yarn in many colors. Awkwardly she handed it to me. She had witnessed my psychotic episodes before. Or "growth experiences," as Dr. Turcotte had labeled them. I'd known June since I had begun to see her father in 1971, and she often kept Chris for me when I had to be away from home for one reason or another.

"Thank you," I said, moved by her thoughtfulness. I didn't tell her that I'd been waiting for a visit from Margaret Mead, who was coming from the land of the dead to visit me. All morning I'd sat waiting for her to arrive. I believed we had much to share with each other.

June sat in a straight chair across from me in the ward lounge, knees together, back rigid, hands clasped on her lap.

Helen was with her. She bent down and kissed me on the cheek. Then she put a stack of my favorite phonograph records from home on the table beside me: the musical *Milk and Honey*, Helen Reddy's

Long Hard Climb, Odetta at Carnegie Hall, the operas *Tosca, La Bohème,* and *La Traviata.* "Did you sleep last night?" Helen asked.

"Yes," I answered. I didn't tell her about the locked room. The experience was still too close to me; I couldn't bear to put words to it yet. "Yes, I slept." She sat down beside me.

I spilled the yarn into my lap and began to twist and knot it, a personal kind of macramé that I can only do when I'm in a state of madness, and then with a strange sense of confidence as if I'd spent whole lifetimes making things of yarn. "What beautiful colors!"

I can see that my working at the yarn was a comfort to June. She wanted the old Margaret back, the Margaret with whom she shared her poems and stories, the Margaret who was friend and inspiration to her. Knowing that she'd done something that pleased me comforted her.

"I've kept the plants watered," Helen said. "You didn't get any mail worth bringing."

The three of us talked while my fingers twisted and knotted the yarn in a frenzy of motion. At each change in the mass of yarn I searched it with my fingertips as if I were a blind woman trying desperately to identify a shape. *There.*

Finally, my heart relaxed in my chest. I took a long breath. Then another. Reverently my fingers caressed the shape in my hand, the sculpture of yarn, the end of my search, even though I'd not known what I was searching for or why. But there—finally—in my hand was a tiny replica of the face of Jesus. It was not the Jesus of the Mexican straw crucifixes with their open and sometimes almost smiling mouths. It was not the face of the stained-glass Jesus in the Baptist church of my childhood. The Jesus face of many colors was very long and thin, and its eyes were closed. Feeling his shape, I thought of the Shroud of Turin. It felt most like that image of Jesus. In knots and twists of yarn in my hand I had found Jesus and was comforted. My eyes filled with tears, and I took several deep breaths before I spoke again.

"Thank you so much for bringing the yarn," I said to June. "That was such a thoughtful thing for you to do." I didn't tell her how deeply grateful I was for the comforting Jesus of many colors. "Thank you so much for the yarn," I said.

"You're welcome, Margaret. I wish I could do more to ease your pain." Her dark hair glistened in the sunlight.

"And thanks to me, too, Margaret," Helen said indignantly.

"Always thanks to you, Helen."

Then my tears began again and I looked down at the peaceful Jesus resting in my palm.

Helen said something to June, and June responded. I was relieved to not have to talk now. Looking at the Jesus was making me remember how when rocking with pain the previous night, I had seen that the veil between the living and the dead was thinner than gauze. It was nothing at all but a veil in our minds. We are all here now, I knew, the living and the dead. You just had to have enough pain or need—or what?—and the mind's veil falls away and there you are with whomever you most need at the moment.

As I had sat on the side of my bed in the locked room, shaking with a deep, inner sobbing, my old friend Joan of Arc was suddenly there beside me, her strong arms around me. I recognized her immediately, though she looked nothing at all like the Joan of Arc that the tall and aristocratic Ingrid Bergman played in the forties movie. She was a short peasant woman with a plain, cleared-eyed face. Still I recognized her and felt her essence. Bernadette of Lourdes was there also, both women capable and compassionate, calm and accepting. Then Saint Francis of Assisi came and knelt before us. He placed his weathered hands on ours while smiling his generous smile, wit and wisdom shining in his eyes. When my own pain was so great I thought I'd be unable to bear it, I was suddenly among those who'd accepted the pain and the unfathomable sorrow so completely that they had grown beyond all human boundaries. I was being comforted by those who had developed compassion and love like nothing I'd experienced in my sane mind. Strengthened by the saints, I no longer found my pain unbearable. What mattered was that I—so flawed and broken a woman, so exhausted and depleted—rested then in the arms of saints.

I say I saw them, but I saw no one at all with my eyes. I saw with an inner vision, but a vision just as real. After I had accepted what was happening to me, the majesty and the mystery of it, I looked up and around me. As far as I could see were suffering human beings ministered to by saints devoted to the duties of love.

Then I saw my own mind as a blossom forever opening. Then I saw a Christ being taken from a cross, comforted and caressed by saints. And through this scene of Christ—a transparency like a slide—I could see another Christ being taken from a cross, and through the transparency of that image was another, then another. For as far as I could see, Christ after Christ was being taken off a cross and comforted. And still the blossom of my mind was opening.

IV

Waking or sleeping? Dream or vision? When I tried to pull it into full consciousness, it floated just beyond my grasp. Vaporous. Tantalizing. In it, we were all words—our entire lives, past, present, and future, were contained in the letters of our names and in the spaces between them. Each name was a living entity. But our names had been shattered, had exploded into millions of letters flung out into the universe like the stars that light the night sky. There were millions of As, Bs, Cs, Ds, Es, Fs, and every other letter of the alphabet. And all alphabets. Each letter had the pulse of an individual, and all the letters of that individual pulsated together. All were filled with the sole purpose of reuniting.

My eyes were dazzled by light from stars strewn across the deep blue-black sky, an enormous net to hold the letters of our names, each star a knot in that net. I stretched my arm, my fingers, as far as muscle, bone, and sinew allowed, but couldn't reach even one letter of my name.

"Margaret!" a nurse called sharply. "Margaret! Keep your mind on what you're doing. You almost spilled your milk. Eat up now before the aide comes to take the trays away."

I looked down at my plate with its boiled potatoes and gravy, slices of baked chicken, carrots, and peas. I thought of all the human beings who'd died and rotted in the earth, feeding the earthworms, the searching roots of trees and grasses. I remembered the painting by Diego Rivera in which you can see a corpse under the earth and the roots of the corn plants searching that corpse for sustenance. Life from death. My head was spinning. I could no longer tell life from death or death from life, plant from person. I could no longer tell human flesh from that of the chicken on my plate, or the boiled potatoes from boiled bones of martyrs.

"I can't eat," I told the nurse. "I feel sick to my stomach."

I pushed the tray aside.

I felt vertigo. My mind was spinning like a kaleidoscope spins before the eye until the hand stops it and a new pattern emerges. But no new pattern had yet appeared. There was only the confusion, the tumbling chaos of my mind.

V

What was I doing to make the nurse look at me with such contempt? Perhaps I was arranging things on the table in some ritualistic way like the artist Joseph Cornell arranged objects in boxes. Or like Carl Jung arranged stones in the sand. Whatever creative thing I was doing, I was doing it in order to guide my mind in its journey back to sanity.

But the nurse knew nothing of my mental, emotional, and creative processes. "Stop your foolishness," she snarled, "and clean up this mess. I've got better things to do than deal with the likes of you."

"Crazy bitch," she muttered under her breath.

I knew that it wasn't what I was doing that made her speak to me with such contempt. She spoke to me that way because to her I was a crazy woman acting crazy. I was crazy and therefore worthless.

My guts churned. I felt that I was about to lose my footing and be swept into a sea of what felt like sheer hatred. How could I endure any more of her belittling behavior and maintain any feeling of self-confidence and self-respect? After days of relating to her I had reached the limits of my endurance.

It was then that I suddenly felt the presence of Grace Clemons. Memories of her came rushing back, filling my mind and heart. I remembered her black satin slippers and her large-knuckled hands. I remembered the many stories of her life she had told me when I was a child. I'd sat in her apartment in Mrs. Forbes's house across the street from Paradise Park in Thomasville, Georgia, eating cookies and listening to her during breaks from drawing and painting with Mrs. Forbes. But in the psychiatric hospital I was no longer a child. I was a woman who, like Grace Clemons, had faced loss and betrayal, and loss again.

There was no time for the old drama, nothing of the theatrical. The woman beside me was straightforward, strong, and capable. She was there because I needed her. Without words, but clearly—mind speaking to mind—she told me that I could not afford the luxury of self-pity or self-condemnation. I could not afford the waste of guilt, the destructive power of shame. She told me that I must be strong, that no matter the obstacles in my way, no matter the losses and the grief, there was life and I must be about the business and privilege of living it.

Then I felt her strong, confident hands pressing firmly against my back, causing me to stand upright and tall. She was no longer only a presence. She was a physical force. I felt my dignity return.

Again without words, Mrs. Clemons reminded me that she would always be with me. "Remember the touch of my hands on your back. When you feel weak, my hands will be there to remind you of your own inner strength. Walk with dignity, my dear. No matter what anyone ever says, remember that the most important thing you can do is to solidly and forevermore *be*, to simply and profoundly *be* Margaret."

VI

The river could have been the creation of Hieronymus Bosch. As I looked into it, I saw that the dark, choppy water was filled with pieces of human beings—streams of bloody entrails, a heart throbbing rapidly in a cold current, a leg, an arm, a wild-eyed head bobbing in the murky water, and many hands and feet propelled frantically by the innate impulse to reunite.

I watched the reunion of parts of people as they struggled to find ways to fit together again. Others required the services of doctors and their attendants from the enormous hospital on the riverbank. The doctors and associates went about their awful, miraculous work with calm, intelligent dedication.

Piece by piece the parts of me found one another.

An aide set my lunch tray on the table before me, a low table stacked with old magazines and boxes of games, not a regular dining table like the patients permitted to leave the locked ward ate at in the dining room. I poked at my food but ate nothing. Looking at it made me feel as sick as looking into the river.

"You've not eaten your lunch," the aide said when she came back to remove the tray. "Do you want to keep it for a while longer?"

"No," I replied. "But thank you for asking." I did not tell her that I couldn't eat because each bite felt like taking a bite out of a human being. All life felt like human life. Or maybe all life was God, and everything had consciousness. Then it seemed to me that I was groping for something too vast for my brain to comprehend. When I tried to grasp it, to articulate it, my thoughts felt like only a snarl of confusion, like the snarl of yarn I'd knotted. But what about the many-colored face of Jesus in the yarn? *Focus*, I told myself, *on the many-colored face of Jesus.*

Experiences in dreams and experiences while awake were beginning to differentiate themselves. My shattered self was starting to come together once more. But I still had a distance to go before I had the clarity and strength necessary to face the doctors and demand that I be released, even against their orders.

PART FOUR

"Hold Fast to Dreams"

Chapter Twenty

I

1981

DR. TURCOTTE USHERED ME INTO HIS OFFICE, WHERE I SAT IN MY USUAL chair across from him. The coffee table, with its clutter of old magazines, books, candles, papers, and boxes of Kleenex, stood between us.

Before taking his seat, the doctor went to the door and called Helen to join us. She came in and sat in the chair next to mine. Dr. Turcotte sat down in his usual chair and reached to pick up a burgundy-colored candle from the floor. He handed it across the table to Helen while looking at me.

"I've given Helen a gift, but I have nothing for you. Are you jealous?"

Why was he trying to provoke me? I remembered how a person who knew him well once told me that she believed he had always wanted to orchestrate a crime of passion. Maybe she was right. He certainly was trying to upset me.

Helen looked at the candle.

"A gift for Helen and nothing for you. What do you think about that?" he asked.

"I suppose it depends on where she lights it."

I understood his game then, his intent to upset me by showing me that he had gained firm control over Helen; that he had wiped out any loyalty she might have had toward me. Even before it happened, I knew the outcome.

He reached across the table and handed Helen a star-shaped candleholder. "Light the candle here, Helen," he said in the same commanding tone he'd used with me in Newport when he'd gestured with his arm and ordered me to come to his bed.

Without hesitation Helen put the candle in the holder, picked up a book of matches from the table, tore one off, struck it, and lit the candle.

"I see, Dr. Turcotte," I said, knowing that he knew that I'd seen through his manipulations, that the veil of denial had finally dropped from my eyes. I crushed my cigarette in an ashtray and got up. Glancing briefly at his self-satisfied face, I left the office.

I knew my relationship with Helen was over. Driving back to Amherst, I thought about it. When Helen had come to stay with me in 1980, shortly after Chris and I moved to the apartment on Dickinson Street, she'd complained constantly of being cold. Even in the warm apartment she wore a wool scarf around her neck.

The doctor explained that she was so cold because she'd been denied affection from her parents. He encouraged me to put my arms around her and hold her as much as possible. Which I did. Eventually she began to sleep in my bed with me. After sleeping with me for over a year, she began to try to seduce me. One night, during a brief psychotic episode, I gave in to her. I can't say whether or not I would have given in to her had I not been psychotic. I can say that, looking back, I sometimes struggle with deep feelings of regret, though I am well aware that regret is a not helpful feeling to nurture.

At the time, our age difference wasn't a problem for me. I was a fan of Charlie Chaplin, who had married Oona O'Neill when she was eighteen and he was fifty-four. And when I was fifteen my boyfriend was nearly twice my age. Then there were Chris and Jim.

I had grown to love Helen, though not in the way I'd loved and still loved Suzanne. The doctor told me that Helen had seduced me into a sexual relationship as an act of revenge toward Suzanne. They had known each other before I had met either, and Helen harbored hurt feelings toward Suzanne, who hadn't given her the support she'd needed when Helen was in high school.

II

I sat at the dining room table and worked on a large watercolor I was painting from sketches I'd done from the roof garden of the hotel where Chris and I had stayed in Puebla de los Angeles, Mexico, in 1969. I still remember the exquisite pleasure of mixing the paints, pigment and water pooling on the white enamel palette of my paint box. The skyline of the city is filled with domes of churches, most of which are topped by crosses. At least my painting is filled with them, and after all these years, the painting is more real to me than any image of the city I might hold someplace in my memory. In my painting, the volcano Popocatépetl rises in the distance, while inside the volcano lies a sleeping woman with long hair made of flames. In a pale purple and indigo sky stands a transparent cross with a transparent angel blowing its trumpet toward the woman as if to wake her.

I no longer remember which of us began to destroy my things first. I only remember the night as the end of our lives together in Amherst.

Helen and I were both psychotic.

There was shattered glass everywhere. I pushed the living Christmas tree in its redwood planter out the door, tumbling it down the back steps onto the snow. Helen picked up the TV from the kitchen counter, lugged it to the back door, and heaved it out, shattering its screen. I took the expensive vase that Chris and Dr. Turcotte's daughter Amy had given me for Christmas and hurled it out the door, sending it skidding across the ice-encrusted snow to rest unbroken against the hedge that marked the end of the backyard.

Then Helen and I stood facing each other in the kitchen. Looking into my eyes, she said that she saw vision after vision unrolling. "My life!" she screamed. "My whole life is in your eyes!"

Not only was Helen psychotic, she was also sick of my depression as well as of me. Now that she had the relationship with Dr. Turcotte that she wanted, I no longer mattered.

Woman in a volcano, I thought, looking at my painting. My head spun, the pressure mounting until I thought that mere bone was not strong enough to keep my brain from exploding and spewing itself all over my dining room.

I picked up a large stone from my collection in a wooden bowl on the dining table. I hurled it at my pen-and-ink drawing of Emily Dickinson that hung over the dining table. The glass over it shattered to small jagged shards, which scattered on the table and floor. I took another stone and slung it at a framed etching of my father, done by the artist who did the drawings for my first book. Another stone shattered the glass covering an O'Keeffe print of an iris.

When Chris walked into the room and looked at me with disgust, I took one of the Wedgwood cups that my beloved Aunt Curtis had given me and threw it against the wall next to him—not *at* him—with all the strength of my adrenaline-flooded body.

Did Helen or I rip the painting of the woman in a volcano down the middle and throw it on the dining room floor with all my other ripped and shattered possessions?

I wasn't aware when Chris and Amy had left the house to call Dr. Turcotte, who made out the papers to have me committed to the state hospital. He called the Amherst police to take me there. I was too absorbed in shattering glass and destroying my paintings and drawings.

Shortly the police arrived.

A policeman put handcuffs on me, while a policewoman silently watched. The doctor had evidently asked June to come with them. She stood beside me in the living room. When the policeman tried to get me out the door and into his car, my body went rigid as a steel rod. He dragged me across the street and tried to force me into the car. I struggled against him as hard as I could.

Of course he won. I gave up and sat down on the backseat. June went around to the other side and got in beside me. She sat upright and silent, hands folded in her lap, eyes straight ahead.

On the tense ride to Northampton State Hospital, Dr. Turcotte's words repeated themselves in my head. "Margaret, your anger is beautiful. Repeat after me: 'Margaret, your anger is beautiful.' Words he'd instructed John to repeat over and over, year after year. Words repeated like the click of the trigger of John's gun night after night.

Then the words in my mind changed: *"Repeat after me: I'll always love you. Repeat after me: I'll always love* you." Words from Gordon Jenkins's *Manhattan Tower,* a record I'd cherished as a teenager dreaming of being an artist in Greenwich Village. *"Repeat after me: I'll always love you,"* I heard in my mind, and I knew it was true that I would always love John. Not in the ways he wanted me to love him, just as he didn't love me in the ways I wanted to be loved. But I knew that despite his faults and mine, despite the anger and the pain, I would always love John even if I never saw him again.

When we arrived at the hospital an orderly got a wheelchair because I refused to walk. Riding, I noticed blood on my right foot. I was barefooted, and the side of my foot was bleeding where it had been cut as I'd been dragged from my apartment and across the street to the police car.

I sat mesmerized by the long red slash as June checked me in to the hospital. Then she was gone and I was alone in that nightmare. The feeling of the ward was familiar—the stench of human bodies, pine oil, stale cigarette smoke. Then, for a flash, it wasn't a ward at all. It was an underground cage where hundreds and hundreds of us had been crammed into that one small space. Hitler wasn't dead at all but had escaped and was concealed someplace in South America from which he ruled this inferno.

Then it was the hospital again and an enraged woman rushed toward me. She grabbed me in her strong hands, shouting words I couldn't understand while she began ripping my clothes off. I yelled for help. Yelled again. Finally, two orderlies wrestled her from me. I went to my assigned bed and sat down, trembling with shock.

How easy it had been for Dr. Turcotte to simply call and have me committed. How easy to avoid facing me. I was filled with fury. I was no longer his patient. I didn't know how I would get away, but I knew I had to. My life and sanity depended on it.

The next morning Helen came with a box of chocolates and a change of clothes. I told her that I wouldn't tolerate being in that nightmare of a hospital again. I asked her to tell Dr. Turcotte I wanted out *now*. I sat on the bed cramming my mouth with chocolates, not bothering to say goodbye as she left.

In the afternoon Dr. Turcotte came with Chris, Amy, and Helen. I was released from the hospital and walked with the group to my car. Helen must have driven it to the office to pick up the doctor and Chris and Amy. Now she sat in the front seat with the doctor, while I sat in the back with the others. I didn't even ask where we were going. I was just relieved to be out of the hospital. I was also in shock. Trees and cars rushed past us. We crossed the Connecticut border and kept going.

Was it in Hartford that we stopped? I have a sense of a city in my memory. Dr. Turcotte drove through a pair of tall gates and down a long drive. He was going to have me committed to a Connecticut hospital! I followed him into the hospital without protest. Chris, Helen, and Amy walked with us.

Dr. Turcotte talked briefly to the admitting psychiatrist, who asked me to come with him into an examination room. I sat on the edge of an exam table while he took my blood pressure, tested my reflexes, shone a light into my eyes, and looked closely into each. Then he pulled up a chair and asked me the predictable questions. Yes, I knew what day it was. Yes, I knew who was president of the United States. Then briefly we engaged in ordinary conversation. Afterward, he shook my hand and accompanied me to the waiting room, where he told Dr. Turcotte that he could see no reason to admit me.

We spent the night in a Connecticut motel. Helen, Amy, and I shared a room. I was quiet. My voice was slipping away from me like it had done after Newport and so many times when I was living with John, upset and afraid. Sometimes then I'd only been able to speak in a whisper for six weeks or more.

Was this happening again?

I took a hot bath while Helen sat on the closed toilet seat and talked with me. The conversation dissolved in the fog of steam from my bath and an emotional exhaustion that dulled my senses. Helen gave me a glass of water and asked me to please take some pills Dr. Turcotte had given her for me. Without arguing I took them.

Then I got out of the tub, put on my pajamas, went to bed, and slept a drugged and dreamless sleep.

III

The next morning we drove back to Northampton and parked in front of the building where the doctor had his office. He and Helen got out of the car. Amy got out of the backseat and, taking the driver's seat, drove to the large old rambling house that served as home to Dr. Turcotte and his wife and children, along with various patients who sometimes stayed there while he was treating them. Sometimes Chris stayed there also. That past October, John and I had signed papers making Dr. Turcotte Chris's legal guardian in order to make it possible for him to attend school in Northampton, rather than in Amherst, where he felt suicidal. We didn't expect him to attend school often in Northampton, but we were hoping he would be able to drop out of school when he reached the legal age of sixteen. The legal arrangement, though, did not affect the frequency of his stays with the Turcottes. He came and went as he pleased.

Amy parked the car, put the key in her pocket, and got out along with Chris. They expected me to come with them into the house. I got out and followed slowly while fumbling in my purse for my car keys. Finding them, I turned quickly, walked back to the car, and slid under the steering wheel. I called out calmly, "I'm just going to the art-supply shop to get a tube of paint." I quickly started the car and drove off. Before either could say anything, I was on my way. But not to Pierce's paint shop.

I headed to Route 9, breathing more easily as the miles accumulated between Dr. Turcotte and me. At the Hadley Howard Johnson's, I pulled up to the outdoor public phone. I got out of the car, put a dime in the slot, and dialed Suzanne's number.

"Margaret?"

My voice was hoarse and weak. I could hardly speak above a whisper. "Yes, it's me, Suzanne."

"Oh God. Just yesterday I'd finally given up on ever seeing you again."

I asked Suzanne to meet me at the College Inn in South Hadley. That was the most unlikely place I could think of that anyone might look for me. She heard the urgency in my voice and promised to meet me.

I hung up the phone and headed for South Hadley. I had no idea what I would do, but I had to find a way to escape Dr. Turcotte for good, and I needed Suzanne's help and support. I parked in front of the drugstore, now long since burned down just as the College Inn was burned down. I walked through the stone-covered patio with its umbrella-protected tables and into the inn, where I took a seat in the small sitting room.

Now that I'd stopped rushing, I realized how drugged I still felt from the medication Helen had given me the night before. I'd noticed a slur in my whisper of a voice. I needed to get the drugs out of my system. I ordered an English muffin and two glasses of water.

I drained one glass and had hardly begun to eat when Suzanne appeared. All the old familiar feelings rushed back when I stood to embrace her. How hard we'd both tried to turn our backs and walk away from the problematical and painful love between us. But no matter what different directions we'd taken in our efforts to terminate our relationship, we always ended up right back where we started—in each other's arms.

Suzanne ordered a cup of coffee from the waitress who'd rushed over when she saw Suzanne joining me at the table. We were the only customers in the small room. Suzanne poured cream into the cup of coffee the waitress set before her.

Looking at her familiar hand performing its familiar motions, I felt like crying. Then my story began to spill from my mouth, my voice grown stronger, words rushing out like water bursting through a dam.

Suzanne wanted to take me to a therapist friend of hers in Northampton. I would follow her car in mine. Together the three of us would talk about what to do to protect me from Dr. Turcotte.

IV

Suzanne's friend welcomed us into her enormous old house. After we sat down in the living room, Suzanne began to tell her the story as she understood it. Overdrugged and uncomfortable, I said, "I'm sorry, I can't sit still, and I really need water."

"Yes," Suzanne's friend agreed. "I think you should drink all the water you can and flush the medication out of your system. And bread. I think you should try to eat. You've really been overmedicated."

I followed her into her kitchen, where she gave me a tall glass of water and put a loaf of bread on the table.

"Just help yourself. And I think the walking is good for you, too."

She joined Suzanne in the living room while I walked through kitchen, dining room, entrance hall, and living room over and over. The more I walked, drank, and peed, the more like myself I felt. I was finally able to sit down.

Having seen Dr. Turcotte harass the patient he had been in love with, and knowing his tenacious grasp on people, I couldn't imagine him accepting my termination of therapy. I could imagine him encouraging everyone in his group to pressure me constantly. Or worse, I could imagine him finding a way to have me committed to some psychiatric hospital forever.

"You need police protection."

I don't remember if Suzanne or her friend made the statement, but hearing it upset me even as I knew I had to accept the truth of it. My poem "Soap Opera" had already recognized it. Police protection.

Suddenly everything felt surreal.

We called several of my friends and my daughter-in-law, Mary, all of whom met Suzanne and me at the police station. After stating my reason for being there, the policeman who'd listened to me assigned my case to Detective Richard Andrews. He was a tall, big-built man with dark hair and strong features. A clerk brought him the account of my seizure and incarceration made out by the Amherst Police Department. He glanced over the papers, then laid them facedown on his desk. I told him about Dr. Turcotte's trying to commit me to a Connecticut hospital.

I told him about Newport.

"Did he penetrate you?"

"I don't know. I kept passing out."

"Try to remember if he penetrated you in any way."

"I really can't say that he did. I remember the struggling and the passing out. I remember regaining consciousness to find him on top of me again."

"And?" Detective Andrews asked.

"I remember how deeply and painfully he dug his hands into my body. I didn't understand what he was trying to do. I was so confused and frightened."

The phone on Detective Andrews's desk rang.

He listened intently. "I'll be right down," he said, and excused himself.

Now that it had come to this, I felt relieved. And I had friends supporting me.

Detective Andrews returned, pulled his desk chair closer to us, and sat down.

"That call was from Judge Allen's office. Turcotte sent a couple of his people over to take out papers to have you committed to the state hospital. We just stopped the papers from being processed."

According to Dr. Turcotte, the district attorney had been trying for years to find a way to put a stop to his practice. He'd said many times that the police were after him because of his independent, rebellious, unconventional nature. I'd heard that a judge had felt that justice hadn't been served in a case involving Dr. Turcotte and an ex-patient, and there were several area therapists who claimed that he had damaged their patients. I wasn't at all surprised that the police welcomed me with open arms. Maybe I was their answer.

But I couldn't remember if he'd actually penetrated me. Would penetration have been that much worse for me than the endless hours of wrestling, fighting, drugs, fear, and confusion? What he'd done to me had nearly destroyed me, but what the police needed was a technical rape charge.

"We have to have a charge against him in order to have the legal power to protect you."

Then a friend spoke up. "Well, I know that according to John Robison, he has a record of insurance covering recorded visits when he was on vacation."

I could see Detective Andrews's brain go into first gear. Behind his brown eyes I could see all his training and experience coming together in an attempt to devise a plan to finally put Dr. Turcotte in his place. Could I give him names of other patients? I told him the names of those patients I knew. Could I give him dates of office visits that he'd reported when I'd not really had appointments?

"But he saw me many more times than recorded on any insurance form." Then thinking of Newport, I added angrily: "He saw me many more times than I wish he had."

"It's better that you don't take the stand anyway. Everything could deteriorate into a circus of a sanity trial between the two of you. He's damn clever with his Bible clutched against his damaged heart. We'll begin the investigation of possible insurance fraud. In the meantime, let me know about any communication you have with anyone connected to him." Then he added, as if an afterthought, "I think it would be a good idea for you to be examined by a psychiatrist now so we could have that on the record in case Turcotte tries anything." He suggested a conventional psychiatrist respected in the community. When I agreed, he called the doctor and made an appointment.

The meeting was over. I drove to South Hadley, where I stayed with Mary and John Elder in their home.

The next day Suzanne went with me to the psychiatrist. We sat together on chairs across from his desk. He began the familiar list of questions. I answered thoughtfully, politely. I felt condescended to but held my tongue. At last he looked me in the eyes.

"Would you say that you believe someone is out to get you?"

I returned his steady stare. "The police tell me that this is true," I replied.

He put his pen down.

The interview was over.

V

We were sitting in the assistant district attorney's office, and Detective Andrews was asking me questions about dates recorded for my visits to Dr. Turcotte. Was I in town on those dates? Did I go to the appointments as recorded? I responded as accurately as possible, given my difficulty remembering dates. I had no interest in having Dr. Turcotte charged with insurance fraud. I knew he had spent more time with patients than Blue Cross would ever reimburse him for. I just wanted to get away from him, and I saw no other way except by getting police protection.

"You're a threat to Turcotte," the assistant district attorney said, repeating Detective Andrews's concern. "He'd like to lock you away in some back ward forever."

"If the police should come to commit you to the state hospital," Detective Andrews instructed me, "ask them to contact me through the highway patrol office. If they won't do that, just go with them quietly."

I remembered being handcuffed, my body rigid against the police car. Was it true, as the Amherst police report stated, that I had tried to grab the pistol out of the officer's holster? With handcuffs on? I only remember the brute force of the man, the coarseness of the fabric of his uniform, the strong smell of leather.

"Remember," Detective Andrews emphasized again, "just go with them quietly this time," he said with a smile, a gentle tease. "We've already drawn up the papers for your release."

I'd heard from Dr. Turcotte about the priest who had fled after his accusations, and of how he believed his first patient was going to kill him. Someone had always seemed to be out to get him in one way or another. Now I was that someone, and I was not going to back down or flee. But I'd been afraid that he would succeed in getting me committed someplace for good. The assistant district attorney had confirmed my fears, and for that I was grateful.

The last time I'd driven Dr. Turcotte home from a meeting in Amherst, I'd taken the back way to Northampton, going past the old Hadley cemetery across from a cornfield, and through the flat farmland stretching to the Connecticut River. The fields with row after row of green, a scene I loved, gave me no comfort, no relief, no cushioning from his words.

His voice was intense. He'd seen the movie *Magic*, a thriller about a ventriloquist who murdered people with his dummy. "After seeing that movie I realized I have a killer running around loose inside of me," he said excitedly. "If people knew what goes on in me, they would be very afraid."

I thought of those words when Detective Andrews handed me

Dr. Turcotte's latest newsletter. For years he'd been writing newsletters on whatever topic he was focused on at the time—world peace, the role of fathers in the family, the importance of expressing anger—and reporting on his latest projects, ideas, and experiences. He sent his newsletters to patients, priests, public officials, and friends.

Detective Andrews pointed out an article that Dr. Turcotte had written about me and my family. In it, he wrote that I was suicidal and would be found dead by the side of the road by my own hand. *I'll not fulfill his prophecy any more than Mary had burned down her house, killing herself and the children, or the priest had burned the parish house as he'd predicted,* I thought.

VI

I knew I could never go back to the Dickinson house. My friend and writing student Jean Sanders rented a truck for me and got my things from the apartment. She stored them in the barn on the farm that she and her partner, Nancy Bullard, owned. Nancy found me a small apartment in Belchertown and, with the help of friends, I moved into it immediately.

My new life had begun.

VII

After we met with the assistant district attorney, Detective Andrews walked with me to my car. He unbuttoned the jacket of his suit so that the gun in the holster strapped to his chest was clearly visible— a message to any of the Turcotte group we might meet. As we stepped down from the curb he took my elbow and escorted me across the street to my car.

He opened the door and I slid under the wheel. "Thanks," I said, fumbling in my purse for my key. I found it, and put it in the ignition.

"Remember," Detective Andrews said, "if you hear anything from anyone in that group, let me know at once." He handed me his card. "I've written my home phone number on the back. I don't usually give it out, but I want to be sure I'm available any time you need me."

"I really appreciate this," I said, putting the card in my wallet, where I would keep it for years.

"Glad to do it. You've had enough trouble. You don't need any more." He gave the roof of my car a friendly pat and raised his hand in a farewell gesture before turning to walk back to the courthouse.

It was a great relief to finally have police protection. Still, there were phone calls in the middle of the night: "Just calling to see if you're still alive. I hear you are. Fucking shame." *Click.* There had been the time one of the Turcotte group stood up and yelled at me during a public poetry reading I gave at the Jones Library in Amherst. And another telling the police I was supervising John Elder and Mary in building a bomb to blow up the Turcotte house.

But now a Belchertown police car was circling my apartment building several times a day. I felt safer until a Belchertown policeman banged on my door in the middle of the night, intent on taking me to Northampton State Hospital at Dr. Turcotte's request. I persuaded him to call Detective Andrews, who told him the Belchertown police were there to protect me, not to incarcerate me.

Now that the investigation of Dr. Turcotte had begun, the police could protect me as a potential witness in a possible insurance-fraud case. Yet he and his followers had not severed their relationships with me. All too often when I drove to the post office to get my mail I had something from one of his followers. I got a postcard from Helen accusing me of being a liar. One day I got a postcard from Dr. Turcotte. I sat in my car in front of the post office and read it. The picture was a pencil reproduction of *A Section of the Magnificent Mohegan Bluffs,* and the description on the back of the card stated, "With treacherous shoals and rocks below, where many sailing ships have met their doom." Above this description Dr. Turcotte had written: "Good Morning America!" Under the description he'd written: "8:00 A.M." Beneath this was a quote from scripture: "I am the vine; you are a branch." The period at the end of the sentence was a large red circle.

I laid the card on the car seat beside me. My heart pounded. Every time I got one of the cards or letters condemning me and using scriptures to back their claims, I succumbed to a feeling of guilt at least briefly, and had to fight my way up to a feeling of self-confidence. Had I been wrong in going to the police? Had I listened to Suzanne and her therapist friend's advice and not my own mind and heart? I agonized. Then I again thought of Newport.

It was years before I could talk about that experience without intense emotion building in my body until I was shaking inside and out. No matter how many times I told the story of Newport, the pressure built inside me to tell it once more. Had it been necessary for him to penetrate my body for him to be guilty of raping me? Wasn't it enough that he had plundered and tormented me? Even if he had penetrated me and I'd remembered, in court it would have been my word against his, the word of the patient against that of the doctor.

"It would be better if you didn't have to appear in court," Detective Andrews had said. I agreed that it would be better to avoid a sideshow with the doctor. I still regretted that my getting police protection resulted in the insurance-fraud charge when my own complaint toward him was his sexual assault. But more than regret, I felt the excitement of anticipation as I looked forward to beginning my life anew.

VIII
1983

Looking back, I realize that my new life as a teacher of children had to begin in Holyoke. I'd been drawn to that city for months after hearing of the icons in a Greek Orthodox church there. One Sunday I went to a service there and sat alone in a pew, quietly taking in the many icons of saints along with those of Jesus and Mary. The smell of incense filled the air.

The stylized figures created by a master icon painter surrounded me on all sides with their rich colors, the thick lines of their features, and their long fingers, full robes, and shining halos. Hearing nothing of what was said, I took in line after line, shape after shape, color after color, filling a hunger deep inside me.

Then the service was over.

Walking back to my car, I stooped to pick up a perfect white bird feather at my feet.

I went back to Holyoke one day the next week, this time to browse in some of the secondhand shops I'd noticed. The first two shops offered no treasures to attract my attention. In the third shop, an old woman, her wild gray hair barely restrained by the few hairpins poked into it, sat behind a counter, crocheting a doily. I asked if she had any rosaries or religious medals for sale. She said she thought she did, then disappeared, shuffling along in her house slippers.

I heard her rummaging through one drawer and then another while I looked with amazement at the chairs piled to the ceiling against the far wall, and the incredible clutter that filled every inch of the little store.

When she finally returned, she was clutching a cigar box to her breast. She set it on the counter and opened the lid. Inside were medals of Saint Jude, Bernadette of Lourdes, and the Virgin Mary; a child's rosary; several crosses and crucifixes; and a small photograph of a little girl smiling out from the oval shape she'd been cut into in order to fit a frame no longer there. Something about the eyes of that child smiling at me from the nineteenth century attracted me, and I placed the photograph on the counter along with several other pictures of children from the nineteenth century. I also picked out several of the medals as well as the child's delicate rosary and several crosses and crucifixes. "How much would these cost?" I asked.

Whatever price she quoted was so low that I added a few more medals to my collection. Then I paid her.

"Thank you," I said taking the small, crumpled brown bag that she held out to me. "Thank you very much."

"Bless you," she responded. Sitting down on her stool, she picked up her crochet hook and began to crochet as I turned to leave.

Driving home I thought of possible ways to use my new treasures. I wanted to create three-dimensional collages in wooden cigar boxes I'd collected.

Home, I sat down in my reading chair and gently slid my new treasures out of the bag and onto the table beside me. Then I began to examine each with care. I was especially drawn to an old crucifix. The cross still held its shape, but the Jesus hanging on it was so worn down that only the vague shape of the body was discernable. All detail must have been rubbed away by the thumb of someone who had caressed it for many years while praying. In my heart I felt the presence of an old woman. Had she prayed for her sick husband as he lay dying? Had she prayed for her children? Had she prayed for enough food to feed them? Had she prayed for herself, that she would have the strength and wisdom to raise them?

I laid the crucifix back on the table. I wouldn't be using it in a collage. I wouldn't be using any of the things I'd bought that day in a collage. They all felt special in a way I was unable to understand.

I looked into the eyes of the little girl smiling out from the oval shape, and of the other children from the nineteenth century. They were children from Holyoke's past, and yet I was as moved as if they were living, our eyes connecting, and my heart moved beyond words. I had no idea that within weeks I would begin to work with children in Holyoke, opening their hearts and minds to writing poetry as they opened my heart to them.

Chapter Twenty-one

I

1983

TWO DAYS BEFORE I BEGAN THE JOB OF LEADING POETRY WORKSHOPS FOR the two hundred children in the Donahue Elementary School, my friend Nancy Bullard and I climbed a hill that rose beyond the old apple orchard on her farm. Brilliant sunlight illuminating the August green of the trees illuminated my spirit as well.

I turned to Nancy. "I need a part-time job, and I need it to be outside the academic community," I said with the clarity that had come to me as we'd walked.

When I got home from Nancy's, Suzanne called and told me that an elementary school in Holyoke was looking for a playwright to replace the one who'd resigned from an arts project at the last minute. Would I be interested in applying? Though no playwright, I felt that the position was exactly what I needed. Ideas of things to do with the children flooded my mind.

The next morning I met with the principal and several of the teachers. The school had never had any sort of arts program before, and the teachers had a lot of questions. I answered with the confidence of someone who had a long history of working with children, though I'd only led writing workshops for adults.

The following day I was in the school as the first poet-in-residence.

In the hall, I met my first two students: Luis and Ramon.

"Are you a teacher?" Luis asked as I raised my head from the spout of the water fountain.

"Yes," I answered. "I'm here to teach you something about poetry."

"Po-what?" Ramon asked, puzzled.

"Poetry," I repeated slowly, searching for a way to make a concrete, understandable thing of the word. Then I remembered seeing a poster-sized copy of Langston Hughes's poem "Dreams" tacked up in the library.

I walked with the boys to the library, where I pointed to the hand-lettered poem. "This is a poem," I said, and asked Luis to read the first verse aloud:

> *Hold fast to dreams*
> *For if dreams die*
> *Life is a broken-winged bird*
> *That cannot fly.*

"Do you have a dream?" I asked.

"I want to be a policeman," Luis replied.

I asked Ramon to read the verse aloud.

"Have you ever felt like a broken-winged bird?"

"No. But once I had a broken collarbone," Ramon responded.

"We're talking about simile, about one thing being like another," I explained. "A broken collarbone is a little like a broken wing."

I turned back to Luis. "Have you ever felt like a broken-winged bird?"

"No. But I felt very sad when my father died."

The three of us sat down on the carpet while Luis talked about his father's death. "I talked to him the day before he died. I loved him very much. I talked to him that day, and then he was dead."

"You might want to write about your father and how much you loved him."

"And how he died," Luis added.

"Yes," I agreed softly. "And how he died."

As we sat talking, a teacher walked by, glancing our way.

"That's our teacher," Ramon told me.

Luis smiled at me. "She thinks you're teaching us."

Ramon smiled.

I smiled, too. "I am," I said. "These are some of the things poetry is about."

II

I felt fortunate to work with a group of children who had few if any strong preconceptions about poetry. If they knew little about poetry, I knew little about them and their city. I did know something about writing. One of the most important things I'd discovered was that my strongest images came when I opened myself to the world around and within me through my senses. Once a fragrance coming through an open window was enough to evoke my book-length poem *Red Creek*. Often simply describing a visual image has become a poem in itself.

I began teaching in the Donahue School by guiding each class in writing a group poem that required the children to use their senses. I instructed them to lay their heads on their desks, close their eyes, and imagine that they could move around anyplace in Holyoke in an instant. Then I called the children's attention to their senses. What did they see? What did they hear or smell, touch or taste? Soon another hand went up, then another. When no more hands were raised, and I felt the poem had come to a natural ending, I asked the children to open their eyes while I read the poem aloud.

They were excited to hear their group poems that served as my introduction to the children and their city, and their introduction to poetry and to me. I learned that one boy's little sister's hair stood straight up before she brushed it down in the morning; that someone else's sister was pregnant; that one boy's uncle worked in a paper mill, while his father worked making guns. I learned the names of some of the streets, and that Saint Vincent Nursing Home was in Holyoke. I learned that the children were aware of food stamps, robberies, house fires, welfare, SSI.

By the end of my first week in Holyoke, I had led all two hundred students in the school of fourth-, fifth-, and sixth-graders in writing their first poems. A couple of teachers commented that they had never seen the children so quiet and involved. I was more surprised at myself than at the children. I'd always found relating in groups difficult. Even small groups had intimidated me, but over the years I'd learned to lead workshops for adults, though there were usually no more than twelve in a group. Now I was leading workshops for twenty to twenty-five children, and I felt more relaxed than ever. I felt confidently at home.

"What's poetry?" I asked the children. "Something that rhymes" was the most frequent answer I got at first. The truest answer came from Greg Thompson, a boy who, raising his arm for my attention, said: "Poetry is something that comes from the bottom of your heart."

The children surprised me with their enthusiasm for writing poetry. Everyone was writing. Poems were tacked up on bulletin boards, published in the Holyoke and Springfield newspapers. The principal had to order more composition books. "Would you like to hear a poem?" a child would ask a complete stranger visiting the school. One newspaper reporter asked a boy what he wanted to be when he grew up. "A fireman and a poet," the boy replied without hesitation. Poetry belonged everywhere, to everyone. The excitement was contagious.

To have their personal feelings and experiences valued and put into a form to be shared was life-giving to the children. It was also life-giving to me. I opened my heart to the girls and boys of the

Donahue School, and in that opening I opened to my strength and power as a teacher. I was learning more about who I was.

Sometimes, when a child seemed to be struggling to express himself, I would spend time alone with that child, asking questions and taking dictation myself when it seemed too much for him or her to try to both express himself and write. This was the case with Jesus Mendez. When we were alone together in the library, he told me the poem he wanted to write while I did the actual writing.

He wanted to write a poem about his baby sister. "She was the prettiest thing I ever saw," he said sadly. Then he told me about going into the baby's room. He described how his mother lifted her hand and how it fell back on the bed. The tension was palpable.

"The baby was dead."

I worked to write with a calm, steady hand, but my heart was racing. When Jesus went back to his classroom, I sat in the library, remembering his words: "She was the prettiest thing I ever saw." I remembered how beautiful my long-dead sister's eyes were. When Jesus told me about the baby's hand falling back onto the bed, and that she was dead, I was once again in the hospital with Mother and Harriet. As I wrote Jesus's poem, my head was filled with my own mother's words: *Ring for the nurse, Margaret. Harriet's dead.* Working with Jesus had reopened that old wound, and I went back into the pain.

When I got home that day, I again wrote about my sister's near death. Again I cried. Listening to the children was an act of healing for me, just as it was for them. I remembered the dream I'd had years before, that all of human history was stored in my mind. In the dream I was panic-stricken that history would begin to unroll in my bloodstream and my heart would burst with the pain. "Don't worry," a voice in the dream had told me. "History will unroll in your heart only as your heart grows large enough to hold it." Teaching the children at the Donahue School, I felt my heart growing larger every day.

———

III

I could no longer endure the relationship with Suzanne. Both when I was leaving my marriage and later when I was leaving Dr. Turcotte, Suzanne was my major emotional support. For Suzanne, I was the major catalyst for change in both her marriage and her relationship with her mother. I don't claim this as truth, only as my interpretation.

I never said that I wanted her to leave Bob. But if she loved me as much as she said she did, if I mattered as much as she claimed, I wanted the respect that love deserved. *When she realizes how she's hurt me, when she finally fully claims her love for me, things will be different,* I told myself. But if Suzanne had entered into our relationship fully, if she had given the relationship the respect and attention it required, she well might have lost her marriage. And above all else, she wanted to keep her marriage intact.

"Do you realize how much pain I've gone through for you? Do you think you're the only one in pain?" Her voice still reverberates in my brain. And yes, she did go through pain. I knew that. But enduring pain solved nothing for either of us.

"Married woman who will neither stay or go," I wrote in a poem at the time. I wrote two books of poetry to Suzanne and destroyed them, crushing poem after poem in my fist. I wrote and discarded page after page of journal entries about the relationship. Yet we continued the same old tug-of-war.

I thought again of how, when I was a girl, Mother's friend Francis told Mother about people asking how she could love her brain-damaged daughter, Kate, with her wild green eyes, nightmarish noises, and violent stomping. Francis always answered that she loved the daughter Kate could have been.

What about the daughter she had? What about Kate? I asked myself many times over the years. Thinking about this once again, I looked at my relationship with Suzanne in a new light—*that light.* I was mourning the relationship I imagined possible with Suzanne, not the relationship we had.

Nothing was ever the same after that.

The deepest truth I knew was that the relationship with Suzanne could never work, and in time I found the strength to turn away. Turning away from Suzanne was a major step toward being kinder to myself. I look back with sadness at the pain that some if not all of our children suffered during the years of the relationship that Suzanne and I loved, fought, worked, and struggled through. Yet, given who and where we were emotionally then, I see no other way we could have lived our lives.

There was always a place where Suzanne and I failed at understanding each other, and as frustrating as it was, it never canceled the love we felt.

Chapter Twenty-two

I RECENTLY CAME ACROSS A PHOTOGRAPH TAKEN IN 1985, ON MY FIRST trip back to Georgia since 1969. It was a simple snapshot of Mother and Mercer on a bridge of gray weathered boards that spanned a body of water in the Okefenokee Swamp. They're crossing the bridge, their backs turned to me. They were walking away from me when I snapped their image with my camera.

How unexpectedly the significance of a thing can change. Mother and Mercer are crossing the weathered gray bridge, and now both of them are dead. Unprepared to see this image of my mother and brother walking away from me, I felt my heart plummet, then fill with emotion.

When Mother had asked me if there were special things I wanted to do while I was in Georgia visiting them, I mentioned going to the Okefenokee Swamp. From as far back as I could remember, I'd been fascinated by it, but I had never been there. Mother's friend Vereen Bell had written a book about it titled *Swamp Water* before he went off to World War II and got killed. Every time we drove past his house in Thomasville, I thought about him drowned in his crashed plane in the Pacific Ocean, starving on a raft with the rest of the crew, or being eaten by sharks.

I was six years old in 1941 when the movie *Swamp Water*, starring Walter Brennan, Anne Baxter, and Dana Andrews, was released. It was terribly exciting to see a movie made from a book written by my own mother's friend. It was also exciting to see a place in Georgia made into a Hollywood movie.

But the main reason I wanted to go to the Okefenokee was my intense fascination with the swamp itself, old and primitive, mysterious and wild, with its alligators, turtles, lizards, diamondback rattlesnakes, cottonmouths, black bears, bobcats, and great blue herons; its red-tailed hawks, ospreys, wild turkeys, woodpeckers, and egrets; and its abundance of fish, frogs, and crayfish.

Islands of peat bog gave rise to trees, shrubs, and grasses, the ground itself trembling underfoot. Indians gave it the name Okefenokee, meaning "Land of the Trembling Earth." Indians who lived and died there as early as 2500 BC; Indians who shared the land and its abundance until de Soto came with his men, bringing with them diseases that killed the natives by the thousands. Finally, the last of the Seminoles were driven into Florida by soldiers. Now the Okefenokee holds its silent history in the roots and wood of its ancient trees.

Cypress trees still stand that were growing there when Dante was writing his *Divine Comedy*, Michelangelo was being born, and Hieronymus Bosch was painting *Ship of Fools*. The same cypress trees were sprouting roots and branches when Henry VIII married Anne Boleyn and Ivan the Terrible died in Russia. The same giant cypress trees were reaching toward the magnificent sky as my brothers and sister and I were born and grew up in South Georgia. I had always longed to see the Okefenokee, where wildness and the wonder of nature existed side by side, where the distant past and present were one.

As important as the Okefenokee was in my imagination, the thought of a trip there was eclipsed by the thought of seeing Mother. During my therapy with Dr. Turcotte I'd cut off my relationship with her. It was only after I'd terminated my relationship with him that I called her again. "Now you realize that I've loved you all your life," she said. For all of Dr. Turcotte's faults and his evaluation of Mother's negative influence on my life, I couldn't let him carry the full responsibility for my cutting her off. I blurted out: "Just because I've cut off my relationship with Dr. Turcotte does not mean that he alone was the problem between us, Mother." I was afraid that I would slip back into old patterns of saying the things she wanted me to say and not expressing my true feelings. "There are still many things that we need to work on in our relationship."

I might just as well have been talking in ancient Greek. The whole concept of working on relationships was incomprehensible to her. Mother's method of relating when hurt or when she disagreed with me was to withdraw in punitive silence. If I wrote something in a letter that she didn't want to deal with, she simply wrote back without responding to whatever it was that I'd brought up. Her silence about my concerns had made me feel invisible.

When the boys were young, Chris said that our dog Cream sometimes acted like his grandmother, whom he called Amah. When something happened that displeased Cream, she turned her chin up and looked the other way. "Just like Amah," Chris would say. "Just like Amah."

After I terminated my relationship with Dr. Turcotte, I wrote Mother a letter inviting her to come up in October to see the fall leaves, a thing she'd often talked of doing once she retired from teaching. She refused my invitation, replying: "I told you I'd like to come and see the fall foliage if John and I still got along well."

I was stunned. When she had first said that, I thought she meant it as an expression of her own lack of security, that she would come for a visit only if she felt herself not to be a nuisance to John. I'd not realized that the statement had been about her relationship with me as well. But now I understood that she was refusing to accept my invitation. During the years when she'd visited us, she spent most of her time with me, but now I saw more clearly than ever her great love of John, their casual way of bantering and the pleasure they both derived from it. She also respected him for his Ph.D., while Daddy had dropped out of college to join the army near the end of World War I. "Oh, Margaret," she'd said in a tone that sounded almost prideful, "You and John make me think so of Scott and Zelda Fitzgerald."

I had groaned inwardly, wondering if she had any idea what she was saying about us. I'd tried and failed too many times to gain her understanding and support. John's abuse of me came in bed, long after Mother had gone to sleep. I knew Mother looked up to John, while she was puzzled by me. But that she so quickly rejected my invitation—and in such a hurtful way—left me in an inarticulate daze. I said a confused goodbye and hung up the phone. After regaining my composure I wrote a note asking if there wasn't enough between the two of us to warrant a fall visit even though I was divorced from John and living alone.

She responded to my letter with silence. There was no more talk about her visiting me, but in time we were once again writing and talking with some ease. Later, I again invited her up. This time she replied: "I am an old woman now and too afraid to fly." The next year I called and asked if she would like me to fly down for a visit. I was hoping to come to a place of resolution with her while we were both still alive. She sounded excited by the prospect of seeing me.

The night before my flight, I dreamed that Mother's house caught fire.

The fire started out back in the bamboo that divided our property from that of Cousin Heinz. I knew that the fire was too huge to be stopped. I rushed into Mercer's room to get my cigarettes, then went outside to stand with Mother and Mercer to watch the house burn. I felt relieved to have rescued my cigarettes. I knew that it would take some time before the house burned to ashes, and I would have been terribly upset to have no cigarettes as I stood watching the blaze.

Mercer's room had been mine before it was his. I'd grown up in that room, had lain in my bed watching the moon rise over the bamboo, had painted at my easel that stood in one corner, had written at my desk between the two south windows, and stored my books in bookcases underneath the windows. Of course my cigarettes would have been in that room, his room now, with its large TV and stereo, and my paintings on the wall. I hadn't been in Georgia in sixteen years, since the year after Daddy's death, and had seen neither Mercer nor Mother since Mercer's brief visit in 1976. Now we were together again in my dream and the house was burning to the ground.

II

Journal entry, June 27, 1985: We are somewhere over the Carolinas. Except for landing in Newport, I've seen nothing at all of the country, only clouds. Have read several of the excerpts from a book titled Transformations *that my friend Janice copied for me and brought when she came to dinner last night.*

Freud's and Jung's mid-life crises especially interest me.

The plane is descending now, 15 minutes early and shakily, through rain clouds, making writing almost impossible. Temperature in Jacksonville: 88 degrees. Reminds me of the bumpy bus ride to Chulua, Mexico, and the shaky line of my pencil as I did pencil drawings of other passengers.

Now the ride has become smoother, but still nothing is visible. Faint patterns appear on the landscape. They look like rivers and lakes, but the fog is thick.

"Ma'am, please put the tray in its upright position now," the stewardess says, and I gather my papers.

Sharp descent and the land comes into view. Suddenly bright sunshine, then clouds again and lightning. We're coming in over acres and acres of pinewoods.

On the ground.

I saw Mother and Mercer before they saw me. They stood at the gate, Mother talking to Mercer. Mother—who had equaled exactly my five feet seven and a half inches in height and had always been heavy—was now a thin old woman, shrunken by inches and with a slight hump on her back. As always, she was impeccably dressed.

Our embrace was almost formal, but Mother had never given or received warm, affectionate hugs. As she'd said to Daddy many years before: "Wyman, you know I never liked to be touched." Embracing her, I was even more aware of how much she'd shrunk. Then Mercer and I hugged each other. He was balding, and the familiar sadness in his eyes had grown deeper.

Mother insisted that I sit in the front seat beside Mercer in the air-conditioned car. It was then that I realized that I had no makeup on at all and that I'd not worn lipstick in years. I wondered what changes in me Mother was noticing.

The South again. Mile after mile of flat land covered with pitch pine. This part of Georgia felt depressing to me. Daddy always called it "the jumping-off place."

Mother and Mercer had made plans. We were to go not directly to Cairo but to a motel near the Okefenokee where we would spend the night, then go to the swamp the following day before driving to Cairo. I began to realize how very large this trip was to them, and that they had arranged it this way to get the Okefenokee "chore" behind them. I say "chore," for listening to them talk, I was realizing more and more acutely that going beyond the parameters of the small town of Cairo was something rarely considered, much less accomplished.

I regretted having taken the special flight to Jacksonville rather than spending the extra time, energy, and money and flown to Atlanta, then Tallahassee. I'd thought it would be a pleasant thing for all of us to see Jacksonville again, but we didn't see the city or beaches at all. It was clear that their aim was to get out of Jacksonville as quickly as possible. Mercer was nervous but drove safely and efficiently. Mother kept telling him how well he was doing, as if praising a child. Realizing that the trip to pick me up was a major challenge for both of them, I felt sad and regretful.

Soon I fell into my familiar role as the unconventional member of the family. We passed a trailer by the side of the road, a large sign beside it on which was painted an enormous palm of a hand, and beneath it the words: PALMS READ HERE.

"You went past so fast. I would have loved having a palm reading," I said.

"Are you serious?" Mercer asked.

"Well, sort of," I responded thoughtfully. I'd been kidding, but in truth I'd always wanted to see the inside of one of those trailers and experience what it was like to have a Gypsy read my fortune. Gypsies in trailers had been advertising their fortune-telling abilities since I was a child.

"I can stop and turn back, sister," Mercer said quickly.

"Yes," Mother added anxiously. "It would be no trouble at all."

It upset me that they were so eager to please me. I would have felt more comfortable if Mercer or Mother had responded, "You *would* want to do such a thing!" Or "You never change, do you?" in a tone of familiar derision.

At the motel, Mother and I shared a room. After we changed into our robes and stretched out on our beds, Mercer came in, sat in a chair facing the beds, and lit a cigarette. He and Mother talked rapidly *at* me for hours. I smoked cigarette after cigarette. Their anxiety filled the room and my mind and body until I could no longer bear it. I went into the bathroom, changed into my swimsuit, and went out and swam laps in the motel pool. After I returned to the room, Mercer said good night to us and went to his room. Mother and I got dressed for bed and turned out the light. She was a tired, anxiety-riddled old woman. I felt like crying.

"Good night, Mother."

"Good night, Margaret."

The next morning after breakfast we went to the Okefenokee.

As Mother was stepping from the dock into the boat for a ride up one of the canals, I reached out my hand to steady her. She jerked back angrily and told me that she was perfectly capable of getting into the boat without my help. Then she sat down beside me.

"Mother," I explained, "you must have forgotten that I was with you that time we were going to the backyard to pick blueberries and you fell down those steep back steps and hurt yourself so badly."

I was in my early teens when that had happened and was terrified to see Mother lying on the ground, unable to get up and crying out in pain. I'd rushed inside and phoned Daddy to come home. Then I ran out and sat beside Mother, wiping her forehead with a damp washcloth until Daddy and the doctor arrived. Mother had damaged her sciatic nerve and was in bed and on heavy dosages of painkillers for weeks.

"Then there was that Fourth of July when you fell from the top bench of the bleachers at the Amherst High School athletic field, and bounced down every bench to the ground. I was scared to death." Somehow she'd escaped injury altogether that time, but the incident had triggered my memory and again I was shaken.

"I guess I didn't realize how upset you'd been by those falls."

"I guess you didn't," I responded, and the boatman pushed the boat from the dock and we were on our way.

III

It had been sixteen years since I'd been down Cairo's North Broad Street. Trees and shrubs had grown large and lush and covered many details of the houses, making them look unfamiliar. Other houses had been torn down or remodeled as office buildings. I turned my face away from Mercer and Mother so they couldn't see me crying. I had no desire to upset them. My feelings had always been too much for Mother. But my feelings were what I had. I no longer had husband or house. John Elder visited rarely, and Chris had moved to San Francisco. My relationship with Suzanne as I'd known it was over.

Despite my losses, I felt a stronger sense of self-confidence than I'd ever felt before. I'd faced Dr. Turcotte and the Northampton Police Department. While the assistant district attorney had been watching for me to break under the pressure of Dr. Turcotte, I'd grown stronger instead. Through my work with children and teachers in elementary schools, I'd discovered my power as a leader and teacher in new ways. Yes, I could bear to come back to Cairo, could bear seeing Mother and Mercer. I could even bear to take this ride down North Broad Street. But not without tears.

Mercer turned into the driveway and parked. Mother and I got out and walked to the house, Mercer following us inside carrying my luggage. Mother insisted that I use her room while she used the small bedroom that Bubba and I shared before Mercer's birth. I declined her offer. "The middle room will be fine, really fine. It would make me feel bad to displace you."

I stood, looking around the living room. The wood gleamed. Bright light poured through the newly washed windows. How hard Mother must have worked in preparation for my visit. I noticed several new chairs and a new coffee table in the living room. Then Mother wanted to show me her room. She was proud of its changes and additions. It looked more like a sitting room than a bedroom. The bed had no head- or footboard, and had a new, blue tailored quilted bedspread. At the foot of the bed stood a teak coffee table on which she'd arranged sand and seashells around a wood carving of a sandpiper. She'd added more bookcases, and a Danish-modern tan leather reading chair with a matching footstool stood in place of the old wicker rocker in which she'd rocked Harriet.

Then I looked up to see the oil painting I'd done of Mercer from memory the first year I was in college. I'd missed him so. How clearly my longing had brought his features back to memory. It wasn't until he was middle-aged that he told me how upset he'd been at my leaving home and how much he'd missed me. We'd expressed so little overt affection in our family.

The three of us went to the breakfast room, the room where we had always sat to talk as well as to eat. The breakfast bar had been replaced by a handsome old round walnut table with matching chairs that Mother had refinished. Between the table and the door to the dining room were three low Danish-modern chairs, leather straps woven over walnut frames, and several small tables and lamps. Ashtrays were everywhere. On the wall hung an old barn board on which I'd painted several ears of Indian corn, a watercolor of a clay owl I'd bought in Mexico, a plaster replica of the Aztec calendar I'd bought at the Museum of Anthropology in Mexico City, and rows of coffee mugs hanging on a wooden mug holder.

Behind the chair in which I sat was the glass door leading to the terrace. It was through that door that Daddy had watched the birds splashing in the birdbath or eating at the bird feeder hanging from a pine tree. I remembered again how one of the last things that he'd done before dying was to feed the birds, and as always, the image comforted me.

I told Mother and Mercer how good the house looked, and how much I liked their new furniture. Both of them talked at me until I was exhausted. It felt like their talking was sucking the life from me. I finally went to bed, unspoken sadness and grief thick as water in the air.

IV

The next day Mother left the house to go to the grocery store while Mercer was still asleep. Desperate to be alone, I didn't offer to go with her. As soon as she left, I began to pace back and forth in the living room. Then I realized I was doing just as I'd done when I was a girl. It had been an act of survival, my way of working off the anxiety that had often been present in my body when I lived there. After a while I walked out the front door, picking a leaf from a boxwood shrub by the front steps. Just as I'd done when I was younger, I caressed the smooth surface of the leaf and traced the curves of it with my index finger. Until then I hadn't realized that touching the leaf had brought me an even deeper, richer comfort than rubbing the satin edging of my blanket when I was a young child. The long-leafed pines were tall and majestic. The azalea bushes had grown to trees. It was the azaleas, the long-leafed pines, banana trees, wisteria vines, fruit trees, flowers, and grass that had given me the comfort and nourishment that my family had been unable to provide.

I felt guilty for not going to the store with Mother. I knew she wanted me to be with her every minute of my visit, but the longer I was with her, the more upset I became. When Mother and Mercer were together, it felt intolerable. It was as though their pain was so great that their bodies couldn't contain it—it filled the whole room.

Mother invited Bubba and his family for dinner. Bubba spent most of the evening lying on the bed with the headache he usually got when he went to Mother's for Thanksgiving, Christmas, or any special occasion that brought the family together. The older of my nieces asked me a question about how I taught children to write poetry. Otherwise, the family talked about things and people of which I knew nothing.

After Bubba and his family left for the night, I surveyed the damage—a table full of dirty dishes and silver and a kitchen full of dirty pots and pans. I began to gather the plates to take to the kitchen. Mother got up from her chair in the living room and began to help me.

"No, Mother," I said firmly. "Just sit back down. I'm going to clean up this mess. You've worked more than enough."

I was still upset from watching how she walked with Bubba and his family to the front door. She'd shuffled along like a hunchbacked ghost. It was as if most of her had already left the physical world, while her husk of a body was so insubstantial she almost floated. It was heartbreaking how soul-weary she looked.

At my commanding tone, she sat down.

"You're talking to me like Florence talked to Sarah just before she died." Sarah was Mother's sister, and Florence was her daughter.

There was more relief than irritation in Mother's voice. I felt a hard lump in my throat. I knew that this was the last time I'd see Mother just as I'd known that I'd never see Daddy again when I said goodbye to him at the Tallahassee airport in 1967.

Grief over the lost years between us flooded through me. Grief, and great regret that I'd expressed so much anger to her when I was Dr. Turcotte's patient, psychotic, and so strongly under his influence. I wished I'd expressed my anger privately, though I don't know how I could have ever found my way to myself had I not broken with her. There had been no way to talk with her, no way to work on the relationship together.

But I wished for the impossible. I wished I'd been mature enough, strong enough, whole enough, to have given her more. She was no longer the domineering mother who threatened my selfhood. She was an old woman, and someone for whom I felt compassion and heartbreak. Mercer had grown increasingly paranoid as the years passed, and the two of them rarely left Cairo. "Sometimes I feel like a prisoner in my own home," Mother said sadly. "And Mercer is so possessive of me, the house, and everything in it."

I remembered the summer years before when I'd begged her to let him stay with me. "I need your brother," she'd said, and I knew there was no hope of his getting away from her just as I now knew there was no way for her to get out from under his control. As difficult as it might have been, they loved and needed each other.

Mother wanted me to have her father's briefcase and my great-grandmother's bedspread that she'd woven herself, but she had to sneak them into my suitcase when Mercer was out. I remembered how often she used to quote "Bars do not a prison make."

Fortunately, she was able to escape through reading her many books, magazines, journals, and—in their seasons—watching football and baseball on TV. Mercer was especially jealous of her reading. He also complained of her habitual coldness, though I expect he could have borne no more intimacy than he had with her. After her death, from time to time he expressed guilt about the way he'd fussed at her when she'd left Comet sprinkled in the bathtub but hadn't completed the cleaning.

"I need your brother." Well, she had my brother and he had her, and there was nothing I could do except to feel sad for both of them.

After the dishes were finished, Mother and I took a walk in the yard. It was a clear night with a sky full of stars. I reached out and put my arm around her. While she didn't respond, she didn't pull away. She didn't feel wispy and ghostlike as much as she felt wooden and hollow, like a tree dead for years, but still standing, waiting for a strong wind to finally topple it.

V

Mercer turned the car into Laurel Hill Cemetery and drove down to the sexton's station. He parked the car, lit a cigarette, and settled down to wait for me. The sexton saw us and came out of his office. He was a kind-looking man with thick white hair.

"I'm looking for the graves of Gem Vaughn Forbes and Grace Downs Clemons," I explained. "The man at the funeral home said you would know exactly where they are buried."

"That's right, ma'am," he replied, and went in to look up the location of their graves in his record book.

Around me in every direction spread acres of tombstones: stone crosses, obelisks, angels with their great stone wings and somber faces, cherubs, columns, urns, and in the far distance what looked like a statue of a Confederate soldier high on a pedestal. I looked down at the red clay. I remembered how, when I was a child, I always hurt, physically hurt, when we'd ride by a place where the road had been cut out of higher ground, leaving banks of clay exposed. It felt like not only the earth's skin but my own had been ripped away, leaving me with raw flesh and exposed nerves. But the clay under my feet was hard-packed earth, tough and enduring.

The voice of the sexton startled me out of my absorption. "Your friends would be buried in section six. That's a far piece from here," he explained. "I'll just walk with you and show you the way." His eyes were lively, his voice warm. I was grateful for his company.

As we started on our walk, he paused and pointed to a stone on our right, saying, "That was Mrs. So-and-So." I've forgotten the names of these strangers now. "She baked the best peach cobbler in the county. I remember it to this day. Yes, I do. And her apple fritters, too." Gesturing to another stone he commented, "Old Mr. So-and-So was mean as a mule but honest as the day is long." Passing it, he gave the man's stone the kind of pat he might have given an acquaintance's shoulder. He chuckled. "Not one of us boys would dare to swipe a watermelon from his melon patch. He'd just as soon shoot us with his shotgun as shoo us off with a shout."

I walked beside him, feeling as if I had stumbled into a Southern version of Edgar Lee Masters's *Spoon River Anthology*. I longed for a tape recorder. The sexton stopped and pointed at a thick, rough stone. "That was the stone old Dr. So-and-So climbed up on to get in his horse-drawn buggy. When he died they just put his name on it and set it at his head. I guess they thought he'd need it to climb up to the first step to heaven."

His voice softened. "There's the grave of little Miss So-and-So. Lord, she loved dancing more than anything. People said she was going to be a famous ballerina someday. Died young though, bless her heart. They buried her with her ballet slippers right beside her."

We walked a bit farther. Then he stopped. "Here's the plot of your friends," he said quietly, almost reverently. Without another word, he turned and walked away, leaving me alone at the bordered plot, pea gravel thick on the ground around the marble slabs covering the graves. GRACE DOWNS CLEMONS, I read. GEM VAUGHN FORBES. I felt relieved to find Grace Clemons beside Mrs. Forbes and not off someplace by herself. They had been a family, not by blood or law, certainly, but by caring and endurance.

I looked at the simple, severe plot. Stones and marble. Had I expected grass and flowers, shrubs, perhaps a tree? But who was left to care for the living things? Theirs was as maintenance-free as a plot could be. There was nothing at all to remind me of Merrie Gardens or Paradise Park.

Grace Clemons's words came back to me then. "If you aren't with me when I die," she'd said to me when I was a child, "go to my grave. The soul has to have a place to come home to." But I don't believe that the soul of the Grace Clemons I had known and loved would ever have recognized such a colorless, lifeless place as home.

I stood a long time looking at the polished slabs of marble. Did I want the sky to open to a chorus of angels? Did I want to hear Grace Clemons's low, husky voice whisper in the warm air that held all the stories of the dead that the sexton had told me?

"If there is a way to communicate after I'm dead," Grace Clemons had said to me when I was a child, "if there is a way to cross over that threshold, I will come back to you."

In the still, humid air of that afternoon, looking down at the plot, I felt the fact of Grace Clemons's and Gem Vaughn Forbes's deaths far more acutely than I felt any evidence of their lives.

Tears spilled down my face. I'd come to Grace Clemons's grave just as she'd asked me to. I'd come out of gratitude, and to fulfill a promise, knowing that whatever life is—imagination, memory, and a great universal force beyond all human comprehension—I'd come knowing that during one of the most painful and humiliating times in my life, when an insensitive nurse in a psychiatric hospital had threatened to break what pride and sense of self I had left, Grace Clemons had indeed kept her word. Grace Clemons had come back to me, and with her came guidance and strength that continue to this day.

I bent down and picked up a few of the small stones and put them in my pocket. I looked a last time at the granite slabs, then turned away and began to walk back to the car.

"Is there no voice, no language of death?" The old familiar words of the poem Grace Clemons had recited to me so many times repeated themselves in my mind as I moved among the monuments marking other lives, other times forever gone, forever living in hearts that remember.

VI

An early-evening walk to town and back with Mother was the loveliest time of my stay in Cairo. In the three blocks to town, we walked past the Wight house, where Mother had spent many childhood hours happily pushing the Wights' latest baby in its carriage. We walked past the King house, where I'd played cowboys and Indians with Johnny King.

We walked past the Butt house, where old Mr. and Mrs. Butt played Chinese checkers on the screened-in front porch on summer evenings until Mrs. Butt was taken away forever to the state insane asylum. We walked past the house that had been Grandmother's until she'd grown old and moved up the street into Aunt Sarah and Uncle Leonard's house. We walked to where The Old Home Place once stood. It had been replaced by a rose garden, and my fig tree was long since gone, its fruit a sweet memory on my tongue.

Side by side Mother and I walked, a comfortable and deep silence between us. Only in looking back can I see that evening walk as one of those experiences when I've felt connected with eternity. Eternity in the distant bark of a dog, in the call of a mockingbird, in Mother beside me. Eternity in each slow step we took, the last pale pink of the sunset dissolving.

VII

Mother, Mercer, and I sat side by side in a glass-bottomed boat. We looked down through the glass into what the tourist brochure called the deepest and largest spring in the world. As we left the dock, thick grasses beneath us swayed in the cold water's currents. The boatman began his own music, and the haunting sound of his chant seemed to have changed no more since my childhood than the call of the mockingbird or the cry of the loon. He called out the names of Wakulla's underwater wonders—aquatic life, schools of fish, and fantastic limestone formations.

It had been nearly half a century since the trips to Wakulla Springs when Mercer and I were children, and many years since I'd seen my mother and brother. Now I was sitting between them and we were all looking down—sometimes as far as 185 feet—through the clear water, too deep for grass, to limestone and sand. There, at the spring's depths, lay a few remaining fossilized mastodon bones. School after school of fish swam over them, flashing silver in the light-filled water. The three of us looked far below a thirty-foot ledge of limestone to the gaping mouth of a cavern. Only there the water was not clear. There, at the spring's source, water bubbled up a milky blue from the underground river that fed it.

Mercer's body tensed. "It feels like my face is a mask," he said. "It feels like my face is just a mask being pulled from the bone."

I thought of how far he'd come and how difficult his struggle had been since he had been flown home from Vietnam to pace circles around me in the psychiatric ward in Bethesda Naval Hospital, barefooted, talking about Daddy and the American flag, then home to Mother and a lifetime on Thorazine, Stelazine, and whatever other drugs the medical world had offered as an answer.

The boat had passed the spring's bubbling source now and was heading back toward the dock, but I was still remembering the way Mercer dragged his feet that day in Bethesda.

Bubba's second baby died that same week. After seeing Mercer, my family and I had driven down to the baby's funeral. Bubba's baby boy was beautiful. So small and perfect, and so like my own son Chris. Both of them looked like Mercer. But Bubba's little boy had been born with the umbilical cord twisted around his neck. Bubba's first little girl is dead too, and our sister, Harriet. And after years of poverty that followed the early years of plenty, our father died and has been dead for so long now that Bubba's daughters and my sons are grown. And still the boatman's chant continued.

I wondered what Mother was feeling, sitting so close beside me after the sad years of distance, anger, and hurt between us. I knew that she would never tell me her deep feelings any more than she would ask about my confinements in mental hospitals. This was the way she had learned to live in order to survive, to turn away in silence from what she could not bear.

The boat nudged itself against the dock, and the boatman looped the rope secure. We climbed out onto the dock and walked toward the Lodge.

I thought of how often Mother had said, "I did the best I could," referring to being our mother. And this was true. I was glad I'd come home that one last time, that last year of her life.

I was glad we'd come to Wakulla once again.

"You couldn't pay me to drive anybody else to this place, Sister," Mercer said, stopping to light a cigarette. "I only brought you here because I knew you really wanted to come and I love you so much. Wakulla has always scared me to death."

"Even when you were a little boy?"

"Yeah, especially then."

"I didn't know that," I replied, realizing that I'd always believed he loved Wakulla the way I did. The ground under my sandals felt like home.

Mother was walking a little ahead of us, stooped and gray, shrunken and tired. Across the front of the Lodge before her—just as they did when I was a child—calla lilies repeated themselves like flames against the wall.

Chapter Twenty-three

MOTHER DIED ON AUGUST 26, 1986, AFTER WEEKS OF SUFFERING IN THE hospital. I had wanted to be with her, but Mercer said my being there would evoke too much emotion in him and he already had all he could cope with. He also told me that Bubba didn't want me to come down either. Of the two of them Bubba seemed to be the one taking the most responsibility for Mother.

Perhaps Mother wouldn't have wanted me there with her. She'd refused my help when she was recovering from that fall down the back steps many years earlier, injuring her sciatic nerve; then there was the time she was badly hurt in a car wreck and I'd wanted to fly down to be with her, but again she'd refused my help. Maybe she felt more comfortable with my sister-in-law, Anne, sitting beside her bed, feeding her ice chips.

But I longed to be with her.

In fact, I might not have been able to fly to Georgia. As soon as I heard Mother was dying, my entire body grew weak. As the days and weeks passed, I became progressively weaker. There were days when I could do nothing except stay in bed. Then Bubba called and told me that Mother, who was kept alive through the aid of a breathing tube,

had scribbled a note saying she wanted to die. In response, they re-
duced her oxygen. I felt frantic to be with her. After a long evening
of suffering, I got into bed and reached for my pen and journal. I
wrote Mother a letter she would never receive in the mail but perhaps
could receive in her heart that night. I wrote:

> You lie in a coma dying tonight, Mother. I spent all eve-
> ning scrubbing floors, down on my hands and knees, with
> a hard cloth and a brush. There was nothing else I could
> do. I couldn't watch the six o'clock news. Or go for my
> evening walk.
>
> Mother, I couldn't read.
>
> You lie in intensive care with whatever comfort ma-
> chines and tubes can give you tonight. They've cut your
> oxygen back. It's late and my own rooms are quiet. I can al-
> most hear your lungs wheeze. I grope for a way to endure
> this night of your dying, and I remember a night when I
> was young and afraid and you sat by my bed and read from
> *A Tale of Two Cities* aloud.
>
> Mother, may the spirit of everything and everyone you
> have loved be with you this long night of your dying: Flan-
> nery O'Connor, Marc Chagall, Latin roots of words.
> Plants and flowers in your yard—camellias, roses, and the
> fragrant mint, pink azaleas grown to trees. You loved the
> long-leafed pines. Lonely Mercer, Bubba and Anne.
> Meridith, and Leigh. The many children you taught. And
> more people than I can name.
>
> Mother, I remember the tick of the clock in the hall,
> the light from the bedside lamp, and the sound of your
> voice as you read to me until far into the night.

After I finished writing I finally fell asleep.

When I woke the next morning I couldn't bear being alone in the apartment, waiting. I took a shower, dressed, and went out and ran errands. I returned home to find that Bubba had left a message on my answering machine telling me that Mother had died.

II

I missed Suzanne terribly.

Half kidding, I asked my friend Sheryl Stoodley, a graduate student in the theater department at Smith College, with whom I taught a women's theater/writing workshop in a prison in Lancaster, Massachusetts, to find me a new lover. Almost as soon as the new semester started, she told me she thought I might be interested in one of her professors, a new faculty member from the South. She suggested the three of us have lunch together. We agreed to meet at Paul & Elizabeth's, my favorite Northampton restaurant.

I was first to arrive. I pulled out a chair, sat down, and lit a cigarette. Then I saw Suzanne sitting at a table yards from me, talking with a friend. It felt awkward, but I didn't want to call attention to myself by changing tables. The room was crowded anyway, and there wasn't an empty table in sight.

Sheryl introduced me to Kendall. Katherine was her first name, but she preferred to be called Kendall, so Kendall it was. She was a tall, slim woman with extremely short, straight, blond hair. And she had a nub where the little finger on her right hand should have been, something I noticed soon after she sat down because she talked a great deal with her hands.

I also noticed that Dr. Turcotte was sitting just two tables down from Suzanne. His daughter June walked past us and sat down across from her father. But when she saw me, she got up and rushed out of the restaurant.

We had hardly begun to talk before Sheryl started to tell Kendall the story of how Dr. Turcotte had sexually assaulted me in Newport, my having police protection, the trial, and about the doctor finally losing his license. I felt uncomfortable, but Kendall listened with acute interest and there was nothing I could do except to sit silently.

I still couldn't talk about or listen to anyone else talk about the sexual assault without feeling intensely upset while trembling inside, and sometimes outside as well. Now I fought to control my trembling as well as my embarrassment in being introduced this way. As soon as we finished lunch, I said goodbye to Sheryl and Kendall and rushed away.

Kendall ran after me.

She caught up with me and said she was interested in getting to know me. We agreed to meet at Paul & Elizabeth's the following week, this time without Sheryl. I was fascinated by Kendall's nub of a little finger. And I was attracted to this woman who gave me hints of having had a Southern Gothic childhood that rivaled mine.

Our second lunch together led to more lunches, dinners, movies, plays, and long walks on the Smith campus. We were rapidly getting caught up in a wildly intense infatuation.

"I make a terrific short-term lover," Kendall announced.

I was shocked by her directness. But her statement turned out to be true, at least partially. Short-term or not, the relationship became an important one to both of us in ways neither of us could have predicted.

We made love and we made war. We lived together and we lived apart.

Once we went to Peg Robbins, a psychic whom another Smith professor suggested we see. Neither of us had been to a psychic before. Peg—or rather "The Ones" whom Peg channeled—told us that we'd been very close in a lifetime centuries before. According to The Ones, I had been killed in a war and Kendall had never been able to get over it. Peg explained that if Kendall could resolve her feelings in this lifetime, I wouldn't have to die again as a part of the present relationship. But we didn't seem to be able to resolve the small daily problems, much less a problem that was centuries old.

———

III

My friend Sally had once taken me out to lunch at the Riverside Restaurant in Shelburne Falls, a small town in the foothills of the Berkshire Mountains. We chose a table overlooking the Deerfield River. After lunch we walked across the Bridge of Flowers, an old trolley bridge the local garden club had turned into a glorious garden. And there was something in the air itself that drew me to the town.

During the most difficult time I had in my relationship with Kendall, I decided I had to move out of the house we shared at the time. I drove back to Shelburne Falls and went to the Riverside Restaurant again. I had thought of the river and town ever since Sally had taken me there. When the waitress took out her pad and pencil and asked what I wanted, I replied that I wanted a bowl of the soup of the day, a roll, a Diet Coke, and an apartment by the river.

In minutes she returned. She placed the soup, roll, and Diet Coke before me. "The apartment will be available in two weeks."

"You're kidding," I sputtered.

She wasn't.

"It's over the restaurant," she said. "The woman who rents it as a studio is going to San Francisco for two months on business. She wants to sublet it while she's gone."

I rented the apartment before going back to Northampton to pack and move. By that time I was psychotic again.

I had moved and was walking around town in Shelburne Falls when I suddenly lost all sense of where I was or how to get back to my new apartment. Frantic, I went into a store and asked to use the phone. I called Mary Gene Devlin, a teacher with whom I'd worked in the Old Deerfield elementary school and who had become my friend. She and her husband, Jim, arrived shortly. Jim drove us to the home of another Old Deerfield teacher with whom I'd also worked, whose husband was a psychiatrist. After hearing Mary Gene's description of my behavior, he called the hospital in Greenfield and had me admitted to the psychiatric unit.

I was relieved to be there and asked that no one be allowed to visit me. I needed to be alone to find my way back to myself. I began to do this by sitting at a table in the ward dining room drawing picture after picture with my colored pencils. Occasionally I talked with another patient before going back to my drawing.

I have no memory of what I was thinking as I bent over my sketch pad hour after hour, but my mind was becoming less psychotic. When the psychiatrist assigned to my case insisted on giving me lithium, I declined with firm determination.

"I know what I need, and it's not medication."

In a few more days of drawing, dreaming, and sleeping, my thinking was once again clear.

I called Mary Gene, who took me home. I was relieved to be back at my apartment and the river.

John, who lived with his wife, Judy, several miles from my apartment, visited me. We talked, as we had off and on since the divorce. He rubbed my back. Then he got up and walked to a window across the room. He stood there looking out at the river.

"I guess we're like Elizabeth Taylor and Richard Burton," he said. "We love each other but can't live together."

"Yes, I guess that's true," I responded. I felt a trace of sadness.

I looked at his familiar profile for a long time.

IV

Chris had moved away with a new lover. First they had moved to the eastern part of the state, where he had intended to get a job in an advertising agency. When that didn't work out, he and his partner moved to San Francisco. He changed his name to Augusten Burroughs and, when he was around twenty-one years old, was hired by a prominent ad agency, where he was recognized for his creative genius.

For the first few months at the agency he called me at least once and often several times a day to work with him on his ad projects. It felt wonderful to be able to contribute to his life in that way.

But I had reached the limits of my endurance with my own work. I was completely burned out. In addition to working with the children, I led private creative writing workshops in my home and had begun to teach in the University of Massachusetts Summer Writing Workshop. The prison project had ended, and the last journal and the play Sheryl and I had collaborated on with several of the prisoners were still to be completed.

One night Chris called, saying that he was terribly upset and was afraid he was going crazy. "There's no one here I can talk to, and I really need to talk. Please come to San Francisco. I need you."

I told him I would get there as soon as I could. I canceled my teaching job for the fall. My mother had left me a small inheritance, and that, together with what money I had of my own, was enough to allow me to take the year off. I packed and left for San Francisco.

As soon as I spent a little time with Chris and his partner, I saw how unhealthy the relationship was for Chris. His partner was evidently more interested in boys than men, and when they were together, Chris acted like a boy. This disturbed me deeply, but I also saw that the relationship was falling apart.

I shall never forget standing with Chris outside his apartment building on Bush Street one windy day, tears streaming down his cheeks. "I'm lost. I don't know who I am anymore."

I wish I could say that I was able to help him find his way home to himself, but we were rarely alone, and he no longer talked about his emotional state. I suspect he was spending most nights drinking. I was staying in a lovely Nob Hill apartment that belonged to the parents of one of Chris's friends at the ad agency. The friend's parents were out of the country for several months, and they were happy to have someone stay in the apartment. Occasionally Chris dropped by to see me after work. Sometimes he sat and quickly typed a poem on my typewriter. He never even bothered to reread it or take it with him, but I kept every poem he wrote.

When we went out with his friend and her sister one night, he enthusiastically told them about the writing workshops I'd led in Amherst when he was a teenager. The workshops were intended for adults, but Chris would often participate in them, and the groups were always enriched by his contributions. Knowing a group would be coming for the workshop in Amherst often inspired expressions of his humor. A cow skull hung on one wall, and I told the sisters how I came downstairs the morning of a workshop to find an apple in its mouth, while an extremely realistic rubber snake lay half-hidden under the hem of the couch.

Chris also entertained the sisters and me by mimicking his father, brother, and me one evening. He captured all of us at our worst, and it was hysterically funny. His co-worker commented that he would be a terrific stand-up comedian. We all agreed.

V

After I had lived for five months in the Nob Hill apartment, the parents of Chris's friend returned from their trip and I had to move to a room in a hotel for women. Chris no longer came to see me except on rare occasions, and the job he had assured me I had in his ad agency had fallen through. I felt sad and depressed. Without a job or a place to live, I could no longer afford to stay in San Francisco, and I lacked the energy to return to teaching in Massachusetts.

I decided to go to Mexico, where my money would go much farther than in the States. Though Kendall and I were no longer partners, I'd invited her to San Francisco and we'd had a pleasant time together. When I told her of my plan to go to Mexico, she suggested that I go to San Miguel de Allende, where many Americans lived and English was understood most places. On vacation from Smith, Kendall went with me.

Before Kendall left Mexico for Northampton we found a wonderful apartment on the outskirts of San Miguel. It had rust-red tile floors, a corner fireplace in the living room, and clusters of banana trees in the courtyard. It also came with the service of a cleaning lady and a woman who did my laundry in a large tub just outside my bathroom window.

I loved San Miguel with its tree-filled Jardín (town square), its locals and tourists wandering the sidewalks or sitting on benches reading, talking, or simply watching the crowds pass by. There was the old man with his cluster of balloons and small tin push toys for sale. Often musicians played in the gazebo. I spent many hours sitting on a bench sketching people or writing letters. Mornings, a tall thin man bent over a broom and swept the steps of the Church of Saint Michael the Archangel across the street from the Jardín. Evenings, glistening grackles by the hundreds rose from its trees.

I often ate dinner at Mama Mia's, where many Americans met to visit with one another and exchange helpful information. I made several friends, some of whom I traveled with to nearby towns.

I also made friends with Gert Dickman, a widow and the aunt of a Smith College student. Gert and her husband had moved to San Miguel from Brooklyn, where she had taught in an elementary school. After her husband's death, Gert had donated time and money to the building and development of San Miguel's American library. She was a member of the Shakespeare Society and for many years was on the staff of San Miguel's American newspaper. She also built a home for homeless Mexican women. She was in her late seventies when I met her, but though she chain-smoked, ate rich, hot Mexican fried foods, and drank liberal amounts of scotch each day, her energy appeared to be inexhaustible.

Gert was an amazing woman. She often invited me for lunch, during which she educated me about how to make my water safe for drinking, what vegetables and fruits to buy and not to buy and where to buy them. She suggested restaurants and sometimes invited me out with her and her friends.

Most important, she lent me her typewriter.

At home I painted, read, and wrote letters and journal entries. I checked my shoes for scorpions before putting them on, as I'd been taught. At night in bed I listened to the radio, and sometimes to rain splattering on the banana leaves.

Mine was an interesting and peaceful life.

Then for no apparent reason I began to feel physically weak. I grew progressively weaker, and Gert insisted that I make an appointment with her doctor. When the time came, she went with me. After examining me, the doctor—a kind, elderly man—expressed serious concern. He said that if he sent samples of my blood to Mexico City, I might never see them again. And he didn't think I had enough strength to go to the nearest town with a hospital equipped to do the blood tests I needed. He believed I had lupus and thought the wise thing for me to do was to return to the States.

When I told Kendall I was returning to Massachusetts, she invited me to stay with her until I found a place of my own.

I hired a taxi to drive me from San Miguel to the Mexico City airport. I asked the driver if it would be possible to stop at the basilica to see Our Lady of Guadalupe, but he said he thought there wouldn't be time. I was disappointed to not see it again. Then my driver turned a corner and I was surprised to see in the distance the ornate, sixteenth-century church, its front even more sunken into the earth than it was the last time I'd seen it.

When the taxi driver smiled, I realized he'd been determined to get me there all along. But I was puzzled when he drove past the building and turned into the parking garage of a round, very modern church. He explained that the old basilica had been condemned, and the new basilica had taken its place. The painting of Our Lady of Guadalupe was now displayed there.

Light poured through the many windows of the new church. The painting hung on a wall under which crowds of people passed on a conveyor belt. I joined them and found my heart moved once again by the image of the Virgin with her gentle face, clasped hands, her robe scattered with stars. And though the feeling of sacred mystery I experienced when I first saw her in the old basilica, with its dimly lit interior, was gone, I was once again reminded that I too am part of the Divine.

VI

While my doctor in Northampton assured me that I didn't have lupus, I knew that something was wrong with me. And going back to teaching felt impossible. Whatever was wrong, I knew I needed more rest.

Memories of Shelburne Falls and the Deerfield River tugged at me. Kendall announced to her classes at Smith that I was looking for an apartment by the river in Shelburne Falls. One of her students knew of such a place and told Kendall. I called the landlady of the apartment building, and we arranged to meet each other there.

The apartment was much too small, but it had a large porch overlooking the river. Because of the porch, and because I intended to stay there for only a year, I decided to take it.

I had left much of my furniture and many of my books at John Elder's, but I brought my favorite reading chair, my computer, and the computer table Kendall had given me. I also brought the antique kitchen table I'd bought when I'd first moved to Northampton. In the new apartment I put it under the window overlooking the river and used it as a desk as well as a place to eat. Then I settled into living in Shelburne Falls, which held the same attraction for me that it had held originally. But I continued to feel tired. And as the days and weeks passed, I found myself growing more and more depressed. I joined the YMCA in Greenfield and swam laps in the pool there four or five times a week. I wrote in my journal. I tried unsuccessfully to meditate. Time after time I tried to stop smoking, only to give in and light another cigarette, which only made me feel more depressed.

I found the most relief from depression during the time I spent in a small store across the river. Just as I had felt something in the air that drew me to Shelburne Falls, there was something in the atmosphere in the store that made me feel secure and spiritually comforted.

In it were many kinds of stones and crystals, beautiful handmade kimonos, and a large assortment of earrings, bracelets, and pins. Most important to me were the books on shelves that lined a wall next to the river. Beside the books was a couch on which I often sat thumbing through one book or another, reading short sections, and occasionally buying one that especially interested me. I bought *Return of the Bird Tribes* by Ken Carey, *Mysticism and the New Physics* by Michael Talbot, and *Out on a Limb* by Shirley MacLaine. In different ways all three of the books contributed to my spiritual understanding. I believe it was Ken Carey's book that stated that in a future time, when our world had dramatically progressed spiritually, people would no longer feel anger but would only live lives of love. I read that passage many times while thinking of all the anger I had expressed in the past.

Maija Meijers owned the store, and sometimes we had brief conversations. Once she told me that when she was going through a difficult time during her youth, she discovered she could channel beings from the spirit world and explained something of how this had changed her life. Sometimes, when I was especially despairing, I went to her for readings. During one reading she channeled a woman who told me that she was once a nun in a convent in which I was mother superior. This interested me a great deal, as Peg Robbins, who channeled and continues to channel The Ones, had also told me I'd been a mother superior in a past life. Perhaps that explained why I was so drawn to rosaries and religious medals, and spent so much time reading about saints.

Maija no longer has the store in which I spent so many enriching hours. But my relationship with her has endured. And over the last twenty years I've continued to read books about spiritual growth just as I've continued my practices of prayer and meditation while the Deerfield continues to flow past my window on its long journey to the sea.

Chapter Twenty-four

I

1989

I'D RETURNED THAT DAY FROM A SHORT VACATION ON CAPE COD WITH Kendall and felt tired from the trip. I drove to Northampton and let Kendall off at her house. Then I drove myself home to Shelburne Falls.

In the middle of our last night on the Cape, Kendall had waked me, telling me that a voice had come to her in a dream, saying: "Tell Margaret to feel the energy passing through you, into her, and back again. This will be only for a little while." Kendall felt the severity of the message and embraced me with the strength of one sealing a pact. Neither of us consciously had any idea what the dream meant.

After returning home I had dinner at the Riverside Restaurant. A white candle burned on the table. Out the window, reflections of the street lamps on the Bridge of Flowers shone on the river's dark water. The owner of the restaurant, Debby Yaffee, sat with me while I ate. I no longer remember a word of our conversation, though that was the last time I ever spoke in my easy Southern drawl.

Sometime during the night, I woke with a sharp pain in a tooth. I would find out later that I'd clenched my teeth with such force that I'd cracked it down its middle. But that night, I only roused briefly to think: *I've just had a seizure,* though I'd never had a seizure before. Then I lost consciousness.

The next morning I woke confused. Walking to the kitchen, I dragged my left foot slightly. At the table I fumbled with a pack of cigarettes, took one out, put it in my mouth, and lit it. When I tried to take a drag, the cigarette fell to the floor. I had no conscious awareness that half my mouth was paralyzed. Puzzled, I bent down, picked the cigarette up, and again put it in my mouth. Again it fell out. I picked it up, thinking, *My God, I could start a fire.*

I put the cigarette out in the kitchen sink and dialed Kendall's phone number. When she answered, I opened my mouth to speak, but what came out was terrifying guttural gibberish. Kendall responded with puzzlement, then alarm. I struggled with the sounds erupting from my mouth until I was able to say the single word, "Help."

"I'll be right there," she said, and hung up the phone.

Waiting for her arrival, I sat at my kitchen table, writing. I wrote that no matter what I might sound like when I tried to talk, I was sane and rational. I thanked her for the beautiful weekend. I pushed my pen across the paper with a cold, calm terror.

When Kendall arrived, we immediately left for the hospital, but just as she was about to turn onto the Mohawk Trail, I stopped her because I'd forgotten to take my living will with me. I was afraid my condition would deteriorate and I would be hooked up to a life-support system that I didn't want. We went back to my apartment and got it. I asked Kendall to call an ambulance. By that time, it had become difficult for me to swallow.

Kendall drove behind the ambulance to the hospital in Greenfield. There the examining doctor said that, because my case seemed to be complex, and because I had such difficulty communicating, he thought I should be in Cooley Dickinson Hospital in Northampton, where my own doctor could oversee my treatment. I was too weak and confused to disagree. The doctor said he would telephone my doctor to tell him I was on my way to his office. I didn't think to ask him why I couldn't be admitted to Cooley Dickinson immediately, for it was clear to me that I belonged in a hospital, not a doctor's office.

No one suggested that I go in an ambulance.

I lay on the car seat, my head in Kendall's lap, as she drove me to Northampton. "Nothing could be finer than to be in Carolina in the morning!" she sang while I looked at the tops of trees speeding by. "Amazing grace, how sweet the sound," she sang as I worked to focus on the music and not what was happening in my newly unpredictable and frightening brain. "Swing low, sweet chariot, coming for to carry me home," she sang while I lay thinking that maybe that was what was happening to me; maybe I was dying. She sang: "Pack up your troubles in your old kit bag and smile, smile, smile."

When we got to Dr. Smith's office, I held on to Kendall's arm as I walked, dragging my left leg, from the car. Dr. Smith hardly had to look at me to know that I should be admitted to the hospital immediately. He asked his receptionist to get a wheelchair for me. She was a woman I'd known years before when her son and mine had been friends. She was visibly distressed. I tried to communicate to her that I didn't want to leave for the hospital until I'd contacted my son or daughter-in-law. I was afraid I might die on the way. There was no answer, so she left a message on the answering machine, saying: "Your mother isn't feeling especially well, so we're going to have her admitted to the hospital." Especially well? I could no longer talk, was leaning uncontrollably to the left, while the left side of my mouth hung open and drooped down. I could hardly contain myself until we got out of the office and into the car. I burst out laughing. I felt I might be dying, and she'd told my family that I wasn't "feeling especially well"?

I couldn't stop laughing.

I don't remember being admitted to Cooley Dickinson. I don't remember that first night when Kendall sat beside my bed all night long, holding my hand and stroking my head. She told me that toward morning, I said that I might have to go—meaning to die—and she begged me: "Please, stay. Please, stay."

I stayed.

She telephoned friends for me.

The next day in Cooley Dickinson, I had a second stroke. I was getting up from the toilet when, losing my balance and the use of my left leg, I lunged for the grab bar on the wall to my right. I remember nothing after that. That stroke completely paralyzed my left side, destroyed my sense of balance, and left me with double vision. It also left me with a condition called left neglect, in which my brain refused to acknowledge anything to my left. I ate only the food on the right side of my plate, read only the page on the right side in a book, talked only to the person seated to my right.

Overnight half of my world had vanished.

Weeks before my stroke I had gone to my doctor with a complaint about my eyes. While examining me, he had commented that I seemed to be depressed. He suggested that I take some of the new antidepressant Prozac and gave me some samples. I said that I would think about taking them, but I doubted I would. I needed a life change, not a mood change brought about by drugs. For my difficulty with my vision, he made an appointment with an ophthalmologist.

I went the next day. I explained that in bright light my peripheral vision bleached out. After the doctor examined my eyes he left the room, returning a few minutes later with a large book in which he showed me a photograph of a scene in which the central image was clearly focused while the surrounding images dissolved in what looked like intense sunlight. "Is this what things look like to you?" he asked.

"Yes," I responded.

He closed the book and smiled at me. "The good news is that there is nothing wrong with your eyes."

He paused like a stand-up comedian about to deliver the punch line. "The bad news is that the problem is in your brain."

He went on to tell me that in his opinion, I was experiencing migraines but without the pain.

Something told me that the difficulty was not that simple. I called my doctor, told him what the ophthalmologist had said, and expressed my concern. He responded that if the problem didn't clear up soon, I might consider having a CAT scan.

Now he stood by my hospital bed looking down at me. He must have examined me earlier, but this is my first conscious memory of him after leaving his office for the hospital two days before. Now I had suffered a second stroke. What I saw of the room had holes in it like Swiss cheese.

My doctor looked puzzled. "Whatever it was that depressed you so severely is gone," he said. "It's as if a shadow has been lifted."

I had no feeling of a shadow being lifted. But it was true—I was not feeling depressed; I was feeling panic-stricken. I was also beginning to face a major life change, not the kind I'd meant when I'd told the doctor I needed a life change instead of the Prozac he'd offered me, but one that would leave my vision forever changed.

II

Kendall sat beside my bed, reading aloud from May Sarton's memoir *After the Stroke,* while I drifted into and out of consciousness. A visitor—I'd already forgotten who—had left a little vase of flowers, and a nurse had just taken my blood pressure. Or was that in the morning? My memory was hazy, fragmented. "Head," I said, touching the right side of my head. "Head."

Kendall reached over and stroked my head. The headache wasn't intolerable yet, only relentless and exhausting.

Before the strokes, I had had one headache in my life that was severe enough to be memorable. That was in 1959, in our first apartment in West Philadelphia. For the duration of the headache I lay on the daybed in the living room, trapped in pain. My maternal grandmother's migraines were legendary—occurrences of terrible mystery, silence, and dark rooms. Though I never witnessed one, I'd heard about them all my life. As a child, I'd felt a sense of awe about them; her inaccessibility coupled with my longing for her attention and affection encouraged my romanticizing of anything that was hers. My mother had also had headaches but called them headaches, not *migraines*, the word that in my child eyes lifted the experience into the realm of the extraordinary. Still, she would moan, "My head is splitting. My head is splitting," or—on occasion—would slam the back of her head against the wall with great force, as if that self-imposed violence might somehow minimize or at least distract her from the less controllable pain of the headache.

My second memorable headache came in the hospital after the second stroke, though I don't remember exactly when or how long it lasted. When I asked my daughter-in-law, Mary, about it, she thought it must have lasted a week or two. She told me that the family was afraid that the stroke had damaged a pain center in my brain and that I could possibly live the rest of my life in that agony. "In that case," she said, "we were hoping that you would die." I knew nothing beyond my attempt to endure from one assault on my brain to the next. Each seizure of acute pain brought a rerun of the film of John Kennedy's assassination—the impact of the bullet exploding the brain. My whole mind was filled with that image.

But what obsessed me afterward was the thought that the headaches that my sister, Harriet, suffered after she was born were even more painful than my headache, without any medication to dull the pain.

III

John Elder stood looking down at me, his right hand thrust open toward me, holding a small gray model of a Mercedes. Later, when my headache finally went away and my mind was clear, I examined the model carefully and saw that it was a little more than six inches long and made of metal. It was exquisite in its fine details—doors that opened, a steering wheel that actually made the front tires turn, and one long windshield wiper that worked. But that day I saw only my son's expressionless face.

Expressing himself emotionally had never been easy for John Elder, but somehow the gift of that model car said all that needed to be said. *Car* was the first word he spoke at eight months, and it was riding in the car that had given him comfort when he was a baby. Cars were one of his major focuses from childhood to the time he made his first drivable car from old car parts to creating his own car business. The Mercedes is one of the cars his company still services and sometimes sells.

Of all gifts given to me when I was in the hospital, it was that car that I treasured most. Over the years since the stroke, I've had many visitors with children, and I've always kept a basket full of toys for them. But until John Elder's son, Jack, was old enough, I allowed no child to play with the little Mercedes.

When I finally gave Jack the car, I was impressed by how carefully he played with it, pushing it across my kitchen-workroom floor, opening and closing the doors, turning the steering wheel, pushing the windshield wiper back and forth. He was especially fascinated by the windshield wiper. As I watched him push it back and forth over the windshield, I remembered the little boy John Elder spending a long time one afternoon pretending to be windshield wipers. He walked all over our small apartment in West Philadelphia, moving his arms back and forth while repeating the words, "Windshield wipers. Windshield wipers." He continued this for a long time before he came to me with a look of concern on his face. "Mama," he asked anxiously. "Am I really windshield wipers?"

"No, John Elder, you're not windshield wipers," I assured him. "You're a little boy."

I gave him a hug and he went off happily to play but no longer pretended to be windshield wipers that day.

"Can I have some water so I can use the windshield wipers?" Jack asked.

IV

John Elder came from South Hadley, and Chris came from New York, where he now lived and worked. Kendall took several photographs of the three of us together. In one, John Elder is seated to my right, the fingers on our right hands interlocked. Chris is to my left, sitting on the bed. In another photograph Chris is supporting my head with his right arm. In both pictures we are all looking into the camera lens. The pose feels formal. But my hair is uncombed and my hospital gown has slipped off my paralyzed left shoulder. The left side of my mouth droops badly. These things make me look vulnerable and sadly comic, while the expressions on my sons' faces are restrained and sober.

Later Kendall took more pictures of John Elder and me. We are seated in chairs at the ward hall. My head is propped on a pillow, and my hair is still uncombed. In the first, John Elder is looking into the lens with a slight smile on his face, while I am looking at him and smiling. In the next John Elder is asleep, his right arm across my bent leg, my right hand on his arm.

Then she took a series of Chris by himself, his expression pensive, his eyes turned away from the camera. His hair is still thick and curly, and his face looks tender and soft. I cherish those pictures. I had no idea then that I would see him only a few times over the next twenty years.

V

My speech was broken, and I felt lost in the wreckage in my brain. Each syllable spoken was an exhausting explosion of breath. Talking was slow, difficult to understand, drained of emotion. I left out words, confused tense, gender, and time, saying *yesterday* when I meant *today*, *today* when I meant *tomorrow*, *he* when I meant *she*, *done* when I meant *did*. Strange inversions of words came out of my mouth uninvited, unexpected. I often used sentence structures that sounded as if I were translating from French. "How many years has she?" I would ask, meaning to say: "How old is she?"

I puzzled about my strange loss of grammar. I thought about how it would have been were my mother alive to see me. Her speech was as precise and controlled as the public appearance she maintained when I was a young girl in the forties—firmly corseted, with high heels and hose, lipstick, rouge. She never used slang. As a child, I lived in dread of making grammatical errors and having her correct me.

Inside me, time collapsed and I was once again twelve years old, sitting on the couch in my parents' living room. Across the room, the large electric fan rotated its caged face, blades stirring the thick August air. Harriet sat in her wheelchair, blond curls damp against her head. While my mother talked with her friend Francis, a small, dark-haired woman with short, tight curls, Francis's daughter, Kate, raced back and forth across the room, terrible guttural noises—great thrusts and heaves of sound—erupting from her throat.

Harriet and Kate, both born with cerebral palsy, were the bond that connected the two women—my mother, restrained and proper, Francis, burning with intensity, chain-smoking Pall Mall cigarettes, and talking rapidly about her husband's heavy drinking, concerns about Kate, or how the world was going to come to an end any day.

Kate must have been eight or nine years old when we met the Hollingsworths. Already she was a tall, big-boned girl; it would be only a couple of years before she towered over her mother. I was upset by Kate's banging on the piano with her fists—a fierce thunderous sound that was often accompanied by her loud guttural noises. Then she would rush back and forth across the living room, flinging her arms out, wildly scratching at the air. It was as if she was clawing at some invisible wall, frantic to escape.

Francis told us that the doctors at Johns Hopkins said that Kate's brain held no capacity for understanding or making human speech. The horror of being without speech haunted me. My sister couldn't speak at all either, but she seemed to be able to understand at least a little of what we said. When one or another of us would ask, "Where's the little boy who looked after the sheep?" she'd close her eyes in response before we'd say, "Under the haystack fast asleep." I clung to that small indication of communication with my sister. But I can't remember an instance when Kate appeared to comprehend what anyone said, though she must have understood some of her mother's communication if not the actual words. Looking back I can only remember her noises and abrupt, disruptive movements. I never saw Kate smile or cry.

I remembered how the first sounds I blurted into the phone receiver when I called Kendall that morning after my stroke sounded like the guttural sounds that I had heard from Kate more than forty years earlier. Hearing myself terrified me. Was that part of my brain that made and understood words being destroyed? Was I going to be like Kate?

Before Mother died, she told me that Kate was living in an institution. She told me that Francis's husband had left her and had later killed himself, and that Francis herself had died of a cerebral hemorrhage. Kate was with her in the car when it happened. Francis's death was instantaneous. Repeatedly over the years, I replayed what that cataclysmic scene might have been like as the blood broke through its walls and drowned Francis's brain in its red fury.

I imagined Kate stunned in the aftermath of that car crash. For the twenty years of her life, Francis had been the only person Kate had. It was Francis who cooked three meals a day for the two of them in that large house, Francis who helped Kate bathe and dress. It was Francis who brushed her straight brown hair. It was Francis who took her to the mall and grocery store and every other place she went. Francis was Kate's world, and Kate was Francis's.

If the two of them had no bond of speech, what they had was

daily life. Whatever of their bond was love, need, responsibility, or making do with what life dealt, I can't say. And I don't know how Kate acted in the tumultuous wake of Francis's death. But I can't imagine Kate in that car alone with Francis's body without imagining rising from her depths a heartbreaking howl of sorrow more terrible than any sound she'd ever made before.

VI

My memory of the early days and weeks after my stroke is fragmented and blurred, and I've forgotten the proper sequence of things. Kendall's presence was a constant. She stayed with me day and night. Friends and family came and went. Nurses came with medication, the blood-pressure gauge, and the thermometer. Aides came with changes of linen, meals, and the bedpan. Lab technicians came with their needles and tubes. Physical and occupational therapists came trying to help me do things I was no longer able to do in the old ways.

Confused, disoriented, and with the acute pain in my head barely dulled by drugs, I repeatedly asked my friends to please bring me pens and notebooks. I'd lost so much of who I was and was frantic to hold on to what I had left. All feeling was absent from my left side. I felt like I had half of the body of a corpse attached to the living me.

Speech as I had known it was gone. But with shattered syntax, senseless repetitions and omissions of words, and bizarre spelling, I could still write. More than anything else, I clung to words.

Kendall brought me a new journal—a sturdy hard-backed account book, green, with lined paper. On May 10, I wrote my first journal entry:

> *I feel so helpless . . . hurt my face trying to sleep . . . I have a bad headache ~~and my head hurts and my head aches~~. Also, I need my glasses.*

I am very sad and feel like crying. I close my eyes and think: I must
learn patience.

Feeling helpless was what upset me most. When no friend or family member was with me and I wasn't engaged in speech, physical, or occupational therapy, I felt like the baby I had been, helpless and alone, screaming in a closed room.

On May 16, I wrote a fragment of a poem in my journal:

> *Spring rain on the windowpane. Trees,*
> *gray sky. And listen—*
> *I can call back the day*
> *that you pushed me in the wheelchair*
> *in the park.* Stones, *I say.*
> *And* moss. Fragrance of fresh earth.

An additional line has been scratched through, and the poem was left unfinished. But I'd discovered what I needed to know—I *could* find a way to comfort and calm myself when I was alone. If the hospital felt unbearable to me, if I felt trapped and anxious in my body, I could "call back the day." I could remember what comforted and nourished me and give it the form of poetry. The outing in the park referred to in the poem was my first outing in the wheelchair after the stroke. Kendall had pushed me across the street from the hospital to Childs Park. Because the muscles were too paralyzed to hold the bone in, my left arm hung out of the socket. To ease the pain and to keep the bone in its socket, a couple of bed pillows supported my arm.

Spring had come since I'd been admitted to Cooley Dickinson, and I was alive. Kendall pushed the wheelchair close enough for me to reach out and touch an open blossom on a Japanese magnolia tree. I tenderly caressed a deep, wine-colored petal the way one might touch the soft spot on a new baby's head. Kendall walked across the new grass to a dogwood tree, broke off a small, blossom-covered branch, and brought it back to me, laying it on top of the pillows. Looking down at the blossoms, I clamped my hand over my mouth and wept.

Sometimes, on days when my own determination was weakened, I remembered the story of Carolina Maria de Jesus, a story I'd shared with the women in creative writing workshops that I'd led. Carolina, with a second-grade education and two children to support, lived in the slums near São Paulo, Brazil, where she made her meager living by collecting and selling used scrap paper that she found by searching through that city's trash. Believing in the power of her own words against all odds, she wrote a journal that was later published as the book *Child of the Dark*. That book, with the exception of the Bible, has sold more copies than any other book in Brazil's history. I told myself that if Carolina could write herself out of a place of poverty and helplessness, then I could write myself out of a place of panic and fear.

During my month in Cooley Dickinson and two months in the Weldon Rehabilitation Hospital at Mercy Medical Center in Springfield, I wrote about any and everything. I wrote about waiting for visitors, seeing a summer-sun-lit sky through my window, my fear of falling in the bathroom, the monotonous drone of the floor waxer up and down the halls. I wrote about other patients and their visitors, the anxiety that kept me up nights and woke me early in the morning; I wrote about my roommate's blue fish in its small cup of water, the wall of leg braces at the far end of the therapy gym, the little paper angel with its bent foot that dangled from a cord on the small TV over my bed.

VII

I wheeled myself down the hospital corridor for my first appointment with Angela Mansolillo, my speech therapist at Weldon Rehab. I stopped abruptly at the doorway to her office. I couldn't make myself cross the threshold into that small, windowless space. *Breathe deeply*, I told myself, trying to do my childbirth breathing exercise, an exercise I'd since used to calm myself before giving poetry readings. *Breathe deeply*. But I could hardly breathe at all. *Maybe*, I thought, *I am suffocating; maybe fear has sucked all the air from my lungs.*

"I can't work in this room," I blurted out.

I don't know what Angela was thinking about the newly paralyzed, panic-stricken woman facing her from a hospital wheelchair, but she didn't attempt to reason me out of my fears. She simply smiled warmly and assured me that she would find a space in which I would feel comfortable. The next day we met in the computer room behind the nurses' station. The room wasn't large, but it was flooded with light from a large window. Every day for the next two months, for thirty minutes in the morning and thirty minutes in the afternoon, I sat next to that window as I worked with Angela, learning to speak again.

Initially there were a lot of written tests, though I can remember nothing of them now except that I disliked taking them. I felt like a little child in grade school, nervous about performing well for the teacher. And I told no one that I could no longer remember the alphabet.

Speaking, I rolled my *r*'s, and at each syllable uttered, I spat like an actor in the No theater in Japan. Though I had spoken with a thick Southern drawl before my stroke, I now spoke with what sounded like a trace of a German accent. And my new speech was squeezed dry of emotion. It sounded flat and mechanical and was punctuated with struggle-filled hesitations. Often I would kid Angela about going on the road to give poetry readings in this style as if it were something purposefully developed for my performance. In truth I couldn't imagine ever again giving public readings.

To lose my ability to walk was to lose all sense of safety. Who would come when I needed to be propped up in the bed so I wouldn't choke on a sip of water, or when I needed a bedpan or a blanket? To lose use of my left arm and hand felt like a cruel amputation. But I have always been in love with the human voice, with its tonal variations, hesitations, cadences, with what it holds of the geography of one's beginnings and of the experiences that lead one to choose the particular words through which one lives. I *needed* my leg. I *needed* my arm. I *needed* my hand. But in a fundamental way I *was* my voice. The loss of that voice felt like a diminishment of my soul.

A booklet explaining apraxia lay under a pile of books where I'd hidden it. As long as I didn't read it, as long as I didn't put words to what had happened to my voice, my own acknowledgment of it didn't have to cut so deeply. In the meantime, I spent evenings in bed, pronouncing the words with which I'd had the most difficulty that day—*countenance, munificent, ignorance, diminished, eloquent.* I stumbled over sounds, slurred, stuttered, began again.

Six weeks after my stroke, I got the booklet out and read its definition of *apraxia:* "A movement planning problem involving a disruption in sequencing of voluntary movements. A transmission problem between the brain and the muscle." *Apraxia,* I said aloud, allowing myself to feel the pain evoked at the sound of that word. I rolled my wheelchair to the empty dining room and parked at a table near a window. Taking out my pad and pen, I labored to write a poem expressing my struggle to find "music to unlock my damaged speech."

One afternoon when Kendall came to visit, as she did most afternoons, she took me out for a ride around the hospital grounds. As she pushed my wheelchair around the parking lot, she began to sing the song "Side by Side." The mood was light, and the words to the song felt poignant, funny, and true. She and I had stood side by side through one of the most difficult periods of both of our lives and were both more than a little ragged from the effort. Kendall continued to sing. Laughing, I tried to join in.

Though what I was doing could hardly be called singing, and though my words were much slower in coming out than hers and were not at all clearly spoken, they were the first words since the stroke that I was able to say without wrestling each syllable out of my mouth.

I knew that the music had made this possible. Perhaps I could get my speech back through reading rhythmical poetry. And as difficult as it was to speak, it made sense to me to practice speaking by reading what I'd loved most.

I have never returned the copy of *The New Pocket Anthology of American Verse* that Kendall brought when I asked her for poetry I could use in speech therapy. A 1955 edition, the book looks much older. The paper is yellowed and brittle, and some animal has chewed through the binding. The second page of Edna St. Vincent Millay's poem "Renascence" has come loose. I couldn't begin to say how many speech-therapy sessions began with *All I could see from where I stood / Was three long mountains and a wood.*

Because of the music of the poem I was able to read it aloud more easily than most things. I would read as far in its six pages of small print as my energy allowed, while Angela sat listening, helping me with pronunciation, making a list of the words with which I had the most difficulty. Then I would take the list back to my room and practice them.

There were other books of poetry from which I read. Just yesterday, when I took my copy of *The Norton Anthology of Poetry* from its shelf, one of Angela's lists fell out. Reading the list—*argument, tedious, chimney, revisions, decisions, scuttling*—I remembered reading T. S. Eliot's "The Love Song of J. Alfred Prufrock," which, until my stroke, I had not read in many years. I also read Gerard Manley Hopkins's "Pied Beauty." *Glory be to God for dappled things,* I read, struggling, spitting, tripping over words until at the very end I was able get out the final *Praise him* with relative clarity.

Sometimes, trying to find my way in my damaged brain felt like trying to find my way in a darkened carnival fun house where nothing at all made sense. More than once I recoiled in shame, silence, and confusion after mistaking Angela's left hand for mine as she turned a page of the book in front of me. My own hand lay in my lap, still and forgotten by my brain, my brain that had also forgotten my son's phone number, many familiar words, what letter came after *Q* in the alphabet, and much of the left side of my world.

Sitting across from Angela in the small computer room next to the nurses' station, I asked: "Will I ever be able to speak without so much effort?" I had spent half an hour reading to her, while she wrote a list of the words I had trouble with. She looked me in the eyes and answered with honesty and warmth: "I don't know."

One day I took Kendall's paperback anthology outside with us. After months of work, I was going to try to read Millay's "Renascence" aloud, and my mind could hold nothing beyond that intention. Kendall pushed my wheelchair outside and parked it facing a bench on which she seated herself. The book opened naturally to that poem into which I'd poured so much of myself. I gripped the pages between the thumb and fingers of my right hand and—after looking into Kendall's clear blue eyes for an instant—began to read.

"*All I could see from where I stood / Was three long mountains and a wood,*" I began. And continued, line after line, page after page, while words from Angela's word lists filled my mind—*shrinking sight, immensity, remorse, undefined, swirled, omniscience.*

"*I know not how such things can be! / I breathed my soul back into me,*" I read. Like Millay's narrator, I too felt that I had tasted my own death, and the coming back. By loss of hope, I too had seen my vision limited. And I had known the heartbreaking beauty of that first spring after my stroke when I wept aloud at the sight of a bough of dogwood blossoms that Kendall broke from the tree and placed on my lap like a prayer. *The world stands out on either side,* I read. *No wider than the heart is wide.* Tears were streaming down Kendall's face. I read the last lines and took a deep breath. The poem was over.

I was still in a wheelchair. My left leg was still paralyzed. I did not have enough balance to stand without help. My left arm hung limp at my side. I was unable to move my hand. But I could read poetry aloud again. Not smoothly, not with the inflection that I wanted, not rapidly enough, and the words weren't always clear. But I had just read all six pages of "Renascence" aloud to Kendall. I felt as if I had been given wings.

VIII

It was early morning, just after breakfast and medications. I waited with other patients in wheelchairs lined up at the door of the therapy gym, some with artificial limbs laid across their laps. Others were paralyzed, mouths wordless and twisted. One old man stared out coldly. He would never look anyone in the eyes again. One young woman could no longer hold up her head. The man with one eye sewn shut talked to the man with a stump where his right hand had been. This could be hell. Or the purgatory of an unkind god. Or simply life. No more extraordinary than oceans. Or a single crab crawling across the sand. Or the last labored breath of the man in 402, his IV and oxygen disconnected, the day nurse coming on duty.

Soon the therapists arrived. Each gripped the handles of a wheelchair and pushed her patient to an exercise mat, a stationary bicycle, parallel bars, or a table filled with objects used in exercises to improve coordination. My therapist pushed me to the standing box. She helped me up from my wheelchair and into the box, where I stood as she locked me in. She told me that she'd be back in five minutes to release me and help me back into my wheelchair. I stood locked in the standing box, watching her walk away.

The standing box was exactly that—a tall, narrow box just large enough for me to stand in without room to fall. It came up to just above my waist. My paralyzed hand dangled at my side, while my functioning right hand steadied me in the box. I'd been locked in it in order to begin to regain the balance that the stroke took away. Here I could observe the other patients. Here I could stand without fear of falling. No one said a word. The room was filled with the thick silence of people whose damaged brains and bodies had no energy left for words as we struggled to do our work.

A gray-haired woman seated at a table moved a stack of cardboard cones one by one from her left side to her right, then back again. Her trembling hand moved like a great iron claw, mechanical and slow. A man in a hospital gown and slippers pushed pegs into a pegboard, took them out again. Another woman raised and lowered her left arm, raised and lowered her left arm. Everything here was done in slow motion and was repeated like an action repeated forever on a factory assembly line somewhere where there was no visible end product. *Theater of the absurd.* The phrase came to mind, and I searched my memories of the sixties to try to remember a play I saw then. But I couldn't recall the play, only the feelings of disorientation and despair that it evoked.

The therapist said I must stand here a full five minutes.

The far wall was a pegboard hung with leg braces and plastic legs, quad canes and straight canes, walkers. Dust motes floated in the slant of afternoon sun that fell through the window, and I was mesmerized by the motion of these thousands and thousands of particles. Watching them, I remembered standing in my grandfather's bedroom when I was young. The window shade was half-closed and, except for one slant of sun, my grandfather's room was dark. I stood there, stilled by amazement at my discovery of the dust particles. Looking at them, I lost all sense of time. It was as if they would be forever suspended there, as I would be left forever standing on the slanting floor in that old house with its wallpaper roses and cobwebs.

"Margaret," the therapist said, and I jumped, startled at the sound of my own name calling me back from childhood. "Margaret. Your five minutes are up," she said, and unlocked the back of the box.

I turned around carefully and took her outstretched hand.

———

IX

Gripping the bar to my right, I walked slowly, swinging my rigid left leg to the side while my spastic left arm drew itself up hard against my chest, hand knotted into a tight fist. Each step required my total concentrated attention. But I could finally walk the full length of the parallel bars that stood at the far end of the therapy gym. Now Loire, my physical therapist, was telling me that it was time to try walking with a cane. I felt terrified.

Immediately after she dismissed me, I wheeled myself to the office of Dr. Jones, the music therapist with whom I'd worked to control the anxiety that woke me mornings and kept me from falling asleep nights. Dr. Jones had bright, kind eyes and a soothing voice. She also had a pleasant office—photographs of flowers on the wall, plants in the window, music and meditation tapes, and a comfortable reclining chair. Being in her office brought relief from the impersonality of the ward's gym, dining room, nurses' station, and the long hall that someone was forever polishing.

Dr. Jones steadied me as I moved from my wheelchair to the reclining chair. Then she put a tape in the tape deck and instructed me to close my eyes and breathe deeply. I had many times led writing groups in similar guided relaxation meditations. It felt good to follow someone else's guidance. I began to relax.

Was the music Bach? Vivaldi? I seem to remember something baroque. As the tape played, Dr. Jones asked me to tell her what images I saw in my mind. The first images were vague and fleeting. Then I saw an image of me in the sky, sitting in Dr. Jones's reclining chair. As I watched myself floating there, the contours of the chair began to soften and blur until it became a chair of clouds. Then the clouds themselves began to shape themselves into hands. The hands began to tip me gently to one side, then the other, back and forth, up and down. They dipped, turned, and tossed me. As they did, the words *benevolent hands* came into my mind. *Benevolent hands.* With the words came the knowledge that I would not fall. I would not fall because the hands wouldn't let me. Then, from somewhere above my head, the sky opened and streamers in bright colors—red, blue, yellow, purple, green, orange, pink—cascaded over me. I felt washed in a sense of pure joy.

The next day I took my first steps with a cane.

X

John Elder and Mary came for me one bright Sunday afternoon after I was finally permitted to leave the hospital for brief periods. John Elder pushed me down the hall to the elevator, and we took it to the first floor. Then he pushed me down another hall and out into the parking lot. Mary transferred me to the car as she had been taught to do. John Elder folded the heavy hospital wheelchair and put it in the trunk. Then he backed the car up and headed north to South Hadley to a restaurant for lunch.

Because the left side of my face was paralyzed, I could not eat without having food spill out of the left side of my mouth as I chewed. In the hospital-ward dining room, I was not self-conscious about the way I ate. I felt more fortunate than patients who spilled even more food than I did, or than the woman who drooled all the time. Especially I felt grateful that I was not like the man who could hardly swallow at all.

I was determined that I would learn to accept my inability to eat in a socially acceptable manner. I would learn to be as much at ease with it as possible. And I would not let it keep me from going to restaurants. And I would simply take one of the large hospital bibs with me. Which is what I did that Sunday.

Mary checked to be sure the restaurant had a handicapped-accessible bathroom that would accommodate my wheelchair. Then she transferred me from the car to the wheelchair. John Elder pushed me to a table outside in the sun, and we ordered lunch.

It was wonderful to be away from the hospital with its hospital food, its rigid regime of medication and mealtimes, blood tests and weight checks, its overworked, rushed, and pressured staff. I was relieved to be away from constant reminders that I was a stroke survivor. My condition was always being mirrored back to me by the other patients with paralyzed limbs and damaged speech, by the sight everywhere of braces, walkers, canes, wheelchairs. I *knew* I was a stroke survivor. I knew also that I was badly disabled. What I needed was to be reminded strongly that I was still myself. I still had a life. And that *somehow,* I would be able to find a way to live it.

I squeezed lemon juice on my broiled fish.

My son looked at me. Then he lowered his eyes. Even though I could not see the expression on his heavily bearded face, or in his lowered eyes, I knew that my being alive mattered to him. But he was silent as Mary and I talked.

After lunch he drove us to the Summit House, an old hotel on Mount Holyoke between Hadley and South Hadley. Jenny Lind stayed there when she sang at the Academy of Music in Northampton. Emily Dickinson came from Amherst by carriage to hear her. Abraham Lincoln was said to have once stayed there too. The road up the mountain ran just above the dairy farm on which I had lived with my husband and sons for a year before we bought our house in Shutesbury. Below us I saw the hill John Elder sledded down that first winter in New England, and the driveway in which he'd stood, head bent over the open hood of his car while his great-uncle Bill Beattie first explained the workings of a car engine.

From the road I could see the apple tree in the backyard where year-old Christopher had stood at the fence feeding apples to the white-and-black cows that grazed there. And I remembered the many apple pies I baked and stored in the large freezer on the back porch.

John drank heavily by then. I struggled with depression. John and I had both brought to the marriage our own family histories, our own damaged childhoods. And it was all that history into which our sons were born and in which they grew up. The price for them was enormous. John Elder struggled with his own unhappiness over his attempts to relate to his peers. I searched for help for him, for myself, for us. There was a string of ineffectual social workers and family therapists. But it was John Elder's own inner resources that saved him. Nine years old, he played with his trains and Erector set. He read the Hardy Boys books, *National Geographic*, the *Encyclopaedia Britannica*. He ran with his dog, rode his bicycle, played with the farmer's son from next door. Sometimes, in his heavy leather boots and carrying his rock pick, he climbed the mountain.

Now the three of us—John Elder, Mary, and I—were climbing the mountain together in John Elder's car; the incline sharp, woods on either side of us.

At the top of the mountain, John Elder parked in the lot just below the Summit House, took my wheelchair out of the trunk, and unfolded it. Mary transferred me from the car. John Elder pushed the wheelchair up the hill until the hill became too steep. Then he turned the chair around and dragged it up the grassy incline beyond the Summit House, while Mary ran along behind it to catch me if I started to fall. Afraid of losing my precarious balance, I gripped the wheelchair armrest hard and sucked in my breath. Then my son dragged the wheelchair onto a large flat rock and locked its brakes.

I hadn't asked him where he'd intended to take me when he'd picked me up for this first outing with Mary and him since the stroke. Nor did I ask why he had chosen to take me to the mountain. But the place was exactly right. Sitting there on that rock high above the valley, my heart still beating rapidly after the excitement of the trip up, I knew it.

Below us, the Connecticut River twisted its way through the valley, the afternoon sun flashing off it. Below us also were the places in which my son, my daughter-in-law, and I had lived for so many years. The farmhouse stood at the base of the mountain, though we could not see it from the rock. To our south lay Granby, where, before her parents' divorce, Mary had grown up. Across the river was Mount Tom, where Mary's brother Dan had died of exposure, and behind us was the road on which her brother Paul had died in a traffic accident.

To the north, the skyscraper library and the residential towers of the University of Massachusetts rose in stark opposition to the pastoral landscape. It was there that John Elder's father taught, and where I had gotten my MFA in creative writing. It was there that John Elder had spent so many hours of his adolescence learning the complex workings of the computer, and where Mary had later studied archaeology.

Farther north still, in the Shutesbury woods, was the house in which we'd lived for twelve years before the divorce. John Elder had hiked and camped in the woods there, and in the yard there he'd played in the snow with his brother, building snow forts and snowmen; lady slippers and bluets mingled there with used-car parts as John Elder built his first car, which he drove over old logging trails near the house. Chris had played in his wing-shaped tree house in those woods, and I'd walked there, learning the names of wildflowers and mushrooms. In those woods, my husband had chopped and stacked the firewood.

It was in that house that I'd answered the phone to John Elder's numbed voice, saying, "Can someone pick me up at the hospital? I've just had my nose sewn back on." And all that evening long, upset and frightened about his brother's motorcycle accident, Chris had scrubbed at the blood that covered his brother's black leather jacket. It was all he could do.

It was in that house, when Chris was in the second grade, that he began to write poetry and short stories.

It was in the house in the Shutesbury woods that John Elder, when he was in his teens, began to build audio equipment for local bands. He also created light shows with strobe lights and worked with his oscilloscope. And as always, he read. It was in that house that I painted paintings, knitted mittens and caps, cleaned and cooked, wept and fought. At night, in front of the living room fireplace, I wrote long letters to my friend Pat King in Turkey, in London, in Houston. It was in that house that we lived, locked together in need, fear, pain, anger, despair, hope. And in love.

But that bright Sunday afternoon, the house was below us in the far distance. We had survived. As we sat on that large rock just beyond the Summit House, that in itself felt like enough.

XI

My old friend Pat King had come from Houston to be with me in rehab. I'd spent the day in speech, physical, and occupational therapy. It felt good to have Pat there beside me reading as I lay writing in my hospital bed. It felt good to see her familiar freckled arm and hand holding the book, her auburn hair still catching the light even though——as she is quick to say——the color has come from a bottle for years now. The effort to talk with her had exhausted me, just as seeing my weak, paralyzed body had exhausted her. Not only seeing me, but seeing the many other patients with their varying degrees of disability and suffering.

Why was it my role in Pat's life to be the vehicle through which she saw so much pain?

The last time she had been in Massachusetts, she had gone with me to the prison in Lancaster to see a performance by inmates who had participated in the theater/writing workshop that I co-taught with my friend Sheryl.

The women in the workshop came from diverse backgrounds. They were black, white, and Puerto Rican. Two of them could neither read nor write. One had a graduate degree. Some had grown up in middle-class environments, while others came from poverty-riddled neighborhoods. One woman had lived for a time with her children in the New York City subway. One woman with no place to live had searched city dumpsters for scraps of food. The women were serving time for a variety of reasons: possession of drugs, murder, embezzlement, and armed robbery.

We had spent months sharing life stories, discussing issues, expressing emotions. By the time of the performance, we had stripped away many of our preconceptions and expectations, and much of the prejudice and fear had dissolved as the women had come together supporting one another.

"I'm reaching for my life," Zeneida de Jesus had said, speaking for all of us, and not yet knowing that she was dying of AIDS.

Years of writing letters to Pat had strengthened me and helped me to see more clearly. Through writing to Pat, I had been able to face the end of my marriage. More than anyone else, Pat had played an intimate role in my struggle to come to words in the first place. Now, when words were so very difficult to speak aloud, and when I needed a strengthened connection with and renewed faith in the power of my words, it felt good and right to have her by my side even for a little while. At a time when I saw a difficult and lonely future, more frightening than any I'd ever imagined, I knew that if I could focus only on Pat's visit, I could allow myself to breathe, and within my new limitations, to simply *be.*

Sometimes Pat walked with me just outside the hospital building where I held on to the handrail along the sidewalk while taking slow, unsteady steps. One afternoon we sat outside and talked, she on a bench, me in my wheelchair. Only when the conversation was finished did Pat point out that for those few minutes, my speech had sounded almost normal.

It was true. I'd been spending two sessions a day working with my speech therapist and not once had speech come easily, or with the clarity of that conversation with Pat.

What was the difference? With Pat I was not conscious of the mechanics of speaking but was intensely focused on communication. This unselfconsciousness certainly contributed to the diminishment of the nervous anticipation that made me more spastic, making speech even more difficult. But there had been many other occasions since my stroke when communication had been my primary focus.

Perhaps relationships themselves have specific locations in the brain. Perhaps my relationship with Pat was located in a healthy and healing area, and in relating to Pat I was able to call on whatever was healing there. And who can say what role emotions play in the functioning and healing of the brain? I can only say that while talking with Pat, I forgot that I could not speak normally; I only knew that I was talking with my friend whom I loved deeply and who had loved and accepted me for many years. And for a few minutes one afternoon with Pat, I spoke almost as if I'd never had a stroke.

Chapter Twenty-five

In August, after more than three months in the hospital and rehab, I was discharged. My daughter-in-law, Mary, drove me home on Friday and spent the weekend with me, working to make the apartment accessible. She put a grab bar next to the toilet, attached a shower hose to the bathtub faucet, and set up a bath bench in the tub. She put small mirrors low over the kitchen sink and bathroom wash-basin so that I could see into them while seated in my wheelchair. She hammered an enormous nail through a cutting board and out the other side, making a spike on which to hold an onion or apple or whatever fruit or vegetable I might want to cut. She took me shopping for groceries, unpacked my things from the hospital. Most important, she was there, supporting me at what was one of the loneliest and most frightening times of my life.

It was also a time of great relief.

I was home.

But I'd lost my left side someplace in my stroke-damaged brain. And without my left side, everything around me felt both familiar and strange.

How was I going to live?

After Mary left, my friend Sally stayed with me for a while. She called social agencies and set up temporary help for me. Soon I was able to get help from Stavros, a national agency for independent living. Through Stavros, I was fortunate to choose my own helpers, who turned out to be marvelous women, and all involved in the arts. Together we worked at my rehabilitation, and—in every way they could—they worked to make my life one of quality.

As I'd done in the hospital, I began each day by writing before one or another of my helpers arrived. I woke early and sat at my table in my wheelchair facing a window overlooking the river. Most of the poetry I wrote was about experiences related to the stroke, and about the process of adjusting to life in a paralyzed body.

White Caps
White caps on the river.
Wind all day. Hard.
You've been dead three years.
Still I write you letters in my head.
And dream some nights of us together.
Indian summer's gone.
When I crossed the river bridge at dawn
a fine powder of snow was coming down.
My aide pushed my wheelchair
while I gripped the handrail. Mother,
I'm learning to walk again.

II

I was walking across the Iron Bridge with my friend Anne Plunkett as part of my therapy in learning to walk again when I first noticed the many spiderwebs hanging between the sections of iron latticework supporting the handrail. In the cold air of early morning, dew sparkled on the webs, making them look like exquisite and delicate creations of spun glass. Walking so slowly gave me the gift of seeing many beautiful things that I'd not noticed in my rapid walks across the bridge before the stroke.

Later Anne was responsible for having a wheelchair ramp built for me. It returned to me a little of my independence by enabling me to roll my wheelchair out of my apartment by myself.

In time I walked across the bridge with the series of remarkable women who served as my PCAs (personal-care attendants) and became my friends. We walked across the bridge in spring, when the river was full from the melted snow, and in summer, when the river was low and slow-moving and small boys stood on the bridge with tackle boxes and fishing poles, fish lines dangling over the railing. We walked across the bridge in fall, when gold leaves floated on the water and bones of trees huddled on the riverbank, anticipating winter. We walked in winter, when the surface of the river froze, and the wind was hard and cold, and I wore holes in my right mitten from its many trips up and down the bridge rail. And all the while I walked, Hart Crane's words repeated themselves in my mind—*The very idea of a bridge . . . is an act of faith.*

III

Sometime after my stroke Chris told me that I was his ruined mother and that he wished I'd died, that it would have been easier for him. It was true that I could no longer walk or use my left arm and hand, and my balance was poor. My speech had improved, though it was still difficult for people to understand me. And to speak at all required great effort.

But I was exceedingly glad to be alive.

And I could still write.

One day I emailed one of my new poems to Chris. He called as soon as he received it. "You still have your same mind," he said with amazement. "I love that poem."

Poetry always mattered to Chris. Even as a little boy he wrote poetry. But once he was an adult working in the advertising world, he stopped. And he drank heavily. However, there was a brief period sometime in the 1990s, after he moved to New York City, when he was sober. During that time, he wrote more than two hundred poems. Even as first drafts those poems were amazing. I typed all of them for him as a way of showing my support, but I don't know if my doing this mattered to him, or if he ever saw what incredible poetry he'd written. By that time he'd begun to write prose.

It was sometime during the years he worked in advertising in New York that I began to write my memoir, much of which I sent to him through email or read to him over the phone. We would continue to exchange and critique each other's work for nearly twenty years.

But he was drinking again and often woke me in the middle of the night.

"Do you know how difficult it is to write in your shadow?" he would yell. Then he would spew out his anger to me about his adolescence after the divorce. He was especially angry that I hadn't made enough money to maintain the lifestyle we had when John and I were married.

I listened. I was still under the influence of some of Dr. Turcotte's ideas, especially that expressing anger was a part of the process of healing. If expressing anger was good for Chris, then I was determined to listen. But it exhausted me emotionally and physically. I woke many mornings after his calls with little energy to start the day.

Sometime during Chris's years in New York City, I gave a reading at the Northampton Center for the Arts. Chris was on vacation on Cape Cod at the time and both pleased and surprised me by hiring a pilot to fly him to Northampton for the reading. I had seen him only two or three times since the stroke, and those visits had been brief.

After the reading, he came up to me and expressed great enthusiasm. He was surprised that despite my physical limitations, I could still give an effective poetry reading. "I never realized until tonight that I got my stage presence from you," he said excitedly. "And you still have it!"

Seeing Chris was the highlight of the evening for me. I told him I would love to go someplace and visit with him for a while. He responded quickly, saying that the pilot was waiting to fly him back to the Cape. As we were talking, my new therapist surprised me by coming up and introducing herself to him. She told him that he must never again disturb my sleep by calling in the middle of the night. She explained that I needed my rest and his disruptions were a threat to my health.

I remember no more of that incident. Did she say anything else? Did he say anything to her? Did she just make the statement and leave? I have no idea.

What I do remember is feeling shocked at what seemed to me to be inappropriate behavior on her part. Inappropriate or not, after her brief confrontation with Chris, he never again woke me at night with a drunken explosion of rage, and for that I was deeply grateful.

IV
1990

"Your new brain," Julia Chevan, my physical therapist, said, referring to my stroke-damaged brain. We were walking around the therapy gym at Cooley Dickinson Hospital, where I went three times a week. My steps were hesitant, slow. *My new brain*, I repeated to myself, and thought of an article I'd just read in *Omni* magazine called "Catastrophes That Shaped the Earth." The article was illustrated by images of floods, earthquakes, and volcanoes. *How long will it take me to learn the territory of this new brain?* I asked myself.

I was afraid of my new brain. Unpredictably and often, the connection between it and my left leg seemed to become momentarily severed, causing my leg to suddenly stop moving, throwing me dangerously off balance. And always my brain was filled with noise that sounded like static from a poorly tuned radio, static that continued for over a year after my stroke. It made thinking difficult. But since the stroke, the most frightening thing about my new and unpredictable brain had been the grand mal seizure that I had recently experienced. It happened almost ten months after the stroke.

Suddenly and without warning, my body had begun to twist slowly and uncontrollably to my right. I was sitting in my wheelchair at my writing table in the kitchen. Marilyn Zelwian, my friend and PCA, stood with her back to me, washing dishes. As my body began to twist, I saw the fingers on my right hand begin to curl toward the palm the way the fingers on my spastic left hand had curled since the stroke.

"Marilyn," I started to shout, but my mouth contorted wordlessly as my head twisted itself on my neck the way a child might twist the head on a doll into some impossible position.

My brain trembled against my skull.

With a shock of terror, I felt like I was being sucked up in a giant, powerful vacuum, leaving my body through the top of my head.

"No, Margaret!" Marilyn cried out as I lost consciousness.

She told me later that I threw my head back and rolled my eyes upward until only the whites showed. All color drained from my face, while bloody saliva ran from the corners of my mouth. My body shook violently and then went limp.

Marilyn thought I had suffered another stroke. In fact, I'd had a grand mal seizure caused, my doctor suspected, by scar tissue from the stroke. An EEG showed electrical activity indicating the probability of future seizures, for which my doctor prescribed the anticonvulsive drug Dilantin. I'd been taking it for two weeks, and all visible effects of the seizure had disappeared.

Except for Julia's comments and instructions, we walked silently. Walking—as always since the stroke—required my total attention. And since I wasn't walking between the parallel bars with their relative safety, I walked close to the wall for security.

Suddenly I lost my balance and began to fall against the wall to my left. As Julia grabbed my right arm, I caught myself, regaining my balance. I gripped my cane tightly. Remembering the near fall, and anticipating a future fall, I began to walk again, my spastic side stiff with fear.

Which increased the possibility of an accident.

I looked down at my feet. How could I focus entirely on the present step without a thought given to the last step or the next? Our great spiritual teachers have always tried to teach us to live wholly in the present moment. How long would it take me to learn to do that with my stroke-damaged brain?

How was I going to learn to walk confidently with my cane and not near a wall for security again?

I was twelve years old when I read the story of a boy who wanted more than anything else to be able to pitch a baseball. He had been born with cerebral palsy that caused him to be spastic. For many years he worked toward his goal of throwing the baseball, years of hard and finely focused effort. And he succeeded—he was finally able to pitch a baseball.

He wrote that while other people might be able to pitch with more accuracy and ease, he felt certain that no one pitched with greater joy. Most people pitched the ball as an almost unconscious act. He, on the other hand, was almost totally conscious of what he was doing. I loved that story. I thought that it would be wonderful to be so mindful of what one was doing. To be that aware.

Looking down at my feet in the gym with Julia at the end of our session that day, I remembered that story. It had been nearly a year since the stroke, and my brain was still unable to get my leg to do what I wanted it to do. Now Julia was telling me that she could no longer work with me. I was not showing enough visible progress to satisfy the insurance company. I went home, doubting my ability to walk again with any reasonable degree of skill and confidence.

To fight my new doubt, and to build something to stand in place of the loss of therapy with Julia, I intensified my efforts to walk across the Iron Bridge. As always when my PCAs and I walked, I thought of the words of Hart Crane: *The very idea of a bridge . . . is an act of faith.*

In the summer of 1992, when I went back to the hospital to work with Barbara Jenkins, my speech therapist, I met Julia in the hall. She said that she could see that my walking had improved since she'd last worked with me; she thought she might once again be able to help. Would I like her to give me a reevaluation?

I felt elated.

While out in my wheelchair almost two years before, I'd met a young woman walking with a brace on one leg. Our visible disabilities drew us together. She told me that a car accident was responsible for her paralysis. I noticed that her brace was hinged at the ankle, where my own brace was rigid. "If it's ever possible," she said, "try to get a hinged brace like mine. It feels so much better to walk in than the one you have. Much more like normal walking."

I filed this information away. I intended to have such a brace someday. With Julia's offer to reevaluate my walking, I saw the opportunity to discuss the possibility. With renewed hope, I set a time to meet with her.

At my appointment, Julia pointed out that I was using my leg more the way one might use a wooden leg than one made of flesh and bone and blood. She noted that my ankle was so stiff it was almost immovable. *But I was able to get from one place to another,* I comforted myself.

However, after I'd spent years walking that way, my knee was beginning to cause me problems, and I often had backaches. These conditions could only become more problematical as I continued to walk this way.

No, Julia said. I could not have a hinged brace. There wasn't enough flexibility in my ankle to make that possible. But if I could regain some flexibility, if I could make some progress . . .

If. The word meant hope, and I clung to it.

Julia was going to be away for the month of August. If, when she returned, I was able to show her a more flexible ankle, if I was able to shift my weight more to my left side, if I was able to master the exercises that she was going to give me, then we would meet with

Frank Twyeffort, who made prosthetic devices for the hospital, and we would talk about the possibility of a hinged brace.

Julia also agreed to meet with Susan and Ellen, two of my PCAs, and teach them how to help with the exercises that she was going to give me. She would also make a video of the two of us doing the exercises while she explained for the camera what she was doing. Both my helpers and I would be able to refer to the film.

"The theme for the summer," Julia announced when we met again to go over the exercises, one of which she told me to do about a million times while she was away, "is symmetry." But how was I going to be able to develop symmetry when half of my body was so deadened to feeling?

Almost immediately Susan left for the Midwest to visit family. She was gone for over two weeks, leaving Ellen and me alone together to struggle with finding ways to do the exercises. I found that my brain could translate some verbal instructions to action more quickly and effectively than others. Extremely sensitive to physical cues, I had grown accustomed to working with Julia, who used the lightest, most articulate touch I'd known. Now I was turning to Ellen to do with me what a gifted and professionally trained therapist had done. And what we were trying to do felt more difficult than anything I'd done since my early efforts at walking. I was easily tired and frustrated. Ellen was patient and acutely observant. With each meeting she grew more confident, directive, and effective than the last. By the time Susan returned from her trip, Ellen and I had developed a successful way of working together. She taught Susan what she'd learned. Ellen or Susan worked with me five days a week.

Afraid that I had not accomplished what was necessary for me to be able to have a hinged brace, I put off making an appointment with Julia. I kept telling myself that I would give myself one more day of exercise before calling her.

I finally made the call in October and was shocked to find that Julia no longer worked at the hospital but had accepted a job at a nearby college teaching other therapists. However, she had left word at the hospital arranging to meet with Frank and me. I was relieved and grateful.

Frank arrived first for the appointment. While I sat on a high exercise table, legs dangling, he removed my left shoe and my brace and examined my foot and ankle. He rotated my foot. Then, pressing against my sole, he forcefully bent my foot back toward the shin. There was a new flexibility in my ankle. Perhaps I was going to be able to get the hinged brace after all.

When Julia saw what I'd been able to accomplish over the summer, she was pleased. I sat in quiet celebration while she and Frank talked about the design of the new brace.

Then Frank looked at me. "Your work is just beginning," he said, fastening the Velcro strap on my old brace and slipping my shoe on. "From now on, you'll have to do your exercises daily. You have to look at it," he said, fastening my shoe and pulling my pant leg over my brace, "as if you're going to be in school for the rest of your life, with no weekends off."

But I will be able to walk bending my ankle, I thought.

In the early weeks following my stroke, Julia and Patricia Jung had both worked with me. Now Patricia agreed to take Julia's place as my therapist. My sense of balance was still so poor that I felt like I might topple over or fall to one side. Even getting up from the exercise table by leaning forward and lifting my buttocks from the table as instructed not only exhausted but frightened me. I still felt relatively safe only between the parallel bars.

But after I finished the exercises in the treatment room, Patricia announced that I was not going to walk in the gym at all. Using my cane as support, I was going to walk in the hall. I had become too dependent on the parallel bars for my sense of safety. Patricia intended to help me move away from that dependency. Walking with me toward the hall, she explained that she believed one learns more effectively if one is not always able to anticipate what's coming next.

I knew Patricia was right. But I was tired of working so hard. Wearing the hinged brace made me feel frighteningly insecure when I walked. To adapt to it was going to require much more time and effort than I'd anticipated. Easing myself off the exercise table and making my way across the treatment room, I remembered again the story of the boy who had worked so long and hard to be able to throw a baseball. But I wasn't a young boy; I was a woman in late middle age.

I looked down the long expanse of carpet leading to the waiting room. I thought of Rilke's words: *If the angel deigns to come, it will be because you have convinced him, not by tears, but by your humble resolve to be always beginning.*

To be always beginning. Yes. The stroke had obliterated my ability to take an ordinary step. Communication between my left leg and brain was no longer the easy, unconscious thing it had been. My brain was struggling to find new ways to reroute messages, to create a new communications system. I remembered Julia's phrase: *new brain.* I would learn to live with this new brain, and to live in the present moment as well.

Each slow step was teaching me how.

V

My grandson, Jack, was born April 12, 1990, at Cooley Dickinson Hospital. As soon as I heard that Mary was pregnant, I was more determined than ever to regain use of my paralyzed left arm and hand so I could hold my grandchild.

Sharlette Risely, my occupational therapist, was so intensely focused on helping me achieve my goal that she sometimes dreamed at night about ways to help me. But despite our efforts, my hand lay limp on the table in the therapy room. And when I stood, my arm dangled useless by my side.

Even so, the day after Jack was born, John Elder laid him against my chest, where, with the help of my right arm and hand, I cradled him for over an hour while he slept.

In September of that same year Mary started studying at the university for her master's degree in anthropology. For the entire school year I, with help, kept Jack for two days each week while Mary attended classes. I delighted in watching him playing and sleeping in his playpen on my kitchen floor. I fed him and even learned to change his clothes with one hand.

When the weather was pleasant one of my helpers pushed me around town in my wheelchair while I held Jack on my lap. We went to the bank and grocery store, through town and across the Iron Bridge that spans the Deerfield River. Wherever we went people were friendly to Jack, who, in time, learned to respond to their waves by waving back. When he was around eleven months old he began to hold my hand and walk beside my wheelchair for brief periods.

While Mary arranged things on the dining table in their home for a party for Jack's first birthday, he pulled himself up and stood holding on to a table leg beside her. Sitting on the couch across the room, I called his name. To my surprise he let go of the table leg and walked to me.

Jack is now a brilliant and handsome young college student studying organic chemistry. When he comes to see me, he pushes me across the Bridge of Flowers and around town in my wheelchair.

After twenty-one years, my left hand still lies limp in my lap, but I am exceedingly grateful to have lived long enough to have watched my grandson grow from the small boy who walked independently on his first birthday to the fine young man he has become.

VI

After a year of working to regain my ability to speak, I was ready to give a poetry reading at Cooley Dickinson. It was important to me to give the staff at least a glimpse of what the experience of recovering from a stroke was like from a patient's point of view, and I had written many poems with that focus. It was also time for me to reclaim my role as a public speaker.

Barbara Jenkins, my speech therapist for the five weeks I was at Cooley Dickinson just after the stroke and again after my five months at Weldon Rehab in Springfield, was working with me. Barbara, a creative writer herself, did videos of me reading my poetry. Then together we watched each video. Sometimes simply hearing a mistake was enough for me to be able to correct myself. Barbara analyzed the mistakes I couldn't correct myself. Sometimes she wrote phonetic spelling over a word that was causing me difficulty. Other times she had to call on her own creativity to find ways to help me pronounce difficult words. For instance, she drew a little pear beside the word *paralyzed.*

Speaking had become much easier over the year, but reading poetry or prose was still extremely difficult for me, and I spent many hours practicing the poems I planned to read at the hospital. By the day of the reading I felt confident that I could get through the reading without an excessive amount of stumbling. Barbara introduced me, emphasizing the difficulty I had had to overcome and the hard work I'd done to be able to read with clarity and expression after having almost lost my ability to speak at all after the stroke.

Rising from my wheelchair to face the audience of familiar faces, I felt like I was coming home to myself.

Chapter Twenty-six

CHRIS HAD BROKEN UP WITH HIS PARTNER AND MOVED TO NEW YORK when he began to write his memoir. He often commented that hearing or reading sections from mine was very helpful in writing his. He called and emailed me frequently to ask questions about his childhood, and about the years covered in what became his book *Running with Scissors*. I answered everything I could remember.

The more he wrote, the less he shared.

As he completed his book, he distanced himself from me. Shortly before publishing it, he asked if I was going to sue him. The question surprised me. I assured him I would never sue him, that he was my son whom I loved and would always love with all my heart. But I understood why he had asked the question when I read *Running with Scissors*.

I was shocked and brokenhearted. I went through a gamut of emotions. Even as I nursed deeply hurt feelings and anger toward Chris, I felt compassion for him knowing the pain from which his dark humor arose. But I also struggled with my ego, which wanted to defend me.

Before newspapers began contacting me with questions—as they did almost immediately after the book's release—I knew I had to make a decision about how I was going to respond to Chris's book publicly. I decided to say as little as possible, and I declined requests for interviews.

Privately, I went through a period of prayer and meditation. I also went through much emotional struggling and journaling. The following are excerpts from my journal of that period.

6-26-02: I've been crying this morning. I felt like I had been hit in the gut and heart again and again. How could Chris do such blatant lying about me? And when he's not totally lying, he's presenting me—the me that he's created—in a hard, cruel, shockingly superficial, light. How can I hold onto my love for him when he's attacking me unmercifully? Of course I can hold onto my love for him. Nothing could diminish it.

But how can I deal with the pain?

6-27-02: I am grateful that my body had no adverse physical response when I read Chris's book.

But my guts are in a knot. What I feel is depressed, depressed and guilty that I'm depressed. I don't even want to write emails to Chris anymore. And yet I long to hear from him.

6-29-02: What can I possibly say to Chris about his book? That I'm sorry he has suffered so much in his life; that I'm grateful that he found a way to be the writer he'd dreamed of being. I can tell him that.

7-2-02: I continue to love Chris, but have great difficulty with living with much of what he is doing in relation to me.

I looked forward to my weekly Tuesday-afternoon massage. My masseur, Brian, had worked for years to relieve the spasticity in my left side. Lying on the massage table he set up in my kitchen, I had relaxed when, from the radio in the background, I heard the announcer saying that *All Things Considered* was brought to us by this foundation and that foundation and "by Augusten Burroughs, author of *Running with Scissors,* a book about ..."

My thoughts spun in shock, giving me a dizzy feeling that blurred the rest of the sentence.

"Was that your son he was talking about?" Brian asked.

"I wasn't listening," I lied.

At the moment of that radio announcement, I felt all safety for me in my village drain away. Though Chris had changed the names of the people in his book, he left no room for doubt about his characters' identities. His egotistical mother—according to his book—who wrote "mediocre" poetry, lived in an apartment by a river in a small town near the Massachusetts and New Hampshire border, and was paralyzed on one side of her body by a stroke.

After thirteen years of walking across the river bridge, or beside the falls, holding the handrail while one helper or another pushed my wheelchair, I was one of the most consistently visible people in town. Strangers have stopped to tell me that watching me inspired them. Townspeople often said that when they had something difficult to face, they would think of me to give them courage. *What will these people think of me now?* I thought. *Or others who read the book, or read about it?* My town was filled with writers and writers' groups. *The New York Times Book Review* was common reading here in this small village tucked between gentle hills, with a river flowing through it.

I thought of standing with Bubba as we took the cards from the wreaths and bouquets of flowers at his infant son's grave more than thirty-three years earlier. Years earlier, Bubba's baby girl had been killed in a collision with a truck on a rain-slicked highway when she was only nine months old. Now his son had just been buried beside her.

The wind blew a wreath of flowers to the ground. Bubba bent and placed the wreath upright again. Then he stood staring at the carpet of artificial grass covering the freshly dug grave.

I looked down at his shoes, shined to a high gloss, black shoes that had become a black mirror reflecting the gold of chrysanthemums.

"If God is punishing me, surely this is enough," Bubba had said. His voice was leaden—a dirge without music.

I'd wanted to hug him and say, "No. God is *not* punishing you. I don't know why these things are happening to you, but I don't believe for a minute that God is punishing you." But our relationship didn't allow for such intimacy even at such a moment, so I just stood silently there with him, my eyes riveted on the gold flowers reflected in his shoes.

If Chris is punishing me, surely this is enough. That was the thought that flashed through my mind, bringing back to consciousness my brother's words spoken so many years before. But I wasn't facing a tragedy like Bubba had experienced. I had two sons, alive and healthy. Yet I had lost the relationship with Chris that had mattered so much to me. I was left with unbearable loss and grief.

II

In *The Washington Post* Chris was quoted as saying about me: "She thinks she's famous. Everything to her is about her. She wonders what she's going to tell her 'press' when they call about the book. I'm like, 'What press?'"

Could Chris hate me so much? I sent him an email saying that I'd read the *Washington Post* article. I told him that I loved him and would always love him. He replied by email saying that it was great that his book had gotten two full pages in the *Post.* He added that the same thing was going to happen soon in the *L.A. Times, The New York Times,* and the *Boston Herald.*

III

On September 25, 2002, I wrote an email to Chris about the pain I felt in being misrepresented in an article in *People* magazine for which

I'd been interviewed. My email went unanswered. On September 29 I attempted to send the following email to him:

> I see that your book is climbing on the bestseller list again. I am happy for you. I appreciate the enormity of your talent, and the disciplined hard work you've put in to develop it.
>
> I'm enjoying these glorious fall days. I hope you're enjoying them too.
> I love you unconditionally.

When I attempted to send the email, the following message appeared on my screen: "This member is currently not accepting e-mail from your account."

Reading those words, I bent sobbing over the keyboard. I felt like a large part of my heart had been torn out. I had lost one of the most precious things in my life—the email connection with my son, that thin, fragile line of communication I had nurtured with such care because it was all that I had with him.

IV
2009

When working on my memoir, I talked with Suzanne about the time Chris overheard us making love. She told me that her memory of the occasion was that Chris walked into the room in which we had just made love and that I asked him to hand me my robe from the foot of the bed. Suzanne said she was already dressed by that time.

My memory was that Suzanne and I were at the kitchen table drinking coffee when I heard Chris walking down the stairs and out the front door. I realized then that Chris must have been in the next bedroom taking a nap while we made love and would have heard us. Was Suzanne's memory at all shaped by details one of her daughters might have told her about the incident as described in *Running with Scissors*? (Suzanne herself has never read the book.) Was my memory shaped by an attempt to ease the pain of what really happened, whatever that might have been?

According to Chris's account in *Running with Scissors*, he walked in on us making love on the living room couch, a thing we would never have done. And his disgusting description of our lovemaking as well as his talk with Suzanne outside the apartment were both fiction, fiction his anger toward me must have inspired. That he was having a sexual relationship with Jim contributed nothing to his understanding and acceptance of me as his mother having a sexual relationship with another woman. After Suzanne left, I sat at the kitchen table drinking coffee and smoking a cigarette. It wasn't long before Chris returned to the apartment and came into the kitchen shouting angrily at me for having had sex with a woman. Instead of recognizing his emotions and trying to talk with him in an understanding, supportive way, I responded defensively. I hope Chris will find it in his heart to forgive me someday for this, and for all the ways I failed him.

V

When John Elder was forty, a doctor friend of his diagnosed him as having Asperger's syndrome. That knowledge changed John Elder's life dramatically for the better. He not only had a clearer understanding of his feelings and behavior from the time he was a boy until he was diagnosed, he learned ways in which he could change his behavior in order to relate to others more effectively.

I didn't learn of his diagnosis and its effects on his life until he was nearly fifty. Once he and Mary were divorced, he rarely visited or called me. It wasn't until he began to write his memoir that he began to call me, and then he called frequently. His editor told him he needed to write more about his experiences growing up. Because he remembered so little, he depended on me to tell him my memories of his childhood. I was more than happy to do this, not only because I wanted to help him, but also because it gave me the opportunity to hear his voice.

His memoir, *Look Me in the Eye*, has spoken to people over much of the world and continues to educate people about Asperger's as well as to inspire them. I am proud of him and his memoir, though I was surprised at some of the things he wrote that never happened. No ambulance, but Ethel Swift, Dr. Turcotte's part-time assistant, came to take me to the state hospital, and John Elder didn't visit me there. He and Chris were in Georgia with his grandparents the entire twenty-one days I was hospitalized. But more important than questioning our different memories is affirming the fact that not only did John Elder survive his past, but that he has created an incredibly successful and fascinating life.

He must have been not more than twenty-one when he began to build trick guitars for the rock band KISS—guitars that were lit in various patterns with dozens of tiny lights blinking on their surfaces, and guitars that shot rockets into the audience. He traveled with KISS for several years while building and working on their sound equipment. After that, he went on to be an engineer designing electronic games for Milton Bradley. He then worked at a company that built and installed burglar alarms and at another company that built computer components. And always he has been involved in one way or another with cars.

After he married Martha, a woman I really never got to know, he built a house on the outskirts of Amherst. Jack lived there while attending the Amherst High School, and spent many weekends with his mother in South Hadley.

Chris and his partner, Dennis, moved from New York City and built a house on the lot next to John Elder's, though John Elder rarely saw or communicated with Chris, who spent most of his time inside writing on his computer. After nine or ten years Dennis terminated his relationship with Chris. In their settlement Dennis kept the house and Chris moved to a small apartment in New York near Central Park. Since both John Elder and Chris are now divorced from their partners, they sometimes talk on the phone or email each other. However limited their relationship may be, I'm grateful that my sons have each other.

Chapter Twenty-seven

I

2005

"I'M DYING, MARGARET," JOHN ANNOUNCED AS SOON AS HE SAW ME IN the doorway of his hospital room. His wife, Judy, waited in the hall. She was to take him home the next day to die.

John was so weak he could barely speak above a whisper. Grateful to have time alone with him, I parked my wheelchair next to his bed. He was struggling to lift a plastic spoonful of crushed ice. He handed me the spoon, and I raised it to his open mouth. Then I continued to feed him crushed ice as we talked.

My husband for twenty-three years, father of our two sons. He was the person with whom I first saw the vivid colors of fall leaves in the North, and, after that, our first snow, the two of us standing in our backyard in Philadelphia in the middle of the night in our pajamas, snow falling on our upturned faces. "Because I experienced these things first with you," John wrote in an anniversary note to me years after our divorce.

I fed him more crushed ice. We said we still loved each other. There was no reason to remember the anger, pain, and sadness, and every reason to remember the love.

"What do you think happens after we die?" John asked, his eyes lit by fear and longing.

"I believe we just continue our journeys," I replied.

He was quiet. Reflective.

He opened his mouth for more ice.

After a while John Elder arrived. I said I was leaving so that they could have time alone together. As I pushed my wheelchair toward the door, John Elder, who stood by the bed holding his father's hand, reached back and grabbed my hand, gripping it tightly. "Stay," he said.

I stayed.

"So your liver finally gave up, is that it?" he asked his father, and began to sob aloud. He gripped my hand harder. "I'll dig your tractor out of the snow and park it so you can see it from your window when you get home. Would you like that? And the Jaguar?"

"Yes, son," John whispered.

Still holding both John's and my hand, John Elder sat down in the chair beside the bed. We talked about happy times during John Elder's early childhood. Especially we talked about our many adventures camping. John was too weak to say many words, but I elaborated on the few images he suggested, and he affirmed the stories I told.

There, for a few precious minutes, at the threshold of John's death, we were a family again.

II
2009

John has been dead for four years now, and Chris has written his sixth book, *The Wolf at the Table*, published in May of 2008. Another memoir, it is a dark, grim book focused primarily on his father. Since reading *Running with Scissors*, I'd read none of his other books. When I scanned them in bookstores and found each to contain more fiction about the woman he called his mother, I didn't bother to read more. However, after reporters from several newspapers, including *The New*

York Times, asked for my response to his new memoir, I decided to buy a copy of it.

I must have read it quickly and put it away, blocking it from my mind. I'd not planned on writing any more about Chris. But after I recently came across an interview with him that I'd not read, I realized that I had to state that John didn't do several terrible things Chris claimed he did, and I read it again. It's true that John did many terrible things when we were married, but he didn't do those things, and I can't find it in my heart to let those things stand as fact when John is not here to defend himself.

John certainly didn't starve Ernie, Chris's guinea pig. As I remember it, Chris gave Ernie to a little girl, a friend of his from school. And John was nothing but kind to Chris's dog Grover. I was the one who took Grover to the vet, who did all he could to ease his pain from throat cancer. When Grover's pain could no longer be eased, John took him to the vet, who put him to sleep.

John never turned Chris's dog Brutus against him. Brutus was a gentle, friendly dog all his life and slept on Chris's bed nights. The only trouble we had with him was when he followed runners passing the house and got lost. He was once lost for several months before someone called and Chris and Brutus were reunited. Sadly, when the time came for us to have to move from the Shutesbury house, the owner of the only apartment we could find in Amherst didn't permit pets. Chris decided to give Brutus to a friendly fireman from the Amherst Fire Department, so he became the firehouse dog.

I was also shocked anew at the fiction he'd written about his father and me.

I don't know why he chose to imagine me telling him about John's and my wedding, but he did, including a false account of my emotional state that day. I felt upset at how he portrayed Lucille, the black woman who worked for my family until I was thirteen years old. I was especially offended by the way Chris said she talked. And she would never have added rum to the punch served at the wedding reception, for mine was not a drinking family. I certainly didn't think the day of my wedding would be the happiest day of my life, as he wrote, and my friends never told me that I should go to New York City and become a model or an actress. Perhaps Chris wrote about the mother he wished he had.

Whether Chris's memoirs are fact or fiction, the stories he's written about his survival have inspired many young people with troubled childhoods to believe that they too can survive and succeed in life. For this I am grateful. Sometimes troubled parents and young people write to me at my website for support because of Chris, and I'm grateful I have had the opportunity to be of help. I send him love and wish him well as he continues to live his gifted and extraordinary life.

III
1938

Three years old, I woke from my afternoon nap. The room was hot and stuffy. I climbed from my bed and went outside to find my mother in the backyard. As the screen door slammed behind me, she looked up from where she was bent over in the flower garden and waved. I climbed down the steps and felt the warmth of the prickly grass on the soles of my bare feet.

Next door the undertaker unloaded a body from the hearse and carried it through the wide back door of the funeral home. I watched as he backed the hearse into its usual parking space and went inside again. Troubling thoughts tumbled inside me. First there were thoughts about Granddaddy's recent death. Then I thought about my own death.

I felt frighteningly alone.

As if instructed to do so, I looked up at the sky.

Above me, three small white clouds floated slowly north——north past Grandmother's house and Uncle Frank's and the filling station; north to Albany and Atlanta; north to New York City, where Daddy went on business trips and bought me a dress from a place called Macy's.

North.

As I stood watching those clouds, I heard a voice speaking in my heart. "Don't worry, Margaret," it said. "You will die in the North when you are very old. By that time you will understand about death and will not be afraid."

My whole self filled with wonder. I felt comforted as never before. All my troubled thoughts dissolved, and I was once again in a world of butterflies and flowers and the heart-shaped fish pool where fish flashed gold among the lily pads.

Now I'm an old woman and live in the North, just as the voice told me I would. And I am no longer afraid of death. It's been a long journey from the Cairo, Georgia, of my childhood to the New England of my old age, and I know that, for all its detours, wrong roads taken, and stops along the way, it has always been a spiritual one. I also know that the all-loving, all-knowing voice I heard in my heart when I was a child has been with me forever, even during the many times I turned away from it. I know now that I've always been coming home.

Acknowledgments

I am deeply grateful to David Kuhn, my agent, who believed in this book from the beginning and sold it almost as soon as he received it, and to Jessi Cimaforte, an associate at Kuhn Projects, who encouraged and inspired me with her enthusiasm and her many positive remarks. I am also deeply grateful to my perceptive editor Cindy Spiegel, whose edits made all the difference, and to Hana Landes, assistant editor at Spiegel & Grau, who worked faithfully on my memoir. I am also forever indebted to Susan Wyant, who was the only person to read every page of this memoir during the ten years I spent working on it between writing several books of poetry. Susan not only gave me her insightful responses and brilliant suggestions, but also had a deep and consistent appreciation of my work that encouraged and inspired me through even the most difficult times of remembering and writing. I am forever thankful for my daughter-in-law Mary Robison, who continues to devote much of her time to doing everything she can to keep me healthy enough to continue my work. I'm grateful to my son Chris (Augusten Burroughs), who critiqued the chapters he read over the years and supported my work until the publication of his book *Running with Scissors*. And to my son John Elder Robison, author of *Look Me in the Eye*, who supports my memoir as well as supports me in my everyday life. I am especially grateful to my grandson, Jack, for his exuberant nature, his helpfulness, his sharing of his many interests, and the joy he gives me by simply being Jack.

I am forever indebted to Katherine Kendall, without whose help I might not have survived the stroke or healed enough to write this book, and to my brother Wyman Richter and his wife, Anne, whose help in telling me long-forgotten dates and places was essential. I'm grateful for the support of Barbara Jenkins, fellow writer and dear friend, whose brilliant and creative approach to speech therapy at Cooley-Dickinson Hospital in Northampton was a major contribution to my learning to speak again, and for all the help she continued to give me long after formal therapy was over. I'm also grateful for the support of Angela Manssolillo, my speech therapist in rehab at Mercy Hospital in Springfield, whose compassion and understanding were major in my learning to read poetry aloud again. Also for Sharlotte Risley, my occupational therapist, and my doctors Charles Brummer, Marci Yoss, and Lawrence Schiffman. I am grateful to Pat Schneider, who published my book-length poem *Red Creek*, and to Bethany Schneider, who edited my yet-to-be-published *New and Selected Poems*. And to Peter Schneider, who helped me learn to drive again after my stroke, and to Paul Schneider, who introduced me to David Kuhn.

I am deeply grateful for the supportive friendships of Dee Waterman, Marilyn Zelwian, Alaina Beach, Mary Jean Devlin, John Hapeman, Pat Bega, Debra Yaffee, Peg Robbins, Kathy Crane, Ruth Gallagher, Maija Meijers, June MacIvor, Mary Julia Richter Coons, Rita Larrow, Brian and Piyali Summer, Delores Culp, Dennis Helmus, Anne Plunkett, Clifton McCracken, Charles Lewis, Henry Lyman, and all of my PCAs over the years.

I'm grateful to my cousin Margaret Rushin Anderson, who became my friend after we met at my fourth birthday party. We were close friends until we graduated from high school and Margaret married and moved to Germany, while I began my freshman year of college. We became close again in 1984 and continue to be close. I am grateful not only for Margaret's emotional support as I spent so many years looking back at my life, but also for all the rich conversations we had about our past as I wrote about it, and our present lives as we continue to experience them.

I am forever grateful to Pat King.

About the Author

A former leader of creative writing workshops in elementary schools, prisons, colleges, and her home, MARGARET ROBISON had a stroke in 1989 that paralyzed her left side and severely damaged her speech center. With many hours of hard work, she regained her ability to speak, but she continues to spend her days in a wheelchair. She is the author of four books of poetry, and an artist who has painted and exhibited many paintings in oils and watercolors. She lives in Shelburne Falls, Massachusetts, where she takes delight in watching the Deerfield River as it flows just outside the window above her writing table.

About the Type

This book was set in Centaur, a typeface designed by the American typographer Bruce Rogers in 1929. Rogers adapted Centaur from the fifteenth-century type of Nicholas Jenson and modified it in 1948 for a cutting by the Monotype Corporation.